Living Wisely in a Foolish World

H. Wayne House

Kenneth M. Durham

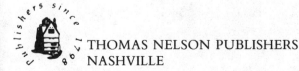

THOMAS NELSON PUBLISHERS
NASHVILLE

Published in Nashville, Tennessee, by Thomas Nelson, Inc., and distributed in Canada by Lawson Falle, Ltd., Cambridge, Ontario.

Scripture quotations are from the NEW KING JAMES VERSION of the Bible. Copyright © 1979, 1980, 1982, Thomas Nelson, Inc., Publishers.

Library of Congress Cataloging-in-Publication Data

House, H. Wayne.
   Living wisely in a foolish world / H. Wayne House, Kenneth M. Durham.
      p.   cm.
   ISBN 0-8407-7460-5
   1. Bible. O.T. Proverbs—Use. 2. Bible. O.T. Proverbs—
Criticism, interpretation, etc. 3. Conduct of life—Biblical
teaching. I. Durham, Ken. II. Title.
BS1465.2.H68   1992
223'706—dc20   92-6209
                                                                     CIP

Printed in the United States of America

1 2 3 4 5 6 7 - 97 96 95 94 93 92

Contents

1. THE WISDOM OF PROVERBS   1

2. FINANCIAL WISDOM   26

3. FAMILY WISDOM   50

4. MARITAL WISDOM   71

5. MORAL WISDOM   85

6. SEXUAL WISDOM   110

7. RELIGIOUS WISDOM   120

8. EDUCATIONAL WISDOM   128

9. POLITICAL WISDOM   142

10. VOCATIONAL WISDOM   162

11. SOCIAL WISDOM   178

12. PRACTICAL WISDOM   198

CHAPTER 1

The Wisdom of Proverbs

ALL OF US want to make the right decisions in life. We wonder what model of car we should buy. Should we borrow money and buy now, or should we wait to purchase when we have cash? Should we co-sign on a loan, or if we have already, do we try to get out of it?

All the decisions we make affect many areas of our lives—our families, our work, our religious lives, our social concerns, our sense of moral style. Some of our decisions may relate to mundane matters and will have minor lasting effects, while others may have an ongoing impact on us and others.

It's no wonder, then, that so many people find themselves in a perpetual quandary over the "right" thing to do in a given circumstance. In fact, we live in a culture that fosters indecision. Every public decision, it seems, is challenged or condemned by someone. Every consequence is second-guessed and every motive questioned. Even within the Christian community, matters from choosing a career to finding a mate to raising children are said to be too difficult for us to handle without "professional" help or extensive, introspective counseling.

Is this what God intended our lives to be? Has He left us here to muddle through as victims of endless indecision? Is the Christian life simply too complex for those who cannot afford therapists and counselors? We believe the answer to each of these questions is No.

God has not left us to discover on our own by hit or miss how to deal with the various issues of life, whether the vitally important or the most trivial ones. The Bible tells us that the Father of all believers cares for the birds that fall from the sky and provides for the flowers in the field. Certainly, then, we know beyond any doubt He also cares for our daily needs. That's why He has provided help and guidance for us in the practical issues we confront every day. This guidance, of course, is found in His Word, and one of the most important sources within the Scriptures is the book of Proverbs.

Look at the headlines in today's edition of your local newspaper. With the exception of natural disasters and "accidents" such as car wrecks and plane crashes, how many of the "bad news" events you read about could have been avoided with wise and prudent decisions? How many would not have happened if the parties involved were godly believers who lived their lives according to the simple wisdom we find in Proverbs? Of course, that kind of world is never going to exist before the Lord returns. But, as we will see, our personal lives can become much more in keeping with the plan and purpose of God if and when we begin to make our decisions and order our personal lives according to the pure and simple wisdom of God.

As in every study of Scripture, the whole counsel of God is crucial to understanding and applying what we find in any one portion, such as Proverbs. But for the purpose of simplicity, an attribute of the Christian life far too often overlooked today, this book will concentrate almost exclusively on the book of Proverbs, one of the greatest guidebooks ever written. Our journey through it together will uncover its gems of wisdom that you can apply to your life beginning right now.

THE PURPOSE OF PROVERBS

Just as every book written today has a purpose—whether to instruct, inform, or entertain—the book of Proverbs was written and compiled with certain objectives, or purposes, behind it, both from the human standpoint as well as the divine. Its two main objectives were to train leaders for Israel and to provide guidance to individuals in avoiding life's personal pitfalls.

Leadership Training

Unlike any other nation, Israel had a direct mandate from God to continually instruct succeeding generations in the things of God and to perpetuate godly leadership. Therefore, the book of Proverbs was written to train future kings and administrators of Israel so that they might provide proper leadership to their

people and serve God's purposes in Israel. Note the first words of
the book:

> The proverbs of Solomon the son of David, king of Israel:
> To know wisdom and instruction,
> To perceive the words of understanding,
> To receive the instruction of wisdom,
> Justice, judgment, and equity;
> To give prudence to the simple,
> To the young man knowledge. (1:1–4)

And the writer reminds us again of our need for instruction as
well as understanding:

> Incline your ear and hear the words of the wise,
> And apply your heart to my knowledge;
> For it is a pleasant thing if you keep them within you;
> Let them all be fixed upon your lips,
> So that your trust may be in the LORD;
> I have instructed you today, even you.
> Have I not written to you excellent things
> Of counsels and knowledge,
> That I may make you know the certainty of the words of
>   truth,
> That you may answer words of truth
> To those who send to you? (22:17–21)

We see in these portions of Scripture that Solomon desired to
teach his sons even as his father David had taught him. Solomon
understood that the real foundation for academic training is
acquiring wisdom in life. By the time of coming of age, the *bar
mitzvah* at age 13, a child should be versed in the wisdom of God,
after which he then should move on to other disciplines of
learning. In this regard, training for leadership in Israel was not
different from what most Christian parents desire for their children today.[1]

Unfortunately education in our country—though it originally
emphasized the priority of spiritual understanding—has degener-
ated to the point where children often aren't instructed well even

---

1. Sons are mentioned instead of daughters since it was they who had greater likelihood to succumb
to sexual sin and be involved in business affairs in society. But Proverbs does provide a
significant tribute to the noble woman in Chapter 31 and isolated statements elsewhere in the
book (11:16, 22 and 12:4).

in basic academics, let alone spiritual truth. From seventeen-year-olds who 200 years ago often knew Latin and could study the Bible in its original languages, we now produce teenagers whose limits of knowledge are challenged by baseball cards and Nintendo games.

How sad it is that we have often forgotten the all-important union of biblical wisdom with the academic disciplines. In our day we have sought to separate wisdom from knowledge, but Solomon wanted his sons to have skill in both the theoretical and the practical. He wanted them to respond to knowledge as well as discernment, to learn from lecture as well as lab.

Though everyone begins life naive, no one should remain naive. This does not mean that people reach a level of absolute or complete wisdom so that they are always wise. At times, in fact, the wise may do something that is foolish and at times the fool may do something that is wise. The book of Proverbs is meant to help us to be foolish less often and wise more often. And it is intended to improve how we live life overall. The crucial issue with which all of us are confronted in Proverbs is whether or not we will move on toward wisdom and not fall into a pattern of foolishness, mockery, or laziness.

Guidance in avoiding life's personal pitfalls

The book of Proverbs is primarily concerned with the ethics of those who believe in God, not those who reject Him. As one writer has noted, "This wisdom is not mere head knowledge, but divinely enlightened understanding of what is good and what is evil (1 Kings 3:9) and experiential knowledge of the Lord personally." If you want to live a godly life and succeed at serving God, Proverbs was written to you. If you are rebellious toward Him and think you can do a better job on your own, you probably will not hear what it has to say.[2]

Because of this distinct slant, the terminology of Proverbs is important—particularly the concepts of "wisdom" and "foolishness." Wisdom is not simply the content of one's head; it is the disposition of one's heart toward God and toward His revelation.

That's why throughout the book the word *wisdom* (and its synonyms) is used as a contrast to evil: "In most of the Old Testament, wisdom is mere skill or sagacity. . . . Proverbs adds

2. I. Jensen, 23.

to the concept of mental acumen the moral rectitude that alone makes intelligence worthwhile."[3]

So even though the proverbs were written to enlighten the princes of Israel, we know that these were also words of God written for His people through all the ages. In 2 Timothy 3:16–17, the apostle Paul wrote that God inspired (literally, "breathed") all Scripture, and that it was written so that the Christian might "be complete, thoroughly equipped for every good work." In other words, any and every believer can turn to this special book to gain advice on how to deal with the various problems in life without confusion or contradiction concerning rightness and wrongness, good and evil. Concerning Proverbs specifically Gleason Archer says: "The constant preoccupation of the book is with the elemental antagonisms of obedience versus rebellion, industry versus laziness, prudence versus presumption, and so on. These are so presented as to put before the reader a clear-cut choice, leaving him no ground for wretched compromise or vacillating indecision." But that's not all we'll find in Proverbs. The reader of the proverbs may learn how to keep out of trouble altogether, which is better yet![4]

HOW TO INTERPRET PROVERBS

Ours is a society of pragmatism and self-sufficiency. In North America we ardently believe in a do-it-yourself brand of life. Perhaps because of our "don't tread on me" heritage, or simply because we are so materially self-sufficient, our attitude generally is: Give me the formula for success, and stay out of my way!

Unfortunately this attitude of formula style living carries over to our interpretation of the Bible. Because of that, there is a tendency among some believers to understand every line of the Proverbs, including statements of cause and effect, or observable consequences, as blanket promises from God. Yet though we may sing, "Every promise in the book is mine, every chapter, every verse, every line," anyone who tries to claim every line of Proverbs (or any other book of the Bible) under a similar pretence will be sadly disappointed.

Not every verse in the Bible is a promise from God. Some statements are statements of fact. Some are general explanations

3. Harris, 553.
4. I. Jensen, 29.

of life. Some are records of history. Some are unique proclamations. Even those that apparently are promises are not necessarily promises to us today. Some are promises to specific individuals. Some are promises to Israel as a nation. And so on.

The Bible is not a wish book. It reveals the character of God, His greatness, His love, and His forgiveness. It is as varied in its methods of communication as is our everyday speech. Therefore, the various verses in the book of Proverbs should not all be taken as absolute assurances from God. Certainly some statements, such as those that reflect a theology of God or His creation, are absolute. But other wise sayings in Proverbs obviously are general principles, rules of thumb as it were.

As one Bible scholar puts it: "In seeking to interpret the various proverbs and apply them to life, one must bear in mind that they are generalizations. Though stated as absolutes—as their literary form requires—they are meant to be applied in specific situations and not indiscriminately. Knowing the right time to use a proverb was part of being wise: 'A word fitly spoken is like apples of gold in settings of silver.'"[5]

As an illustration, many parents have been bewildered by the proverb that says if parents will rear their children properly the children will not depart from their teaching (see 22:6). Though there have been many ways to explain "the way they should go" and whether they will never depart or whether they will return when they are old, the important thing to understand is this cannot be an *absolute promise* in the light of everyone's freedom to choose the way they will go. The passage does teach, however, that careful diligence on the part of parents brings rich rewards that benefit their children. And the fact that being taught well is not an absolute guarantee of an offspring's godliness should definitely not deter parents from seeking to obey this admonition!

As another example, there is an even more confusing combination of opposites in Proverbs 26:4–5:

> Do not answer a fool according to his folly,
> Lest you also be like him.
> Answer a fool according to his folly,
> Lest he be wise in his own eyes.

5. Heater, 557–58, see Prov. 25:11.

Instantly we can see that obeying both of these instructions is not possible if they are performed at the same time. Instead of being absolutes to be followed at all times, they provide wisdom on how to act according to the nature of the situation. Specifically, sometimes it is best to let the fool go his way and not attempt to answer his many frivolous questions. There is an old saying that a fool can ask more questions in a minute than a wise man can answer in a thousand years. Sometimes it is better to avoid the debate. By the same token, sometimes it is best to answer a fool with an answer that reveals his foolishness, lest he—and others—believe what he says. For example, at times it's appropriate to debate a militant atheist concerning the existence of God so that he will be less effective in turning others away from God, or so that he will be accountable to God for the truth he's heard. Simply stated, circumstances and wisdom will determine which of these two options we should exercise.

Let's consider, then, several helpful suggestions on how to interpret the proverbs.

First, we must understand that these instructions are not merely secular maxims, but they come from the Lord. The personal name of God, Yahweh, is found at least eighty-six times in the book.

Second, we need to be aware that *wisdom* refers to heart attitude toward God and righteousness, not simply head knowledge. "To be a fool" is not merely a description of ignorance—it is a description of willful rebellion or wickedness.

We can see this in the contrast between the sage and other leaders in Israel, between the prophet and the priest. The prophet would speak to the people and declare that righteousness is just and sin is disobedience. The priest would say that righteousness is commanded and sin is defilement. But the wise man would say that righteousness is prudent and sin is foolish. It is another perspective and it is as true as the first two, but it is not delivered in the same form. Together all three offered guidance and instruction to Israel. The prophet pronounced the judgment of God. The priest prohibited the unrighteous from participating in sacrifice or worship. And the sage proclaimed that the practicalities of life would prove him true and there would be consequences for the person who followed or rejected his advice.

Third, we need to understand that references to the foolish woman (for example, 9:13–15) refer also to spiritual folly rather than simply to a person. Though the people portrayed in Proverbs definitely are people, not just figurative representations, they can also typify or epitomize the foolishness they display. The foolish woman in Proverbs 9, for example, is the epitome of such wickedness, a contrast to "lady wisdom" found in the first several chapters.

Fourth, we need to remember that when a proverb is unclear, we should consult surrounding verses or parallel passages for possible clarification. Because the proverbs occur in disjointed, short sections, we sometimes need to read similar verses in other places in the book for insight. Proverbs 16 is an example in which the immediate context is helpful. Here we find a series of proverbs on "man proposes, but God disposes."

Close attention to the use of common Hebrew parallelism is also helpful in interpreting a proverb. At times biblical Hebrew will use similar words or ideas to express the same thing in the same verse or verses. At other times, contrasts may be revealed the same way.

Fifth, when a proverb seems to contradict another passage of Scripture, we need to look for a deeper meaning. Examples of this would include the seeming conflict between Proverbs 10:27 and Genesis 4:8 or between Proverbs 6:7 and Acts 14:19.

Sixth, if a proverb is unclear in the Bible version or translation you are using, consult another version. Because all of Proverbs is translated from the Old Testament Hebrew into English, different translations—and word choices—vary. Quite often a word or phrase that has us stumped in one translation will become more clear in another.

Seventh and finally, let the key verse of Proverbs control all your interpretations of the book: "The fear of the LORD is the beginning of knowledge" (1:7).

Proverbs was never intended to cover *every* situation we will ever encounter. It does, however, express the basic principles which most often will hold true. In other words, all other things being equal, a particular principle will be true.

THE TYPES OF PEOPLE DISCUSSED
IN PROVERBS

Since Proverbs is about real life and real people, we need to understand what types of people are presented there. Are we faced with different personality types, such as those that are so popular in some Christian circles today? Are these the "key" to living a victorious Christian life? Are we faced with various birth orders? Or dysfunctional personalities? Or codependent personalities? Or developmentally impaired persons? In what terms does God Himself describe the human race on the most practical level of all?

If you are looking for new and exciting concepts to intrigue you, you will be disappointed with Proverbs. When God speaks of life at the grassroots level, life that is lived either wisely or foolishly, He uses terminology that is plain and simple as well as convicting and revealing. His terminology is so simple, in fact, that every person's ability to understand it is taken for granted—except possibly the fool.

Let's consider some of those terms.

The Simple

In Old Testament Hebrew, the word "simple," *peti*, means "naive" or "gullible." In its verb form it means "open," and describes how the simple person is open to deceit and is easily misled.

The simple person lacks judgment (see 7:7; 9:4, 16), believes anything (see 14:15), and blindly stumbles through life without giving consideration to his actions and their consequences (see 22:3; 27:12). Because the simple person loves his ways (see 1:22), he often strays into folly (see 14:18). His thoughtlessness allows him to drift aimlessly onto the path of fools (see 1:32) and mockers (see 1:22). He also falls quickly into the trap of seduction because he has no discernment (see 7:7). He carelessly rushes toward his own destruction (see 22:3; 1:32).

We might say this person lacks common sense, not because he isn't capable of acquiring it, but because he is either apathetic or rebellious toward God's instruction concerning discernment. This person is like the high school student who laughs under his breath at his parents' advice from Scripture or the college woman who ignores her friends' pleas for her to avoid a romantic relationship with an unbeliever. They are convinced they have a better view of things than God's Word has, that they know what they're doing.

The good news is that the simple can acquire wisdom if they desire it (see 8:5). In fact, one of the stated purposes of Proverbs is "to give prudence to the simple" (1:4). Wisdom calls for the simple to come to her and realize understanding (see 9:16). Because the simple person is so aimless, he may need to witness strong punishment of the sinner in order to be turned toward wisdom (see 21:11).

In a family setting, the "simple" may be the young child who is unwary of the dangers of the sinful world. Whether that child is reared in the fear of the Lord or is left to his own sinful inclinations will usually determine whether he will follow after Christ or yield to the foolishness of the fool and mocker. This puts a great responsibility on parents. We need to be carefully diligent to teach our children the ways of God, especially as they are presented to us in Proverbs.

The Fool

The fool is defined by three Hebrew words. The most common word is *kesil*, which refers to one who is dull and obstinate, not in the sense of being unable to be wise but in stubbornly clinging to foolishness. The fool ignores the pursuit of wisdom (see 17:24) thinking he can simply buy it (see 17:16), though in his heart he has no desire for real knowledge (see 1:22) or godly understanding (see 18:2). He enjoys his foolishness and constantly returns to it "as a dog returns to its own vomit" (26:11).

The wise man is instructed to avoid a fool because the fool is quick to quarrel (see 18:6), enjoys evil (see 10:23) and fully vents his anger (see 29:11). It is "better to meet a bear robbed of her cubs than a fool in his folly" (17:12 NIV). To those who cannot avoid him—usually his parents—the fool brings deep grief (see 17:25) and personal ruin (see 19:13).

The Hebrew term *ewil*, also rendered "fool," is one step lower than *kesil*. This brand of fool moves beyond simple foolish stubbornness by adding moral indecency. He feeds on folly (see 15:14) to the point that all his actions expose it (see 13:16). When he opens his mouth, he can only gush his foolishness (see 15:2). He refuses any advice (see 12:15), preferring instead to recklessly revel in sin (see 14:16), even going so far as to mock sin's consequences (see 14:9). The only hope for this fool is to drive his foolishness from him at an early age (see 22:15). Otherwise, "though you grind a fool in a mortar, with a pestle along with crushed grain, yet his foolishness will not depart from him" (27:22).

The biblical term *nabal* is used only three times in Proverbs, but it adds "an extra weight of boorishness" to the baggage of the fool. This kind of fool is completely closed to reason; nevertheless he insists on speaking out in public (see 17:7). A perfect example of *nabal* is Nabal, Abigail's husband: "For he is such a scoundrel that one cannot speak to him" (1 Sam. 25:17). To observe this trait today, we need only look as far as contemporary "teachers" in the religious realm who advocate every form of sin from homosexuality to abortion, then turn and hiss accusations of ungodliness at true believers.[6]

The Mocker

Moving in a downward spiral, the mocker falls one step lower than the three previous descriptions for a fool. The *mocker*, sometimes translated "scoffer," appears seventeen times in Proverbs. He is not only foolish and proud, he also displays open contempt for wisdom and instruction. Anyone who tries to correct the mocker is asking for trouble (see 9:7; 15:12). He deliberately brings strife (see 11:9) because it's the only fruit his pride can bear (see 21:24). And at the mention of making amends for his sin, the mocker only ridicules (see 14:9). It's no wonder that nobody (nobody within the believing community, that is) likes him (see 24:9)!

Recently one of the popular daytime talk shows presented what it called an "open forum" on abortion. Present for the discussion were a proabortion doctor, a woman who had had two abortions, a "clergy" member who was openly proabortion, and an evangelical pastor. An abortion activist later admitted that the audience had intentionally been filled with proabortion activists from several organizations.

Besides the predictable Christianity bashing by the three guests as well as the host, one of the most obvious elements of the show was the air of hostility and open hatred toward the evangelical pastor's point of view. Rather than listening with open minds, which they all professed to possess, if the pastor dared make any mention of righteousness, biblical standards, or moral accountability, the guests and the proabortionists responded with mocking, shouting, and general disruption. This is an accurate portrayal of what the Bible associates with mockers.

An even more graphic example would be the numerous instances in recent years of homosexuals invading church gatherings, meetings, ordinations, even family picnics in order to shout

6. Kidner, 41.

obscenities and throw condoms at Christians. Not too far removed from this illustration of mocking is our national media
which label such demonstrations as "peaceful" and "coura-
geous."

With this insight into the Old Testament concept of mockers,
we can understand afresh Peter's warning, "Know this first of
all, that in the last days mockers will come with their mocking,
following after their own lusts, and saying 'Where is the promise
of His coming?'" (2 Peter 3:3–4 NAS).

The Wise

The wise are the heroes of the proverbs, set forth more than
100 times as examples of skillful living. "Wise" is as much a
description of one's heart attitude toward God and God's Word
as it is a description of intellect or ability. The wise are wise
because of positive, open, willing, obedient heart responses toward God based on information gleaned from His Word. The
wise know how to live, and live what they know.

The wise long to be with the wise (see 13:20) so they can hear
and observe instruction (see 6:6). Rather than refusing rebuke
like fools do, the wise person receives correction (see 15:31) and
pays attention to biblical commands (see 10:8). He understands
that even the punishment of God reflects God's loving desire to
move him to wisdom (see 3:11–12 and Rom. 8:28–30).

A "wise man" ("man" refers generically to men and women
alike through this book) is one who seeks knowledge (see 18:15)
so he can both store it (see 10:14) and share it (see 15:7). A wise
man learns discipline by pondering the failures of others (see
24:30–34). He gathers strength through counsel and understanding (see 8:14). He is marked by discernment (see 16:21), prudence
(see 14:8), humility (see 11:2), and righteousness (see 10:31).

At the very heart of the wise man's wisdom is his reverence for
the Lord: "The fear of the LORD is the beginning of wisdom"
(9:10). He recognizes that the essence of wisdom is in knowing
God. Discernment, understanding, counsel, and discipline all
flow from God's throne to the wise man. A wise man finds
reward (see 9:12) because wisdom teaches him (see 4:11), delivers
him (see 28:26), honors him (see 3:35), and gives him self-control
(see 29:11).

Wisdom to the wise man is more priceless than rubies (see
8:11) and more precious than gold or silver (see 16:16). As
Charles H. Spurgeon once said, "Wisdom is the right use of

knowledge. To know is not to be wise. Many men know a great deal, and are all the greater fools for it. There is no fool so great a fool as a knowing fool. But to know how to use knowledge is to have wisdom."[7]

THE WISDOM OF THE WORLD VS. WISDOM FROM GOD

Throughout the Bible, a sharp contrast is drawn between the wisdom of the world and the wisdom that comes from God. In the Old Testament, wisdom is portrayed primarily as the capacity to make the right decisions. We all desire this ability, but our concepts of the source for that wisdom may vary. Some of us may search for wisdom by consulting friends. Others might look for wisdom within themselves. Still others might search for wisdom from some spiritual counselor. And some might see all of these sources as viable places to obtain wisdom.

Interestingly, the Bible portrays only two types of wisdom. The first form of wisdom is from below, or from the world around us. It represents the best job human intellect can do to understand and execute life. The book of Ecclesiastes records the thoughts of King Solomon as he evaluated this form of wisdom— and found it all vain, or empty.

The second type of wisdom, the kind that comes from God, is truly satisfying. As a matter of fact, Solomon said that the starting point for all proper wisdom is the fear of Yahweh, the true God. Again, this is not an arbitrary wisdom based on subjective religious experience; rather, it has its source in God's revelation to man, His Word. It is the wisdom "from above," God-breathed and recorded in written form.

The New Testament has similar contrasts between wisdom from above and wisdom from below. In his first letter to the Corinthians the apostle Paul spoke of the wisdom from the world that is "fleshly," and of spiritual wisdom that is from God. His point was that the spiritual person will rely on spiritual wisdom, while those who are unspiritual will follow after carnal ("fleshly" or senses-based) wisdom.

This distinction is demonstrated by four large murals that hang on the wall of the Rockefeller Center in New York. The first painting shows a primitive man working with his hands trying to survive. The second portrays man as the creator of

7. Spurgeon.

tools and some of the comforts he can make with his tools. The third mural depicts man as both master and servant of the machine. The last mural—seemingly mismatched with the other three—shows Jesus Christ giving the Sermon on the Mount and the masses struggling to reach Him.

With an inspiration born from true wisdom, and knowing that the ability to respond properly to God's revelation, not the reliability of our own efforts, will determine the future of mankind, the artist finished his work with these words: "Man's ultimate destiny depends not on whether he can learn new lessons or make new discoveries or conquests, but on his acceptance of the lesson that was taught over two thousand years ago."

ADMONITIONS TOWARD WISDOM

When we look closely at the Near East of ancient times and its culture, we find that wisdom was treasured in many settings and societies besides Israel. The Bible itself alludes to wise men of Egypt (see Acts 7:22; 1 Kings 4:30; Isa. 19:11–12), of Edom and Arabia (see Jer. 49:7; Job 1:3; 1 Kings 4:30), of Babylon (see Isa. 47:10; Dan. 1:4, 20), and of Phoenicia (Ezek. 28:3; Zech. 9:2).

The written records from Egypt and Babylon also show a high regard for human wisdom. Egyptian "proverbs" say:

> Do not talk a lot. Be silent and thou wilt be happy. . . .
> Thou shouldst not express thy [whole] heart to the stranger.

Babylonian instruction included these teachings:

> The poor man is always curious about what he will have to eat.
> Tell a lie, [then] tell the truth—it will be considered a lie.
> A shepherd should not [try to] be a farmer.

Citing these pagan teachings doesn't suggest that the biblical authors necessarily agreed with all of the ideas found in them. Derek Kidner points out: "While the Old Testament scorns the magic and superstition which debased much of this thought (Isa. 47:12, 13), and the pride which inflated it (Job 5:13), it can speak of the gentile sages with a respect it never shows toward their priests and prophets. Solomon outstripped them, but we are expected to be impressed by the fact; and Daniel excelled the wise men of Babylon as one who stood at the head of their own profession (Dan. 5:11, 12)." Solomon's wisdom was clearly portrayed as being vastly superior to the wisdom of the people of the east and of Egypt. In fact, he was considered to be the wisest of all men (see 1 Kings 4:30–31, 34).[8]

But the presence of a certain degree of reverence for wisdom even in cultures other than Israel's—which possessed the special revelation of the true God Yahweh—demonstrates that men can still "think validly and talk wisely, within a limited field, without special revelation."[9]

According to Kidner, one explanation for this phenomenon may be the way in which God has chosen to bestow general, limited revelation through creation. Solomon, in fact, encouraged people to look to nature to gain wisdom (see 1 Kings 4:32–33).

THE PLACE OF WISDOM IN THE SCRIPTURE

The Old Testament word translated "wisdom" is usually a form of the Hebrew *hokma* or *hokmot*. In the biblical context it is directly related to the work of God's Spirit and God's Law. This basic word of wisdom is found not only in Proverbs but also in Job and Ecclesiastes.

In Israel the concept of wisdom was related not merely to having knowledge or living skills, but also to having a relationship with God. To know Yahweh was to know wisdom. Unlike "wisdom" in Greece, where Socrates taught that Greeks needed to "know themselves" (does this sound familiar?), a follower of God in ancient Israel would make knowing God his primary goal. Essentially human wisdom was a goal and a responsibility, but the ancient Israelite would be the first to admit that wisdom is not attainable without first knowing God.

Therefore wisdom sayings occur in the books of Proverbs, Job, and Ecclesiastes both as a human attribute and as a gift of God. A few times Proverbs even represents wisdom in the form of a person, all in the first nine chapters.

More than this, however, the Bible personifies wisdom in intimate association with the Person of God. In Proverbs 8:22–23, for example, wisdom is depicted as being in the beginning with God. Interestingly, its use in the Old Testament was understood by some early church fathers to be references to Christ.

8. Scott, 28, 29, 37, 38; Kidner, 17.
9. Kidner, 17.

In the New Testament, both Paul and John seem to confirm this idea of Christ as the personified wisdom of God. John's gospel refers to Jesus as the "logos" (Word) of God, which may well refer to the Hebrew concept of the wisdom by which God created the universe, rather than the Greek philosophical terms for reason or logic.

Similarly, the apostle Paul wrote to the Colossians about Christ as the one in whom is "hidden all the treasures of wisdom and knowledge" (Col. 2:3). Paul also referred to Jesus as the "wisdom of God" (1 Cor. 1:24).

Carried to its logical conclusion, all of this means that the Lord Jesus Christ has to be the perfect "wisdom and knowledge of God" in physical form. While He was on earth He portrayed that wisdom at different times and in different ways. At the age of 12, for instance, He astounded the learned men in the temple. Later, He confounded the Pharisees when they sought to trap Him. He silenced the arguments of the lawyers when they questioned Him about the Torah and about justice.

Not only was Christ a wise man, He also relied on proverbial sayings to share His wisdom. An example of this is found in Luke 14:8–10 where He quotes from Proverbs 25:6–7:

> "When you are invited by anyone to a wedding feast, do not sit down in the best place, lest one more honorable than you be invited by him; and he who invited you and him come and say to you, 'Give place to this man,' and then you begin with shame to take the lowest place. But when you are invited, go and sit down in the lowest place, so that when he who invited you comes he may say to you, 'Friend, go up higher.' Then you will have glory in the presence of those who sit at the table with you." (Luke 14:8–10)

> > Do not exalt yourself in the presence of the king,
> > And do not stand in the place of great men;
> > For it is better that he say to you,
> > "Come up here,"
> > Than that you should be put lower in the presence of the
> >   prince,
> > Whom your eyes have seen. (Prov. 25:6–7)

Even Christ's style of teaching reveals an affinity for wisdom-type communication. He often used short, pithy statements that were designed to live long in the memory of His hearers. And He recognized two kinds of wisdom—the true wisdom which brought men to God (Luke 7:35), and false wisdom, which He seems to reject in Luke 6:27–38 (a proverb found in Sirach: "Give to the godly man, but do not help the sinner. Do good to the humble, but do not give to the ungodly").

Again, in the writings of Paul we can see that he believed in only two kinds of wisdom—that from God and that from the world. The first would give life; the other would cause separation from the truth and life of God. The wisdom Paul spoke of referred not only to pure doctrine, but also to the association of the Christian with the life and ministry of the Spirit of God (1 Cor. 2:10).

THE WISDOM FROM ABOVE

"Wisdom," confirmed James, "comes from above." In his most notable mini-treatise on wisdom, James lists seven characteristics of godly wisdom. He tells us wisdom is pure, peaceable, gentle, easy to be entreated, full of mercy and good works, without partiality, and without hypocrisy (see James 3:17–18).

Let's briefly consider each of these characteristics separately.

Godly Wisdom Is Pure

We shouldn't be surprised that purity is listed as the first attribute of godly wisdom, since the Bible continually emphasizes the absolute purity of God's nature. When Isaiah received a vision of God (Isa. 6:1–5), he heard the angels of God cry out "Holy, holy, holy is the LORD of hosts." This statement of God's holiness is an expression of the superlative nature of God's holiness: He is inexpressively holy.

A major dimension of God's holiness is His moral purity. God cannot sin, nor can He be influenced to sin. This is a difficult concept for us to grasp, since we live in a fallen world where even those things we consider pure can be polluted or defiled. And, of course, even in our desire for moral purity (a desire all believers should have, according to the Word of God), we can be influenced in the other direction by the many impurities of the culture around us.

But God is not subject to any influences of impurity. Therefore His wisdom is unaffected by the weaknesses we often experience. As a result, His decisions will always be right and pure. His judgments will always be morally sound. And His perception of reality will always be untainted by sin or bias.

Do you want to make decisions that are morally right and ethically pure? In light of the mixed signals we receive every day of what is right and what is wrong, do you want to be sure you are living a life that is consistent and upright? Then live according to God's wisdom. Make Proverbs a foundation for your decisions.

Godly Wisdom Is Peaceable

We live in a world of turmoil. Click your television to any one of the news channels, and in 30 minutes you can see visible evidence that our world is a world of conflict, of dissent, of disagreement, of animosity and aggravation.

Not only is this true among nations, tragically it is also true in churches, in families, and in many of our interpersonal relationships. This is not what God desires for His people. The writer of the book of Hebrews admonishes believers to "pursue peace with all people" (Heb. 12:14). One facet of the fruit of the Spirit in Galatians 5:22–23 is "peace." Jesus Himself bears the title "Prince of Peace" indicating that He alone can bring peace to human hearts today, and peace to the earth when He returns.

Because our God is a God of peace and reconciliation, godly wisdom causes us to seek solutions to our difficulties rather than escalating them. We also seek to reconcile differences with our fellow Christians and acquaintances rather than aggravating them. Obviously, this does *not* mean believers are to turn a blind eye to sin and unrighteousness, as some false teachers would have us believe. Those who love God will hate sin, and will not shrink back from calling it what it is.

But those who desire to live according to godly wisdom will also seek ways to lead the sinner to reconciliation with God. One who seeks the path of wisdom will seek the path of peace. He will, as the time-worn saying goes, "hate the sin, but love the sinner." He will condemn sin openly, while just as openly calling sinners to repentance.

Godly Wisdom Is Gentle

Wise believers will be gentle believers. Strife and harshness is the way of the world's wisdom. Our corporate structure today often advocates a "dog eat dog" kind of upward movement in the business world. Unfortunately, some Christian circles foster admiration—even hero-worship—for professing Christians who carry their baggage of a "shrewd," "hard-driving," or "uncompromising" business disposition over to church or ministry leadership.

Nothing could be farther from God's concept of wise leader! According to James, true Christian wisdom includes gentleness, forbearance, and forgiveness.

Forgiveness is one of the most difficult of all virtues in both a Christian as well as a non-Christian environment. In our world of harsh scrutiny, to err not only is human, it is unforgivable! The attitude of godly wisdom, however, is one of gentleness toward each other. We are expected to turn aside wrath with kind words. Consider from your own experience how difficult it is to continue expressing anger at a person who shows unconditional kindness and gentleness!

By contrast, anger only justifies more anger. Hatred only opens the door for more hatred. And—as hundreds of thousands of divorce cases illustrate for us every year—once the vicious cycle of animosity begins, it is not long before it begins wheeling out of control, destroying everything in its path.

But God instructs us in a better way. Ultimately, the Lord Jesus is our example, who though reviled He reviled not. Though He was hated for the truthfulness of His message, He responded to his assailants with love. James alludes to this type of attitude when he says, "Therefore, my beloved brethren, let every man be swift to hear, slow to speak, slow to wrath; for the wrath of man does not produce the righteousness of God" (James 1:19–20).

Godly Wisdom Is Willing to Yield

The next characteristic of wisdom from above is that it is willing to yield or "easy to be entreated," as the Authorized Version translates it. This Greek expression was used in the language of the military and referred to someone who was entirely willing to take instructions from the commander-in-chief.

Stubbornness and inflexibility are natural traits in all of us. It wasn't too long ago, in fact, that some Los Angeles motorists moved from their traditional lane-squeezing to outright warfare, settling right-of-way disputes with guns instead of words! Like stubborn drivers who refuse to obey "yield" signs, in all of life we tend to think we're right and that others should yield to our views.

In matters of biblical truth, of course, it's true that we should encourage others to agree with God's viewpoint (which also should be our own predisposition). But in the inconsequential matters of everyday life, our attitude should be one of godly wisdom. We should reflect a willingness to listen, to truly hear others' views, to be willing to assent and be a team player when issues of God's truth are not at stake.

Godly Wisdom Is Full of Mercy and Good Works

James continues his description of godly wisdom by saying it is "full of mercy and good fruits" (3:17). "Who is wise and understanding among you?" he asked. "Let him show by good conduct that his works are done in the meekness of wisdom" (3:13).

If you profess with your mouth a commitment to God's standard of wisdom and understanding, but then live your life differently, you are displaying foolishness. Believers who are wise with the wisdom from above must display that wisdom in the way they live. Not only will this lend harmony to the body of Christ, it will also help draw unbelievers to faith in the Savior.

We should live our lives under the pressure of being the "books" read by the unsaved. Every day we live our lives in a spiritual fishbowl looked into by those who wonder at our manner of existence. We can be beautiful to behold, or we can reflect poorly on our Father.

Granted, this view exerts a certain amount of pressure on us—it makes us *responsible*? But this is our calling. We were "created in Christ Jesus for good works" (Eph. 2:10) as we see confirmed in numerous other passages:

And God is able to make all grace abound toward you, that you, always having all sufficiency in all things, may have an abundance for every good work. (2 Cor. 9:8)

. . . that you may have a walk worthy of the Lord, fully pleasing Him, being fruitful in every good work and increasing in the knowledge of God. (Col. 1:10)

Now may our Lord Jesus Christ Himself, and our God and Father, who has loved us and given us everlasting consolation and good hope by grace, comfort your hearts and establish you in every good word and work. (2 Thess. 2:16–17)

... in all things showing yourself to be a pattern of good works; in doctrine showing integrity, reverence, incorruptibility... who gave Himself for us, that He might redeem us from every lawless deed and purify for Himself His own special people, zealous for good works. (Titus 2:7,14)

Remind them to be subject to rulers and authorities, to obey, to be ready for every good work. (Titus 3:1)

All Scripture is given by inspiration of God, and is profitable for doctrine, for reproof, for correction, for instruction in righteousness, that the man of God may be complete, thoroughly equipped for every good work. (2 Tim. 3:16–17)

And let us consider one another in order to stir up love and good works. (Heb. 10:24)

Godly Wisdom Is Without Partiality

A person who is impartial is equally fair to all people. He doesn't use his position to take advantage of people, even when it is his "right" to do so.

One of the chief features in the life of Solomon, who asked God for wisdom and received it in full measure, was that he could judge fairly. He exemplifies the need to listen to all sides of the question and to judge equitably without prejudice.

Part of that responsibility for the Christian in cases of accusation or implication is to judge according to the Bible's standards and procedures. Rather than trusting in our own fallible discernment, we should be careful to require the verification of two or three reliable eyewitnesses, and thus short-circuit the potential chaos that can easily be wrought by gossip and false accusations.

Godly Wisdom Is Without Hypocrisy

No one likes a phony, yet any of us can fall into the folly of the double standard if we are not careful. The lack of integrity we can observe today in Christians—even Christian leaders—is alarming. We should be straightforward, saying what we believe, and living what we say.

Throughout the book of Proverbs, one of the most visible characteristics of the person who is wise and discerning is consistency. There's no double-mindedness, no hypocrisy, no vacillation in the life of the godly wise.

THE FEAR OF THE LORD IS THE BEGINNING OF WISDOM

Throughout the Scriptures there are many statements and passages concerning the wisdom God gives, but the major portion is the book of Proverbs. In Proverbs we find the statement which can best be amplified, "The fear of Yahweh, the true God, is the beginning of wisdom" (see 1:7; 1:10). But what does it mean to fear God?

In our low-commitment society, *fear* is interpreted by many Bible teachers as our concept of *respect*. In that context, to *fear* God is to stand in awe or to reverence Him. "In a few prominent passages [to fear God] means simply obedience to the divine will, and it is in this sense that the teachers, too, seem to have understood the term. The modern reader must, therefore, eliminate, in the case of the word *fear*, the idea of something emotional, of a specific, psychical form of the experience of God. In this context, the term is possibly used even in a still more general, humane sense, akin to our 'commitment to,' [or to describe] 'knowledge about Yahweh.'" While this understanding of *fear* is surely one aspect of the *fear of God*, is anything else involved? Is there more to it than that? Because some teachers believe a stronger meaning of *fear* would cause us to have an unhealthy view of God, we are told we should see God as a God of love, not as one whom we should fear.[10]

This point of view is not consistent with Paul's teaching in 2 Corinthians 5:10–11. The translation of Paul's inspired words in the New King James Version is perhaps the best we can find: "For we must all appear before the judgment seat of Christ, that each one may receive the things done in the body, according to what he has done, whether good or bad. Knowing, therefore, the terror [*fear*] of the Lord, we persuade men; but we are well-known to God, and I also trust are well-known in your consciences." (See 14:26–27; 16:6.) Without doubt, Paul's concern for the judgment he would receive by Christ gives us a much more profound concept than mere respect. Is this our concept of God today? Do we live with a sense of serious responsibility before Him? And do we seek to broaden our wisdom in this life because of our accountability before Him in eternity?

Almost anyone who has enjoyed a successful career in the

10. von Rad, 66.

military can verify that the first step toward understanding one's role and executing it well is to fear—in a healthy sense—the commanding officer. That's because understanding the seriousness of consequences, both good and bad, is a wonderful motivator!

Our relationship with God is no different. To understand who He is, and to fear the consequences of living outside of His will and approval, truly is the beginning of wisdom. It is also the watershed between the wise and the foolish. Throughout Proverbs, wisdom is equated first and foremost with submission to God, while folly always includes a heart that is ignorant, apathetic, or rebellious.

Proverbs phrases this concept in various ways, but the point is always the same:

> The fear of the LORD is the beginning of knowledge, but fools despise wisdom and discipline. (1:7 NIV)

> He whose walk is upright fears the LORD, but he whose ways are devious despises him. (14:2 NIV)

> A wise man fears the LORD and shuns evil, but a fool is hotheaded and reckless. (14:16 NIV)

These verses show us that if we desire to be wise, we will build our knowledge on a spiritual foundation, and we will remain open for correction from the Lord.

Just as "wisdom is vindicated by her deeds," the moral dimension of wisdom in our lives is made evident by our righteous lifestyle. Just as John emphasized in his first epistle, a righteous walk is proof positive of one's relationship with the Lord.

The foolish, on the other hand, despise wisdom and discipline. They may be mentally smart, but they are morally deficient because they reject the spiritual aspect of their lives. Without God's perfect standard, they have no solid guide for the moral and spiritual decisions they encounter every day.

Proverbs presents all people with the only means by which we can avoid evil (see Prov. 16:6). If we long to avoid bad decisions, sin, and the consequences of foolishness day by day, wisdom— God's wisdom—is our only hope. And wisdom begins with fear of the Lord. To fear the Lord is to hate pride, arrogance, evil behavior, and perversion. It is only when we begin from a point of forsaking self and looking to God that we can ever hope to learn a godly skill for living.

According to God's Word, those who reject the fear of God hate knowledge. They willfully spurn God's rebuke and reject His advice. Such hardening of heart, says Proverbs, will only bring trouble (28:14), and those who choose to go their own way rather than God's, will receive the results of their own wisdom (Prov. 1:29–31).

ACQUIRING WISDOM

For those who have ears to hear and eyes to see, the Bible presents an airtight case for the lifelong process of acquiring wisdom. In terms that can be understood by the most simple-minded, God reveals wisdom's benefits both in positive terms as well as negative. Rejecting God's guidance has disastrous effects, while fearing God has many benefits. The fear of God will bring "health to your body and nourishment to your bones" (Prov. 3:7–8 NIV). In general and intently practical terms, following wisdom can add many years to our lives: "The fear of the LORD adds length to life, but the years of the wicked are cut short" (Prov. 10:27 NIV). And parents who fear God will be helping their children do the same (Prov. 14:26).

In the book of Proverbs, the wise man gives three conditions we must meet in order to acquire wisdom (Prov. 2:1–4). He gives each condition twice in different words, using a literary device called "synonymous parallelism."

We find the first condition in four equivalent phrases: "accept my words," "store up my commands within you," "turn your ear to wisdom," and "apply your heart to understanding" (Prov. 2:1–2 NIV).

These involve absorbing the principles of wisdom so thoroughly that our lives and personalities automatically express them. The second condition involves a verbal commitment to obtaining wisdom (Prov. 2:3). And the third condition involves a dedication to looking for wisdom in earnest, the same way we would search for hidden treasure (Prov. 2:4).

"People's searching for wisdom," writes one scholar, "includes persistent inquiries, attentive listening, and diligent looking for the purpose of acquiring it. Wisdom is far more valuable than all of the material wealth of the world."

Simply understanding these three conditions should cause us

to remember the words of Jesus, who asked, "What will it profit a man if he gains the whole world, and loses his own soul?" (Mark 8:36). No matter what premium the world might place on its own brand of wisdom, it will be of no profit whatsoever if, in our process of seeking, we do not seek the wisdom that comes from above.

By God's grace, the book of Proverbs enables each of us to have God's insight on how to live lives that will glorify Him; how to build up others; and how to be at peace with ourselves. Following its precepts will bring success in business and in the home. Through heeding its advice, we can avoid those regrettable pitfalls that can make life so difficult.

If we listen to God's wisdom, we will experience joy and laughter rather than feeling the sorrow and despair that are so much a part of those who heed the "spirit of the age."

Proverbs speaks to every area of life we will ever encounter. No stone is left unturned; no path not taken. The only issue in question is whether we will consider its ways and follow its advice.

CHAPTER 2

Financial Wisdom

FROM GOATS AND GOLD
TO PAPER AND PLASTIC

ASK FOR A book on financial wisdom today—even in a Christian bookstore—and you'll likely be pointed toward a volume that speaks in terms of net worth, liquid assets, individual retirement annuities, mutual funds, and so forth. You are likely to read about how to think and grow rich, about the power of thinking successfully, about an attitude that says, "See you at the top." And, providing you are a middle-class white American with a steady salary and more income than obligations, some books like these may be helpful.

On the other hand, the kinds of financial information we are accustomed to in our materialistic, twentieth-century culture don't help us much when it comes to really *understanding* money—why it exists, what it can do, what it can't do, and what it might or might not do to us. Financial journals provide little help for those who find themselves locked in a poverty cycle, and business magazines give us even less with which we can educate our children concerning money.

Even our churches tend to downplay the truth behind price tags and dollar signs, perhaps because any discourse on God's view of money is eyed by suspicious congregations as a prelude to asking for more of the green stuff. Thus our working reservoir of biblical financial wisdom consists of a couple of verses like "The love of money is a root of all kinds of evil" and "God loves a cheerful giver." With nothing more than these in hand, we battle the bondage of money, being careful not to love it as we strive to accumulate as much of it as possible, being equally careful to never give when we can't do it cheerfully![1]

Fortunately God has revealed in His Word, especially in Proverbs, a wealth of real truth about wealth. Why? Because the inevitability of financial burdens and entanglements was as real when Proverbs was written as it is now. In that day, as in ours, people had businesses to keep alive, bills to pay, jobs to keep, and families to maintain. Many of our most valuable archeological artifacts and clues to the past, in fact, are inscriptions outlining financial receipts, inventories, tributes, taxes, salaries, and debts. And, just as surely as money brings out the best and worst in people today, it has always been so throughout history.

Long before actual coinage appeared in the ancient world (sometime before 540 B.C.), personal wealth was based upon two things—material possessions and an accepted medium of monetary exchange. That is not to say that people did not "spend money." They did. They conducted their purchases in one of two ways: either by barter or by bullion weighed out in the scales.

Probably the earliest unit of barter exchange was livestock, since so much could be provided through ownership of domestic animals and the animals themselves could yield long-term "dividends" through reproduction. Ownership of livestock, in fact, was the way in which Abraham's prosperity was calculated (see Gen. 13:2) along with his possession of bullion. Because livestock could be easily assessed and transported, it was an ideal medium of barter in the ancient world, as it still is in some parts of the world today. Other units of barter among people for whom bullion was either too scarce or too precious to use included oil, agricultural produce, foodstuffs, and even clothing and household goods.

For those who possessed more personal wealth but needed to conduct transactions without that wealth present, precious metals filled that void. Without going into a philosophical treatment of exactly *why* silver, gold, and jewels are considered to be valuable assets, we can see that at least from the time of Abraham and possibly earlier, bullion weighed out in standardized measure has served as money. And, logically, the exchange of bullion for items one might otherwise barter has stimulated commerce and has motivated the pursuit of profit as well.

1. 1 Tim. 6:10; 2 Cor. 9:7.

How does this relate to today's paper-and-plastic society?

Because we generally don't barter our possessions today, we often miss out on key points of Scripture when it speaks of an abundance of these bartering units or when it makes reference to the methods of trading. Specifically, since we don't own cattle or goats, we conclude that a verse about cattle or goats just doesn't apply to us. Or because we don't weigh out our payment for groceries, we skip over verses that refer to scales and balances. Because we trade in paper notes that only *represent* real money, and because we flash plastic cards that merely *represent* our ability to make enough money later on to pay for what we are purchasing now, the biblical concepts of "barter and bullion" are lost on us.

Yet we're in no different position today than were our Old Testament counterparts. We are subject to the necessities of earning, buying, and selling just as they were. We are as frustrated as they were when faced with more need than money or by running out of paycheck before running out of month. We are just as tempted as they were to set righteousness aside in order to gain wealth, to disregard the poor who have had no say in their status, or to resent God and the wealthy because of our own needs.

That's why we need the simple wisdom of Proverbs in relation to finances. When it comes to money, sophistication has not replaced God's truth! Changing terminology—from "dishonest" to "shrewd," from "borrowing" to "leveraging," from "greedy" to "aggressive"—has not changed the consequences of actions against which God's Word has warned us for centuries. We need look no further than the newspaper to find examples aplenty of those who have violated the clear precepts of Proverbs for the sake of financial gain, and have suffered the consequences.

An example is the story published a number of years ago by a Dallas magazine about one of the "movers and shakers" in that city. The man was incredibly wealthy, possessed enormous assets, and managed several multi-million-dollar business enterprises. Trying to discover what drives a person like this, the interviewer asked the businessman about his source of motivation.

"I'm driven by two things," he replied. "Love and fear—the love of money and the fear of going broke." Interestingly, within six years this man had filed for bankruptcy.

Even more telling are the lives of those who are "lucking" into sudden wealth through state-run gambling called lotteries.

Though some people take their earnings and quietly disappear into obscurity, others stay in the public eye long enough to reveal what the Word of God has taught us all along—wealth in any amount does not change a person's character. But rags-to-riches-to-rags stories are not new.

Many years ago a gentleman named Keith Nicholson won the then amazing sum of more than $426,000 in the British soccer pool. As he and his wife set out to spend, spend, spend, they first spent more than a tenth of the money on a luxury home. They then proceeded to throw elaborate parties, sometimes every night for days on end. At the end of only four years, they had managed to spend $196,000. "We had oodles of money," Mrs. Nicholson recalled later, "but we lost our friends. The people we had known in the old days, and who we really wanted to see, never came around." Finally, in 1966 Nicholson was killed in an expensive car purchased with his winnings. From what was left of the money, $107,000 went to the government in taxes. The remainder was invested—half in a trust for his children, and half to provide Mrs. Nicholson with an income of $25 per week.

Obviously it is incumbent on all of us to look into God's financial primer. The book of Proverbs was not designed to impress the wealthy, nor will it discourage the poor. It contains harsh words for some of the rich, but it offers equally stern words for some of the poor. It does not condemn wealth for those who handle it wisely, nor does it teach that a lack of wealth is shameful.

In context, the wisdom of Proverbs in relation to finances should make all of us equally uncomfortable.

WHAT MONEY SHOULD MEAN TO US

P. T. Barnum, who was no stranger to money or the pursuit of it, once said, "Money is in some respects like fire; it is a very excellent servant, but a terrible master." To say that money has become the master of Western civilization at large is an understatement. Perhaps it is because we are so consumed by the acquisition and dispensing of material wealth that we do not see how much it rules our lives.[2]

That's not to say that money is master over every one of us. Money means many different things to many people. For some people it is the ultimate measure of success, the ultimate source

2. Attributed to P.T. Barnum; original source unknown.

of joy, the ultimate resource for fulfillment in life. For others, however, money may merely be a means to an end, a necessary inconvenience, a God-given resource for accomplishing His work, a source of frustration, a cause for worry, or a fixed factor in an organized life.

Regardless of what money actually means to us individually, we need to understand that God has some clear ideas of what it *should* mean to us and what it should have meant to His people in the Old Testament. In order to understand the terms in which God addresses the issue of finances in Proverbs, we need to understand a little about the role of prosperity in the relationship of God's people of Old Testament times to Him.

In all ancient cultures and religions, wealth, prosperity, and security were inextricably connected to the deity or deities a culture worshiped. And because the prosperity of most ancient cultures was dependent on the fertility of the land in producing crops and livestock (remember the barter system), various deities and religious practices tended to develop according to the themes of the fertility of the land, storms producing rain, the flooding of rivers, and so on.

In light of this, imagine how revolutionary it was for the true God to call out of Ur—where the fertility of the Tigris and Euphrates rivers guaranteed a prosperous culture—one man, Abraham, who was to dwell in a land where prosperity would be much more tenuous. God promised Abraham that He would make him personally prosperous, and also that He would bless his descendants in the land He promised.[3]

Although the promise to Abraham that his descendants would dwell prosperously in a bountiful land would never be rescinded, in Deuteronomy 28–30 God made it clear to Israel that any generation of Abraham's descendants could, through disobedience, miss out on God's blessing in the land. In other words, obedience would lead to blessing, while disobedience would lead to a lack of blessing and would even bring harsh discipline. Prosperity in the land, therefore, was an outward sign of the nation's faith and obedience. In the same way, poverty in the land was a sign of God's blessing being removed. This principle, properly understood, should have motivated the nation to keep itself pure, devoted to the covenant promises of God, and obedient to His Word. And at times it did.

3. Gen. 12:1–3.

A problem arose, however, when people within the nation of Israel began to apply the principle of Deuteronomy as the measurement of whether or not God approved of individuals. In other words, some people began to look at the poor and say, "God is not blessing them; they must be in sin or spiritually inferior." Likewise, they would look at the rich and say, "God is blessing them; they must be holy or spiritually superior." Worst of all, they would look at themselves and think, "I have every reason to strive for riches in order to prove God's approval of me."

Of course this outlook went far beyond material wealth or poverty. It included physical infirmity or well-being, mental health versus mental illness, and even marriage or widowhood. This was precisely the view held by the Pharisees at the time of Christ, the popular view that every misfortune in life is the result of God's judgment for some sin. Even Christ's disciples had been influenced by this outlook, as seen in their question to Jesus concerning the man born blind, "Rabbi, who sinned, this man or his parents, that he was born blind?"[4]

This problem, then, is one of improper, or reversed, priorities. The incorrect formula for financial priorities was *prosperity equals God's approval which equals happiness*. This attitude is actually no different from the teaching of the health-and-wealth hucksters of our generation. One prosperity preacher has gone so far as to assert that God can't give you what He doesn't have; God doesn't have money problems—so if you do, they aren't from Him.

The effects of this incorrect way of thinking were as devastating to the Israelites of old as they are to us today. To help His people, the Israelites of old as well as Christians today, God provided *real* wisdom, the *real* truth about prosperity and poverty, through the wisdom book of Proverbs.

According to the Word of God, the proper formula is *God's approval equals happiness*. The end result of God's approval on an individual's life may or may not include prosperity. To be sure, there are certain virtues that accompany the life of faith, and as we will see, some of these can result in material security. But as far as God's approval and our spiritual position are concerned, the material is essentially immaterial!

First and foremost, the wisdom, or skill for living, given in the book of Proverbs is "better than rubies." This automatically places the value of God's wisdom in the highest possible

4. John 9:2.

category—beyond the level of bartering goods, even beyond the level of weighing out bullion. Jewels like rubies were too precious to use for everyday transactions. They were treasures, part of a family's legacy, the crown jewels, or a rich daughter's dowry.[5]

That's precisely the way we should view the acquisition of wisdom from God's Word. Since all the things we might desire cannot even be compared to God's wisdom, acquiring it should get the lion's share of our time and attention. Why? Because the wealth that wisdom promises is one that lasts forever. When wisdom personified says, "Riches and honor are with me," we would be foolish to think this refers to material gain. Not only would that be contrary to God's character, it would mean that the more godly a person gets, the richer he or she should become![6]

But that's not the kind of wealth God wants us to achieve. The riches wisdom offers are enduring, or "non-perishing," riches, and they include righteousness. This was precisely Christ's point when He admonished His listeners to "lay up for yourselves treasures in heaven, where neither moth nor rust destroys and where thieves do not break in and steal." Knowing we naturally relate to that which is valuable in earthly terms, the wisdom of Proverbs proclaims, "My fruit is better than gold, yes, than fine gold, and my revenue than choice silver." What would the Christian community in North America be like if it really believed this proclamation of God's truth—we who are so busy working fifty or sixty hours per week, we who have double incomes and triple debts, we who are too busy pursuing careers to pursue the lost?[7]

God's wisdom, God's priorities for living, God's righteous standards, and the understanding of His Word should be more precious to His people than any type of monetary gain. The formula should be *God's approval equals happiness*, with or without the material trimmings. We should so covet the skill of choosing Him that we seek after it in the same way we would mine a mother lode of silver in our backyards or the way we would dig for a buried treasure.

It is interesting to watch the news for items about companies who have found new ways to extract precious metals from old

5. Prov. 8:11a.
6. 8:11b; 8:18a.
7. 8:18b; Matt. 6:20; Prov. 8:19.

mine tailings or, better yet, to hear of treasure hunters who have found a long-lost, unsalvaged Spanish ship. If there is one trait common to each one of these treasure-seekers, it is that *nothing* will keep them from reaching their goals. They know the treasure is there, and they are willing to do anything to recover it.

The great attraction of gold, silver, and precious gems, of course, is not just their inherent beauty and value, it is the profit, or personal gain, that comes from them. The sage uses our understanding of that simple truth to remind us that the profits of wisdom are even better. We read in Proverbs 3:13–15:

> Happy is the man who finds wisdom,
> And the man who gains understanding;
> For her proceeds are better than the profits of silver,
> And her gain than fine gold.
> She is more precious than rubies,
> And all the things you may desire cannot compare with her.

Clearly this passage speaks of priorities. Since words like "better" and "more precious" are comparative terms, they should cause us to compare corresponding factors in our own lives. God's wisdom is *better than wealth*. Understanding God's Word is *more precious than rubies*. If these things are so, then what in our lives should get the better part of our time? What elements of our schedules should we consider more precious than others?

If it is true that "the blessing of the LORD makes one rich" —spiritually, it would seem we would make the pursuit of His blessing our highest priority, not just in word as many do, but in deed, in schedule, in commitment, in study, in real life. The result, says the sage, is that "in the house of the righteous there is much treasure," clearly referring to the immaterial fruits of righteousness, while "the revenue of the wicked is trouble." Another passage, "Better is a little with the fear of the LORD, than great treasure with trouble," states the same wisdom in slightly different words. If your focus is material treasure, and you sow the seeds of unrighteousness to get it, you will get the material wealth you wanted—and plenty of trouble to go along with it.[8]

How much better to make God's priorities your priorities, and to enjoy the greater, imperishable treasure of righteousness along with whatever He chooses to give you, whether it is a little or a lot. Most of us believe that we only have to choose which we

8. 10:22a; 15:6; 15:16.

will put *first*, God or mammon. Seldom do we consider that we will have to choose one *or* the other! Sometimes, however, God allows our options to bring us face-to-face with an exclusive choice of righteousness *or* riches, integrity *or* income, wisdom *or* wealth. In those cases, God's instructions are clear: "How much better it is to get wisdom than gold! And to get understanding is to be chosen *rather* than silver." If it comes down to a choice, there is only one choice to make![9]

For some Christians, that choice has meant sacrificing a promising career, a secure job, national status, or any one of a number of "perks" in order to stand firm rather than give in to spiritual compromise. A Christian salesman may choose to resign rather than "wine and dine" his clients. A Christian accountant may choose to give notice rather than falsify company records or file erroneous tax returns. A Christian model or actor may head for the door rather than compromise morals. The possibilities are numerous, and they occur every day. The point is that if an either/or choice ever arises, God's advice is to *not* take the money—and run!

We cannot leave this aspect of financial wisdom without noting that God's Word clearly teaches that making God's wisdom the priority of your life *can* have a direct impact on your material well-being. Just as surely as the negative traits of wickedness, laziness, and dishonesty will have their lasting effects on your life, generally speaking, righteousness and wisdom also can have positive effects on your material well-being.

The most obvious example of this is the Proverbs 31 "excellent wife," whose internal righteousness is manifested in her diligence and success at a cottage industry of buying a field and earning a profit from it. For her, the gaining of profit was simply an outgrowth of her commitment to righteous wisdom, and it was directed toward provision for her family. She was not a career woman out to "find herself"; rather, she personified the spirit of Proverbs, which is "by humility and the fear of the LORD are riches and honor and life."[10]

In recognizing that living wisely can have material benefits, however, we must never fall into the error of assuming that the lack of material success automatically signifies a lack of wisdom.

9. 16:16.
10. 31:16; 22:4.

WHAT WEALTH DOES AND DOES NOT DO

Wealth does not guarantee security or happiness in life.

Turn on the television, watch a few commercials, and it's not hard to see that the message of our society revolves around all the things wealth can do for us—the possessions it can purchase for us, the places it can take us, the leisure time it can afford us, and the security it can guarantee us, or so we are led to believe.

The tragic result of the message that wealth guarantees happiness and security has been accurately summarized by Frank A. Clark, who observed, "Modern man is frantically trying to earn enough to buy things he's too busy to enjoy!" Most Christian families, no matter how committed to spiritual priorities, have at times felt as though they have been pulled into a whirlpool of financial interdependency as they continually try to make enough money to afford the "necessities" and "luxuries" they have acquired for themselves. For example, no sooner do you begin making enough money to replace the old, beat-up family car, than a little more is required to make the monthly payments, pay larger insurance premiums, keep up the warranty-required maintenance, fit the new beauty with a car alarm, and so on. Or consider the couple that finally scrapes enough money together to afford their first house. Along with the dream home comes a mortgage payment they planned for, and a raft of other things they perhaps didn't anticipate, such as tools for working on it, appliances and furniture to fill it, materials for fixing it up, a lawn mower and yard tools, hoses and sprinklers, service calls on the air conditioner and furnace, and who knows what else!

On a little more sophisticated plane, consider the plight of the financial wizard who parlays his earnings into an impressive and ever-growing investment portfolio. With an increase in wealth comes an increasing need to keep that money working for him. He must invest, speculate, buy, sell, and manage. With increased diversity comes increased concern, increased worry, increased stress, increased risk. Sometimes it all collapses like a house of cards; but even when it doesn't, the anticipation of what *might* happen is almost as bad.

Granted, these are facts of life. So why mention them here? Because too often we incorrectly assume money and possessions can do for us some things they can never accomplish, and we fail to recognize other things they *can* do if we will only let them.

For example, we are indoctrinated in our culture to believe that the key to happiness and security is a successful career. Through stereotypes shown to us in the media, we are taught that the intelligent, upscale, successful business person is the one who spends extra hours at the office each night, who is not "burdened" by family obligations that might interfere with his work, who spends days, or even weeks, traveling and working endless hours for the company. This person, of course, reaps success in the form of raises and promotions, and thus can afford the hallmarks of success, like a new German-built car, the finest wine, and a gold credit card!

Make no mistake—the Bible places a high premium on character traits like diligence, perseverance, and sincere effort. But Proverbs is just as clear that these traits should be an expression of our desire to please God, not to acquire wealth in order to guarantee our future. Proverbs 23:4–5 warns us against setting our eyes on wealth:

> Do not overwork to be rich;
> Because of your own understanding, cease!
> Will you set your eyes on that which is not?
> For riches certainly make themselves wings;
> They fly away like an eagle toward heaven.

Does this mean we should not work for pay, or that we should not seek to advance our careers? No, not at all. It means that those who make career advancement more important than the things of God, including home and family, and those who place all their confidence in their financial reserves, may be in for a huge disappointment. Money really does have a way of making wings for itself and flying away! Moreover, to trust in a corporate entity to provide those things which only God can provide really is setting our eyes on that which "is not." As one Christian businessman stated after rearranging his personal priorities to place his relationship with God and his family above the corporate will for his life, "I suddenly realized this company won't feed me soup after I've had a stroke. It won't come visit me in the rest home. It won't make sure I'm warm and well-fed when I can no longer do those things for myself."

Though we won't hear many motivational talks on how to be content with what we have, we should think carefully about the prayer of Agur found in Proverbs 30:8–9:

> Give me neither poverty nor riches—
> Feed me with the food You prescribe for me;
> Lest I be full and deny You,
> And say, "Who is the LORD?"
> Or lest I be poor and steal,
> And profane the name of my God.

Money, success, and climbing the corporate ladder are not evil in themselves, but they are no substitute for the security and well-being only God can provide for those who live according to His wisdom.

The best possible avenue to security, according to Proverbs 3:9–10, is to:

> Honor the LORD with your possessions,
> And with the firstfruits of all your increase;
> So your barns will be filled with plenty,
> And your vats will overflow with new wine.

Wealth does not guarantee—nor disqualify—righteousness or spirituality.

This point might seem obvious, but remember the context of God's plan for the descendants of Abraham. Their obedience as a nation would produce God's blessing; their disobedience would bring His discipline. This truth was perverted by some to include the notion that personal wealth was a sign of God's approval, while personal misfortune was a sign of His curse or disapproval. Therefore, some people would equate wealth with righteousness or superiority and poverty with sinfulness or inferiority.

Is this concept really that far removed from the way we think today? Or is it the "logic" behind the practice of loading church boards with the most wealthy and influential people in the congregation? Do we really select spiritual leadership for Christian organizations based on godliness, or do we sometimes succumb to the false standard of God's supposed seal of approval based on someone's bank book? And what about the modern practice of making celebrities of those who profess Christ and happen also to possess great wealth?

It is clear from Proverbs that at least some "ruthless men retain riches." Proverbs is also clear that one who is "greedy for gain troubles his own house," and that there will always be those who have gained their wealth, at least in part, through dishonesty. In other words, wealth can reveal the fruits of godly character, or it can reveal an inordinate desire to accumulate wealth through any means. The question is: How do we tell the difference?[11]

According to Proverbs, we must look beyond a person's material status to the more important aspects of character and virtue. The next time we select a board of elders, perhaps we should remember that a poor man who walks in integrity is better than a rich man of questionable character. And we should examine ourselves as well, making sure that our motives and methods in relation to the making and spending of money are in line with God's Word. We should recognize that a person's financial position neither ensures nor eliminates spiritual depth and quality.[12]

Wealth often reveals the means by which it was acquired.

For the person who has acquired wealth by integrity and because of God's blessing, this is not a threat. For the person who has accumulated wealth through deceit or dishonesty, however, this is a chilling concept.

Proverbs is clear that ill-gotten or unwisely acquired prosperity has a way of exposing its beneficiary. Consider, for example, those who take advantage of the poor. Our society is filled with these kinds of people. In some cities "slum lords" charge impoverished immigrants outrageous rent for substandard accommodations, only because they know they can get away with it. Drug dealers prey on the boredom of poor teenagers, giving "free samples" of addictive drugs in order to guarantee desperate customers a week or two later. "Reputable" business people encourage the poor to collateralize homes and possessions, looking forward with relish to subsequent repossessions and evictions.

No matter what has brought the poor to their position of poverty, God has strong words for those who would take advantage of them. He warns that the person who "oppresses the poor to increase his riches . . . will surely come to poverty." Likewise, the person who increases his wealth by usury and extortion of the poor is actually collecting wealth to be given over to those who pity the poor. And, if that were not enough, the Lord Himself will plead the cause of the poor who are robbed simply because they are poor, and He will "plunder the soul of those

---

11. 11:16; 15:27; 20:10, 14, 17, 23; 21:6.
12. 19:1.

who plunder them." By contrast, the person who freely gives to the poor, says the sage, "lends to the LORD," and the Lord Himself "will pay back what he has given."[13]

The Law of Moses made provisions for the poor of Israel to be taken care of by those who had plenty, so caring about the poor in the land was a sure sign of obedience to the Word of God. And God would not let that go unrecognized. This is certainly true today, especially when applied to caring for those in need within a local fellowship.

Another way in which ill-gotten wealth might reveal the true character of the one who has acquired it is through eventual consequences, or cause and effect. The vivid picture in Proverbs 1:8–19 of those who seek wealth through criminal activity concludes with the destruction of the criminals themselves (v. 19). Whether we see this in the fatal shooting of a teenager robbing a liquor store or the jailing of a white-collar embezzler, it is a true principle that should cause us to resolve ourselves to absolute honesty and integrity in all our financial affairs. Because the "treasures of wickedness profit nothing," we should seek the day-to-day "righteousness" that "delivers from death." Because "wealth gained by dishonesty will be diminished," we should stick to hard work to earn our increase.[14]

Whether through trickery, dishonesty, unfair oppression of the poor, or usury, the end result of our quest for wealth will often reveal the way it was obtained.

Wealth has absolutely no bearing on our relationship with God or how we will spend eternity.

How wonderful it is that God does not accept us into His kingdom based on how much wealth we can acquire! This was a point about which many were confused even at the time of Christ. One's financial status was often looked upon as a harbinger of an individual's status in the kingdom of God. That's why the rich young ruler went away sorrowfully when he was challenged by Jesus to make good on his profession of obedience to God's Word. Christ instructed him to "sell all that you have and distribute to the poor, and you will have treasure in heaven; and come, follow Me."[15]

Contrary to what the Pharisees taught, material wealth was

13. 22:16; 28:8; 22:22–23; 19:17.
14. 10:2; 13:11.
15. Luke 18:22–23.

not and is not a measure of one's acceptability before God. Or, contrary to what the prosperity theologians teach today, wealth is not a measure of one's faith in Jesus Christ. Quite frankly, material wealth in and of itself has nothing to do with one's status in relation to salvation. "Riches do not profit in the day of wrath," wrote the sage, "but righteousness delivers from death." For those who might arrogantly think that material prosperity covers a multitude of sins, he also wrote, "He who trusts in his riches will fall, but the righteous will flourish like foliage."[16]

Acceptability before God comes for us just as it did for the Old Testament believer—by grace, through faith, based on blood. A fat checkbook does not prove one's acceptability before God, nor does a luxurious house or an expensive set of clothes. It should be said, too, that a lavish, impressive church building proves nothing about a congregation's relationship with the Lord, even if some claim that a massive monument of architecture is a "good witness" to the community. Wealth simply does not equal righteousness.

SOME FACTS ABOUT LIFE AND DEBT

It's amazing, isn't it, that debt was as much a problem in the ancient Near East as it is today. Why else would the sage pass along God's wisdom concerning indebtedness, surety, and over-obligation?

The popular Christian view of what the Bible has to say about debt is that the only kind of debt the Bible speaks about negatively is that which is unpayable. In other words, debt that is within a person's ability to repay is not true debt; debt beyond a person's ability to repay, however, is condemned.

The book of Proverbs makes a number of statements about debt and borrowing that are relatively simple to understand. The clearest statement, in fact, apparently passes no moral judgment on the practices of borrowing or lending. It simply tells us the way it is: "The rich rules over the poor, and the borrower is servant to the lender." Restated, we might say that those who have money generally exercise power over those who don't, and those who borrow money are controlled by those who lend it.[17]

This twofold statement obviously is true whether or not the

16. Prov. 11:4; 11:28.
17. 22:7.

borrower has the ability to repay. Consider a home mortgage, for example. The bank able to lend the money necessary for a home purchase is in a superior position, and the person seeking the loan definitely is in an inferior position. Moreover, if the loan is approved, there is a very real sense in which the borrower will "serve" the lender. A significant percentage of the borrower's energies will be devoted each week to earning enough money to pay a portion of the debt, along with massive interest charges. What the purchaser plans for the future will revolve around the ability to keep paying on the loan, and any potential for a move to a different location will hinge on this ability to sell the house and retire the mortgage or to put together financing on a new home. In our day, borrowing in this manner is practically the only way to own a home. However, that does not make this principle any less true. The borrower is still servant to the lender.

Looking beyond the practicality of buying a house or car, our Christian ranks today are filled with those whose debts have far exceeded the boundaries of reason. Stemming from a pursuit of those things money can buy, there are borrowers who are chronically enslaved to the lenders of consumer credit. If all our debt service was totalled, our collective average hourly salaries were figured into our total monthly debt obligation, it could be that we are working five or six hours a day just to pay off our consumer loans. The greatest tragedy is that we are servants of our lenders for most of the day, servants of ourselves and our families for the bulk of the remaining time, and servants of the Lord least and last of all.

What is the answer? Since we cannot wish ourselves out of debt tomorrow (wouldn't that be nice?), perhaps the best first step would be to cultivate a true view of that concept we call "credit." Like many misnomers in our culture, "credit" is not credit at all. In fact, it is just the opposite!

What is true credit? Consider, for example, that you want to buy a new stereo from an electronics store. You can't come up with the purchase price right now, but the owner agrees to let you drop by each payday and pay $100 toward the price. He will keep the stereo, he won't charge any interest rate or layaway fee, and when the stereo is entirely paid for, you can take it home. Each time you drop by the store and pay $100, what is it you come away with? You come away with a receipt showing $100 more *credit* toward the purchase price. Your account is *credited* with the money you pay, and when the *credit* you've paid equals the price of the stereo, the merchandise is yours. That is credit.

What, then, is this thing we call "credit"? Simply put, it is debt—or at least the potential for it. A "credit line" of $1,000 is actually a "debt potential" for that amount. When you buy something "on credit," you are actually buying it "on debt." Carrying the terminology all the way through, we could say that a "credit card" in reality is a "debt card."

Why play with the terminology in this way? To remind ourselves that the credit so readily available and easily obtained in our economy today is waiting to put us more and more into the position of the "borrower," who in turn is a servant of the lender.

The concept of Proverbs 22:7 is so simple even a child can understand it. But just in case a child has a problem understanding the truth behind credit cards, try this experiment. Show a child your wallet with $5 in it and ask, "How much money do I have?" The child will answer, "Five dollars." Then show the child a credit card, explain that it has a "credit limit" of $1,000, and ask again, "How much money do I have?" If the child answers "A thousand and five dollars," it's time for an explanation of the difference between true credit and debt. If he answers, "You still have $5," let him handle your finances!

For those who do have debt service to pay, Proverbs has some ready advice concerning promptness of payment:

> Do not withhold good from those to whom it is due,
> When it is in the power of your hand to do so.
> Do not say to your neighbor,
> "Go, and come back,
> And tomorrow I will give it,"
> When you have it with you.

The godly person will pay promptly; if promptness of payment is simply not possible, he will handle all his accounts with absolute honesty and candor. Interestingly enough, creditors often respond favorably to those who cannot pay but are entirely honest and straightforward. (If you think you need help in this area, please seek counseling!)[18]

There is one other area related to debt that the Scriptures repeatedly warn us about, and that is the area of becoming "surety," or "security," for someone else. Proverbs 6:1–5 not

18. 3:27-28.

only warns us of the folly of this move, it also gives us sage advice about how to attempt a remedy. The situation itself is characterized by words normally used to describe a fowler's snare and the hapless bird caught in it. In this case, the snare is that of guaranteeing someone else's loan with your own assets. Why is this such folly? Logically speaking, it includes the same principle of the borrower serving the lender, only in this case the one providing "surety," the co-signer, has no control over his own destiny. Instead of being dependent on his own integrity and ability to repay, the co-signer has placed himself entirely at the mercy of someone else's character and resources. The co-signer may become a servant of the lender without ever getting to use the money, or services, or goods, or any other benefit of the loan. Horror stories abound when it comes to relationships that have been ruined, families that have been split, friendships that have been ended, and assets that have been lost because of the unwise practice of co-signing. Unless we are absolutely and intimately familiar with someone and their ability to repay, we should never collateralize our own assets for the benefit of another borrower. And even then—even in the case of a friend—we should think twice![19]

The remedy for the situation is not pretty, nor is it a sure thing. What it involves is swallowing our pride, humbling ourselves, going immediately to the lender, and pleading with heartfelt request to be released from that obligation. That is the only solution once the bad move has been made, and it remains to be seen whether it will work.

The best solution, of course, is prevention. If we don't want to suffer the consequences of becoming surety for a stranger, we should hate even the thought of doing it.[20]

WHAT ABOUT POVERTY?

With the upsurge in compassion for the homeless of our country, a debate has begun to rage among religious leaders. At one end of the spectrum are those who contend that all poor are victims of society and should be attended to with gifts of money, food, and shelter, and that all who claim to be Christians are responsible for taking care of all poor and homeless. At the other extreme are those who claim that all the impoverished are there

19. 17:18; 22:26–27.
20. 11:15.

by their own doing, that they need to pull themselves up by their own bootstraps, and that if their situation does not improve, it is because of their own laziness and lack of initiative.

Fortunately, God's Word is more balanced, realistic, and equitable than either of these extremes. Before we consider what Proverbs has to say about the poor, we need to remind ourselves again that the Mosaic law made provision for the poor of the land through the generosity of those who were more fortunate. Corners of the fields were to be left unharvested, fields were to be left for the poor to glean, and every sabbatical year was to include the forgiveness of unpayable debts. In other words, the people of Israel were to care for the poor of Israel. It is significant that God never gave laws that mandated care for the poor outside the community of faith, though—as we will see—compassion on all the poor is a manifestation of godliness.

Now let's consider some of the wisdom found in Proverbs concerning poverty.

Poverty does not disqualify anyone spiritually.

In a nutshell, poverty does not preclude godliness. In fact, Proverbs seems to teach just the opposite: that poverty may enhance godliness, while wealth may take the edge off godliness. For example, while the wealthy person may answer people with roughness and insensitivity, the poor person will learn how to use "entreaties," or gentle persuasion. The poor can walk in integrity, they can possess great spiritual "riches" in spite of their material lack, and they deserve the dignity of not being mocked, which is actually an affront against God.[21]

In short, though poverty is not desirable, it is not a spiritual disqualification. There will even be cases, according to Proverbs 28:11, in which the poor man will have discernment exceeding that of the rich.

Poverty is not desirable.

There are two ways in which people become impoverished. Some are poor through no fault of their own, while others are poor because of their own doing.

The facts revealed in Proverbs concerning the realities of poverty are useful in both cases. For those who are impoverished through no fault of their own, the cruel facts should cause those

21. 18:23; 19:1; 13:7; 17:5.

not trapped in poverty to respond with more understanding and compassion. For those who are impoverished by their own doing—or *might* end up in poverty by choosing the way of foolishness—the harsh facts about poverty's hardships should cause them to think twice about the way in which they conduct their lives.

What do we learn from Proverbs about a life of poverty? We learn that it is destructive. Proverbs 10:15 probably refers to the way in which the poor are the first and most plentiful to die in times of crisis. Epidemics, wars, and natural disasters always seem to cause more of the poor to die than any other class. We also learn that poverty is lonely, that the poor man is hated even by his own neighbor, and that he is separated from his friend. And we learn that the poor person is perpetually at the mercy of the rich.[22]

In light of these disadvantages, it is not surprising that God requires the righteous to respond to the poor with sympathy.

Poverty can be the consequence of laziness, indulgence, excess, or immorality.

Many are poor by no choice or will of their own. On the other hand, however, the ranks of the poor include many who are suffering the consequences of bad choices, of living foolishly, of rejecting God's wisdom. In addition, many of the "innocent poor," in fact, are products of the "willful poor." Many women and children who are genuinely trapped in a poverty cycle, for example, are poor because of the foolishness of someone else.

The Bible never condemns the status of being poor, but it does warn sternly against behavior that can result in poverty. The point here is that we *not* look at someone in poverty and assume that they are guilty of violating these principles, but that we be warned away from behavior that will result in poverty and that we properly advise those who want to escape the poverty they are in. Clearly the presentation of God's principles for avoiding or escaping poverty is never justification for condemning or ridiculing the poor.

What kinds of decisions and behavior can result in poverty, and how can we escape its clutches? Above all else, the best way to avoid poverty is to work hard. Proverbs encourages individual effort by reminding us that "in all labor there is

22. 10:15; 14:20; 19:4; 22:7.

profit," while by contrast "idle chatter leads only to poverty." These two statements do not oversimplify but place the greatest hope for escaping poverty squarely on the shoulders of the individual, not in handouts and giveaways.[23]

As a matter of fact, Proverbs seems to indicate that a welfare society (one which provides giveaways beyond the sustenance level) will kill an individual's incentive to work because "the person who labors, labors for himself, for his hungry mouth drives him on." By contrast, working to provide for one's own needs will bring a satisfaction that can never be found on the receiving end of perpetual, non-motivating handouts. The sage tells us that it is the one who cultivates his own land who will be satisfied with the bread it produces and that the payment earned by a man's hands will be given to him.[24]

What is the widest avenue to poverty? There are several, not the least of which is laziness. Laziness involves more than a realization that working for one's livelihood involves effort and toil. It is a total disdain for work. It is the mistaken belief that work is part of the curse of the fall—an idea which some misinformed Bible teachers continue to teach.

The truth is that even before man's fall and God's curse on the earth, Adam and Eve were given meaningful work to do. They were to "subdue" the earth and "have dominion," or rule, over it as God's representatives. Moreover, God placed Adam in the garden to "tend" it and "keep" it. In an unfallen world, work was not foreign to the human race, nor was it troublesome. It was divinely ordered and meaningful.[25]

The fall of the human race, however, changed all that. Because of man's sin and God's curse on an earth which was now under Satan's dominion, work would involve "toil" and "sweat," though through that process it would yield a livelihood. Because man chose Satan as a taskmaster rather than God, the task at times would be troublesome and would involve much effort. But God promised that toil and sweat will, indeed, provide bread to eat.[26]

The problem with laziness is that it disdains the process necessary to receive the product. The lazy man wants the blessings of God without accountability to God. That is why Proverbs so

23. 14:23a; 14:23b.
24. 16:26; 12:11.
25. Gen. 1:28; 2:15.
26. Gen. 3:17–19.

often associates laziness with character traits that are contrary to righteousness. That is why in society we can observe a certain "morality of laziness," a mind-set that resents righteousness, dodges accountability, revels in immorality, and expresses continual rebellion. Laziness is not only a problem, it is a symptom of the more serious problem of rebellion against God. And one of the consequences of laziness, immorality, and excess is poverty (though we need to remember that poverty does not automatically indicate the presence of these problems). This is the plight of the "sluggard," who is also a "fool" or "slothful" man. He is not lazy because he is poor; he is poor because he is lazy, rebellious, and self-centered.

The status of the lazy poor does not keep them from wanting the best in life. "The soul of a sluggard desires, and has nothing," we are told, while "the soul of the diligent shall be made rich." But it does not make the fool any more receptive to correction: "Poverty and shame will come to him who disdains correction, but he who regards reproof will be honored."[27]

As we have already seen, the lazy man degenerates further, to the point where he will not even prepare the food he has foraged or lift his hand from the bowl to his mouth. All he is interested in is logging more "rack time," turning on his bed like a door on its hinges. Rather than pounding the pavement looking for a job, he will spend his time in front of the TV, watching movies late into the night (when, interestingly enough, most ads for employment agencies and trade schools are aired). And when he does get a job, his "slack hand" loses it for him, and returns him to his sorry state.

Among this category of poor we will also find those who have at one time gained wealth through dishonesty, through deceit, or through an early, easy windfall. This includes people who throw money away on state lotteries, hoping to get rich from a process that is far less likely to hit them than a bolt of lightning or a meteorite! Isn't it interesting, particularly in light of Proverbs 28:22, that some of those who win lottery jackpots are broke again within a year or two?[28]

The lazy always have an excuse for not working, and they believe their troubles can be solved only by others giving them what they want or need. Ultimately, the foolish, unwise, rebellious disposition of the lazy poor can lead to death, as Proverbs

27. Prov. 13:4; 13:18.
28. 13:11; 21:6; 20:21.

21:25 warns: "The desire of the slothful kills him, for his hands refuse to labor."[29]

The only real answer for this person is repentance for his hatred for the way God has ordered the world and the pursuit of the one true God who can repair his life. Though it will not guarantee material security, it is the only hope for contentment in this life!

Poverty should be looked on with compassion and understanding.

After so much discussion of money and finances, this is an appropriate point on which to conclude a discussion of poverty.

There may be no easier way to become proud and haughty than through the accumulation of material things. Our culture assumes that wealth equals superiority, and few believers escape that indoctrination. The Bible, however, sternly warns against condemnation and oppression of the poor. As we have observed, while many are poor because of their own foolishness, there are many who are poor because of unavoidable circumstances. The wise person recognizes this fact and seeks to respond appropriately.

While the fool may take advantage of the poor to gain wealth, the wise person recognizes that the sovereignty of God is as much responsible for the poverty of the poor as for the security of the affluent. Therefore, the righteous person "considers the cause of the poor," extends a hand to the poor and needy, and displays righteous generosity that becomes part of the solution rather than perpetuating the problem.[30]

Some years ago in central California, there was a Christian businessman whose furnishings and appliance business flourished. Interestingly enough, a large part of his clientele were the poor of the community. They were not the lazy poor, but the working poor—migrant farm workers, minorities, those in manual labor jobs. They flocked to this man's business not because they would receive a handout, but because they would receive fair treatment and consideration no one else would give them. And from the profits of his business, the businessman supported dozens of missionaries and various ministries in the community.

What made this man—who has long since gone home to be with the Lord—so compassionate toward the working poor?

29. 21:17; 22:13; 26:13; 30:15.
30. 22:16, 22; 29:13; 29:7; 31:20; 11:25–26.

One look inside his wallet would have provided the answer, for it contained an old, black-and-white photo of an impoverished child, standing in the dirt of a Depression-era farm labor camp. He was that child.

> The generous soul will be made rich,
> And he who waters will also be watered himself.
> The people will curse him who withholds grain,
> But blessing will be on the head of him who sells it.[31]

---

31. 11:25–26.

CHAPTER 3

Family Wisdom

THE PRIORITY OF FAMILY

THERE'S A MOVEMENT in evangelical circles today that expresses deep concern over the effects of public education on our children—and rightfully so. Over the past 30 years, public education has become a stronghold for humanism, evolutionary thought, anti-religious bias, and moral relativism. At the elementary level, children are exposed to curricula that may include New Age philosophy, Eastern mysticism, or even occultism in the guise of "values clarification" or "progressive education." At the high school level, sexually explicit material, contraceptives, and abortion referrals are far more welcome than the moral precepts of the Bible.

It is a grave situation. According to experts, classroom experiences amount to about *7 percent* of the influence on a child's life from birth to adulthood. By contrast, church and Sunday school account for only *1 percent* of the influence in a child's life during the same period of time. What is most startling, however, is that home and family life account for the remaining *92 percent* of influence on a child from the cradle to college! In other words, if priorities need to be chosen in campaigning for more positive influences on our homes and families, the overwhelming majority of our time, thought, effort, and work needs to be applied to the family itself.

Obviously public education, public ministry, and public politics are important, especially in today's world. But God's Word clearly indicates that the foundational building block of every society—in every age—is the family unit. The family is the incubator of every culture, breeding in a self-contained microcosm that which will determine the course of future morality, philosophy, and spirituality.

This means that even more important than conducting campaigns *for* the family is conducting campaigns *in* the family. Before we begin to lament the direction our country or culture is going, we'd better be ready to look inside the walls of our homes and learn in what direction our families are going, because, as the title of Charles Swindoll's book so astutely suggests, "Home is where life makes up its mind."

From the very beginning, God has emphasized the priority of the family. In Genesis 2:24, precisely between the creation of Eve and the consummation of the first marriage, we are told that for the perfect completeness of husband and wife "shall a man leave his father and mother and be joined to his wife, and they shall become one flesh." Not only does this verse show us God's idea of the sanctity of sexual oneness, it also shows that from the very beginning He has considered the family unit—starting with husband and wife—to be a sacred priority. Even before the fall of the human race, the continuation of God's pinnacle of creation depended on *leaving* as well as *cleaving*.

By killing one or more animals to provide clothing to cover their nakedness immediately following the fall, God taught Adam and Eve that blood must be shed to cover the shame of their sin. Not only did they understand the significance of this, they apparently instructed their sons Cain and Abel in the matter, as we can see in the episode in which both sons brought an offering before the Lord. Apparently each son responded differently to the family instruction, as shown by God's response to their offerings and attitudes before Him. Nevertheless, what they knew about God they learned within their family.[1]

The rest of the book of Genesis traces the genetic line of God's people—but even more importantly, it traces the legacy of faith in God's covenant promises that are preserved and perpetuated in *families*. Salvation in the Old Testament, as in the New, was by faith in God's covenant promises. It was not automatically inherited by birthright. Jacob got confused on that point and sought to scheme his way into the inheritance by bloodline or legal heirship rather than by faith. But for all his faults, he had been instructed well enough within his family to know that what God offered was what he wanted. Faith in the true God was perpetuated from Abraham to Isaac, to Jacob, and on to Joseph and the other children of Israel.

---

1. Gen. 3:21; 4:3–8.

As the nation grew in size and spent 400 years in Egypt, it was the family unit that kept it distinct and separate from the Egyptian culture around it. Even though the children of Israel lost much of their knowledge about God during that time, they preserved their distinctiveness in family units, so much so that when the time of the Exodus came, they proceeded "in orderly ranks," most probably according to family units (or "armies") in contrast to the "mixed multitude" that was also with them.[2]

Thereafter, every time God acted on behalf of the nation of Israel, He commanded that the event—as well as what it meant—be "remembered" to each generation afterward. When God instituted the first Passover, for instance, He said: "And you shall observe this thing as an ordinance for you and your sons forever . . . and it shall be, when your children say to you, 'What do you mean by this service?' that you shall say, 'it is the Passover sacrifice of the LORD, who passed over the houses of the children of Israel in Egypt when He struck the Egyptians and delivered our households.'" This same command was given in regard to the eating of unleavened bread, the consecration of the firstborn, the memorial at the Jordan River, and numerous other testimonies and memorials in the Old Testament.[3]

Not only were the families within God's people to actively teach their children about the great deeds of God, they also were responsible to teach them the Word of God. As Moses proclaimed to the nation in Deuteronomy 4:9–10, "Only take heed to yourself, and diligently keep yourself, lest you forget the things your eyes have seen, and lest they depart from your heart all the days of your life. And teach them to your children and grandchildren, especially concerning the day you stood before the LORD your God in Horeb, when the LORD said to me, 'Gather the people to Me, and I will let them hear My words, that they may learn to fear Me all the days they live on the earth, and that they may teach their children.'"

How would godly parents perpetuate faith in the Lord from generation to generation? First and foremost—more than through the ministry of the priests or the proclamation of the prophets—it is by the example and instruction provided in the home.

Even circumcision—the sign of faith in the covenant promises of God—was designed to remind parents of the importance of continuing the legacy of saving faith within their families. The

2. Ex. 13:18; see Ex. 12:38, 51.
3. Ex. 12:24, 26–27; 13:8, 14; Josh. 4:5–7.

influence of parents on their children, not the cutting of flesh, would pass on to the next generation a predisposition toward faith. The faithfulness of families to do this would allow Israel to stand, or the failure of families to fulfill their role would cause Israel to fall into apostasy and idolatry. And just like today, it would take only one generation of God's people becoming comfortable and complacent in order to guarantee that the next generation would become spiritually numb.

Therefore, the faithful saints of the Old Testament took it upon themselves to order their families as the primary institution of life, where saving faith in the true God was cultivated and godly maturity was harvested. It was not a matter of family for the sake of family, or family for the sake of success, but family for the sake of giving glory to God, not only in the present generation, but also in the next, and the one after it, and so on.

And because God had covenanted that through Abraham's offspring all the nations of the world would be blessed, preservation of faith in those covenant promises included a vision for being a "light to the Gentiles," a sentinel for righteousness in an unrighteous world, the place to learn how to live wisely in a foolish world. The mission of the family has always been, in the words of one organization today, "to know Him, and to make Him known."

It was in precisely that spirit that the Proverbs were given. The book of Proverbs is the epitome of family instruction, not only as a guidebook for parents, but as a resource for children and a primer on family interaction in general. Not only does Proverbs contain the words of a godly father to his son, it echoes advice given by godly parents a generation earlier. It provides God's perspective on family life from many angles, including childhood, youth, maturity, and old age. Most importantly, it is His "family counseling," not for the sake of comfort or success, but for the sake of godliness, righteousness, and witness. It is designed to glorify Him, not the family.

God's priority is the family. He commanded it, Proverbs proves it, and Israel ultimately experienced the consequences of ignoring it.

This connection between God's intent for families, the content of Proverbs, and the balance of Israel's history is not imaginary. Proverbs contains a warning that eventually was not heeded, and that cost the children of Israel discipline at the hands of Gentile nations:

> There is a generation that curses its father,
> And does not bless its mother.
> There is a generation that is pure in its own eyes,
> Yet is not washed from its filthiness.
> There is a generation—oh, how lofty are their eyes!
> And their eyelids are lifted up.
> There is a generation whose teeth are like swords,
> And whose fangs are like knives,
> To devour the poor from off the earth,
> And the needy from among men.[4]

Today, as in Israel's day, the first and greatest responsibility for changing the world around us does not lie with Christian schools and church programs, it does not depend on "pro-family" legislation or parachurch groups, and it does not even rest with those who sacrifice their families for the sake of public ministry. According to God's Word, the divine priority for perpetuating a legacy of "knowing Him and making Him known" lands squarely within the confines of the family. The more we concentrate our efforts there, the more results we will see. The more we ignore it or try to work around it, the less we will reap in terms of lasting rewards.

This, in fact, is why the New Testament is so adamant about the qualifications of godly leadership, including a godly family life: "For if a man does not know how to rule his own house, how will he take care of the church of God?" If you want to know what anyone's spiritual life is really like, catch it at home! Follow it around while it does its chores. Listen in on it during family spats. Watch it when it's tired.[5]

And if we want to know what family life can really be like—and should be like—we need to look into the book of Proverbs.

THE PURPOSE OF THE FAMILY

Most believers are familiar with the name of Jonathan Edwards, whose pioneer faith influenced the earliest years of America. Some even know Edwards was the product of a godly home. What few Christians have heard, however, is the way the Edwards family continued to nurture that faith long after its famous patriarch was gone.

More than 400 of Edwards' descendants reportedly have been

4. Prov. 30:11–14.
5. 1 Tim. 3:5.

traced. Among them were 14 college presidents and 100 professors, and at least 100 Christian ministers, missionaries, and Bible
teachers. More than 100 became lawyers and judges, some 60 or
more doctors, and more than 50 notable authors and editors.
And it is said that nearly every significant American industry has
benefited from one or more offspring of Edwards' lineage.

God's assigned purpose for the family is to honor Him and to
perpetuate faith and obedience. As parents, we have no higher
calling than to build our offsprings' trust in God and to construct
a solid foundation upon which they can do the same for their
children and their children's children after them. And there is no
question that He will honor our efforts with lasting results.

Of course, there are a lot of other wonderful things family life
provides. Regardless of the unfortunate and inaccurate stereotypes propagated by tasteless television shows ranging from "All
in the Family" to "The Simpsons," God designed the family to
provide refuge, fulfillment, completion, and satisfaction in life.
But if the purpose of the family is to honor God and perpetuate a
legacy of faith and obedience, then the nature of the family
(especially in regard to parents) should reflect the nature of God.
The family should be a living, instructive model of God's relationship with His people.

If God loves and thus disciplines, the family should love and
thus discipline. If a righteous, mature life makes the Father glad,
then righteous, mature offspring will make their parents glad. If
a wise saint heeds the instructions of God's Word, then a wise
son will heed his parents' words. If the Father continually desires
the best for His children, then parents should continually desire
the best for their children.[6]

We learn from Scripture that God desires from His people the
same kind of faithfulness that exists between a husband and wife.
He cares for His people like a father cares for his son. He
cherishes His people like a nursing mother cherishes her baby.
And He admonishes and corrects His people just like a loving
parent will admonish and correct a child.

Basically, then, it is the purpose of the family that gives
meaning to the principles of family life. The instructions of
Proverbs, ripped out of their biblical context and applied arbi-
trarily with no view toward the purpose of building and perpetuating a righteous faith in God, might have some effect, but

---

6. Heb. 12:6; see Prov. 3:11–12.

they will not have the effect God desires. They will be nothing more than rules without reality, which will produce superficiality rather than substance.

Too many "Christian," or more accurately "religious," parents desire a rule book or an instruction manual that will tell them how to "straighten out" their families. Having lived their lives in a steady state of spiritual lukewarmness, they suddenly find their families are in trouble and begin to scramble for a quick formula for success or a place to dump their kids for reform. Unfortunately this is the wrong place to begin. The Bible doesn't offer quick-fix solutions. What it does offer, however, is the best first step: "The fear of the Lord is the beginning of knowledge." Total personal commitment to Him is the place to start. After that, the observations, admonitions, and instructions of Proverbs and other passages offer a wealth of information which—with the overall purpose of family squarely in focus—can help us on our way.

Does the Word of God guarantee success for families? No, no more than it guarantees spiritual maturity for individuals. We simply cannot make spiritual decisions for our children, nor can our children make spiritual decisions for us. Adam and Eve lost Cain. Isaac and Rebekah lost Esau. David lost Absalom. Even the words of Proverbs maintain a conditional tone: "My son, *if* you receive my words . . . *then* you will understand the fear of the LORD, and find the knowledge of God."[7]

Yet Proverbs does provide an optimistic outlook—far more optimistic than some "Christian" writers today! The popular message today is that every failure, as well as every success, is the ultimate result of environment and influence. If children fail, it is their parents' fault. If parents are inadequate, it is the fault of their family background. And so on. This places an enormous burden on parents to be perfect, and they live in perpetual fear that somehow they might create a dysfunctional environment that will cause the downfall of their children. It also provides an oft-used escape hatch for rebellious adult children to blame their spiritual shortfalls on someone beside themselves and their own sinfulness.

By contrast the message of Proverbs revolves around parents' loving cultivation of faith in the true God and the wisdom of obedience to Him. These are the essentials of life, and they are best learned within the context of the family. Rather than dwell-

7. Prov. 2:1, 5.

ing on personality types, birth order, emotional scars, or any other outside influence, Proverbs talks about real thoughts, real actions, real decisions, real accountability, real consequences, and real rewards. It teaches us about the responsibilities of parents, but it also addresses the willful choices children (both young and adult) can and do make.

Proverbs' point of view might seem terribly naive and simplistic in our sophisticated society, but it is the best wisdom the God of the universe has to offer.

The principle of instruction

> If a man has a stubborn and rebellious son who will not obey the voice of his father or the voice of his mother, and who, when they have chastened him, will not heed them, then his father and his mother shall take hold of him and bring him out to the elders of his city, to the gate of his city.... Then all the men of his city shall stone him to death with stones.[8]

This may seem like a harsh place to begin looking at the specific principles of Proverbs, but stop and think about it. This was part of the law of God which formed the national constitution of Israel and governed Jewish life at the very time the Proverbs were written. That means that every Hebrew couple who gave birth to a child would at some time look down at that precious little life and realize, *if we don't teach this child faith and obedience, it could cost him his life*. In other words, the warning of Deuteronomy 21 was given as much for the parents of infants as it was for adult children in rebellion. Just think: capital punishment was imposed then for the same rebellious attitude our culture glorifies and revels in today!

While none of us would advocate a return to considering rebellion against parents as a capital offense, imagine how much more seriously parents would take the responsibility to instruct their children if they could see the consequences that lay ahead. If you ever have the chance to sit in on a felony trial, make a point of finding out where the parents of the accused are sitting and take note of their expressions and appearance. In most cases, few people reflect more pain and sorrow than parents who must sit and watch their children suffer the consequences of foolish living.

That is part of the purpose of Proverbs—to provide for parents

8. Deut. 21:18–19, 21.

some sneak previews of what becomes of children who either are not instructed in the narrow way of wisdom or willfully reject it. These snapshots of the future, in fact, are some of the best and most memorable teaching texts parents can provide for their children. And just as these vignettes frequently appear in a contrasting couplet (i.e., "The wise son... *but* the foolish son..."), parents should not rob their children of the full counsel of God by giving the positive side without the negative. Both are essential for acquiring a working knowledge of life.

The value of this kind of instruction is the pervasive theme throughout the book of Proverbs. In addition to addressing his son directly as "my son," the sage frequently reiterates the value of the instruction he and his wife have provided throughout their child's lifetime. This shows us that the responsibility of parental instruction is the corporate responsibility of both parents.[9]

Further, when we understand the descriptions in terms of that culture, we realize God considers godly instruction to be of greater value than anything else an adult child can take from the home. The "ornaments on your head" and "chains about your neck" in that day were signs of wealth and status obtained through inheritance. This tells us that nothing could be of greater value than sending an adult child out into the world with a steadfast faith in the true God, as well as a conspicuous skill for living.[10]

Though many parents might see this as a mandate for their children to listen to them and remember what they say, it really speaks more strongly of the commitment God requires from the parents. Wise parents make instructing their children in the way of the Lord a priority. Nothing is more important than teaching children about life from God's perspective. No matter what they do or where they go, parents are always looking for methods for communicating to their offspring the realities of wisdom and folly, of righteousness and wickedness, of truth and error.

The wonderful, liberating truth is that this can be done as easily on a fishing trip as during family devotions. It can be done at church or at a football game. Whether the illustration is a pastor's sermon or a drunken baseball fan's undeleted expletives, wise parents use the world and all its illustrations as a living laboratory and the Scriptures as the textbook. Of course, this requires that parents know what the Word of God has to say.

9. Prov. 1:8; see 6:20–21.
10. 1:9.

Don't make the mistake of thinking that "my commands" and "my instructions" mentioned in Proverbs refer to material parents simply pull out of thin air. The instruction, wisdom, law, teaching, sayings, understanding, and commands given in Proverbs were nothing less than the Word of God itself.

For his part, then, the wise child will not forsake the spiritual instruction he has received from his parents. He will "bind them" around his neck, and "write them" on his heart for safe-keeping, just as an heir wears his prized heirlooms for security and protection. He will "treasure" them "within," and will "retain" them both in his sleep and in his waking hours. He will carry his godly parents' instruction with him for a lifetime for the "length of days and long life and peace they will add" to him.[11]

The principle of correction

If parenthood were simply a matter of sitting children down and giving them a good pep talk every day, of filling their minds with instruction, and then turning them loose in the world, we would all be much happier! The truth, however, is that along with instructing them in the *right* way, we must also warn them about the *wrong* way and correct them when they stray. In putting this parental responsibility in perspective, it helps to make a distinction between *correction* and *discipline,* even though sometimes in Scripture the two are synonymous.

Generally speaking, *correction* is instruction in how not to live life wisely. It is advice against a certain way of thinking or acting. It is a course correction or change in route. *Discipline,* on the other hand, is the method of correction that sometimes must be used. It is the weight behind the advice, or the less severe consequence that will bring about a change in order to avoid the more severe consequence.

On one major league baseball team, a highly paid player of superstar status went into a terrible batting slump. Game after game went by, but he failed to reach first base in more than twenty times at bat. His manager's first attempt at a remedy was *correction*—he ordered long hours of work with a batting coach, stints in the batting cage, slow-motion videos, and other forms of instruction. After a week or so of no change, the manager noticed that the player's problem seemed to be one of teach-ability not technique. His problem was not action, it was atti-

11. 3:3; 6:21–22; 2:1; 3:2.

tude. So the skipper sat him out—benched him until further notice. For someone used to the fans' adoration and attention from the press, that was *discipline*. The results were almost immediate. In practice, the player was a changed man. His apathy was replaced by intensity and concentration. And it wasn't long before he *earned* a spot in the team's starting lineup.

In Proverbs many passages draw a line between these two methods of instruction. Correction is offered most frequently in the form of negative examples. Some of these are brief one-liners, such as "a foolish son is the grief of his mother," while others are more lengthy, like the episode involving "a young man devoid of understanding" and the crafty harlot. Anytime one of these corrective verses is taught, one of the first questions that comes to mind is *whom is this speaking to—the parents, or the child?* Probably the best answer to that is *both*.[12]

Consider Proverbs 10:5: "He who gathers in summer is a wise son, but he who sleeps in harvest is a son who causes shame." If taken seriously by parents, it is a verse that should motivate them to teach their children the value of personal industry and the fulfillment that comes from hard work. If taken seriously by adult children who desire to live life wisely, it might motivate them to get off their duffs and find a summer job while the finding is good. Probably what God did *not* intend, however, is for a mom and dad to quote it in front of other adults who happen to be in the living room when Jason or Jenny rolls out of the sack at noon on Saturday!

The corrective value of Proverbs is what keeps us coming back to it again and again. When we read that "a wise son heeds his father's instruction, but a scoffer does not listen to rebuke," we may be convicted that as parents we need to teach obedience to our children while they are young, or we may become convicted that God has a pretty low view of an attitude that scoffs at rebuke or correction. Our own receptiveness to correction can be revolutionized when we understand that "he who disdains instruction despises his own soul, but he who heeds reproof gets understanding." And it would seem that no parent can remain passive if he or she really understands that "a foolish son is a grief to his father, and bitterness to her who bore him."[13]

As for the truly dismal picture of what awaits those who ignore the narrow path of God's wisdom, Proverbs is both

12. 10:1; 7:6–23.
13. 13:1; 15:32; 17:25.

graphic and simple in its language concerning those who not only reject their parents' correction, but reject their parents themselves. We find that "he who mistreats his father and chases away his mother is a son who causes shame and brings reproach," meaning that a rebellious child who turns on his parents brings shame to the entire family. And "Whoever curses his father or his mother, his lamp will be put out in deep darkness" is the warning that total rejection of one's godly upbringing then could have resulted in the dire consequences prescribed by the Law in the Old Testament, or today can become a "sin unto death" in the language of the New Testament.[14]

For the parent who begins with his or her own relationship with the Lord, however, and makes a priority out of knowing Him and making Him known, there is good news. Understanding that it is our responsibility to seek God, and that it is His responsibility to bless our children, we can put a great deal of confidence in a principle like the one expressed in Proverbs 20:7: "The righteous man walks in his integrity; his children are blessed after him."

The principle of discipline

As we have already mentioned, discipline is a consequence of not heeding correction. It is an unpleasant consequence, though not nearly as unpleasant as that which awaits the person who either ignores it or never has the opportunity to benefit from it. But because it is unpleasant, and because it often hurts, those who receive it mistakenly think that it is incompatible with love. In other words, "If you love me, you won't discipline me."

The message we find in the Bible is precisely the opposite. Both in the nature of God and in the nature of parenthood we find two sides to the same coin: love and correction. In the nature of God, we see a perfect coexistence of love and correction in the truth that God hates sin but loves sinners in the statement "Whom the LORD loves He chastens, and scourges every son whom He receives" (Heb. 12:6). These two facets of His character are in perfect harmony. To perceive either one without the other leads to error. Love requires discipline, and discipline must be administered by love.

The book of Proverbs assumes these two sides of the same coin in application to family life. Very simply, *there is no love*

14. 19:26; 20:20.

without correction; and there should be no correction without love. If we miss this point, we miss the wisdom of Proverbs!

As we see in Proverbs, God is not squeamish about parents disciplining their children. In fact, it can be stated no more plainly than it is in Proverbs 13:24: "He who spares his rod hates his son, but he who loves him disciplines him promptly." This was not written as a sorry attempt at self-justification! It was not given by "the God of the Old Testament," who somehow is different from "the Jesus of the New Testament." And it was not included in God's eternal Word as a principle that would become archaic or outdated. It is eternal truth given to us by an eternally unchanging God.

Parents' natural love for their children presents the unfortunate paradox of wanting them to "turn out" righteous and happy, but it also causes parents to be reticent when it comes to discipline. So God was good enough to lay out the principle for us in black and white! If you love your children, you will discipline them. If you don't discipline them, you must hate them, because you are doing the worst thing in thing in the world for them.

For children that translates, *"If your parents discipline you, they love you. If they don't care what you do or don't discipline you, you'd better start to worry about whether or not they really love you".*

Regardless of the abusive caricature some activists portray as the Bible's teaching on corporal discipline, it is interesting that the book of Proverbs provides the most healthy and balanced picture of parental discipline we can find. It makes it clear that the purpose of discipline is instruction and correction, not punishment. Initially the purpose was to spare the child the grave consequences that were prescribed by the Law, and though we do not live under the Law today, the consequences can be just as fatal, (although they may take longer to have an effect). When the sage says that a spanking will "deliver his soul from hell," he was literally referring to *Sheol,* or the grave. Both Sheol and the grave are *the place of the dead,* which is where the rebellious son would end up if he continued in his rebellion as an adult. Proverbs 23:13–14, therefore, might be paraphrased, "Whatever you do, don't hesitate to correct your child. If you spank him now, he won't die from it. In fact, it may save him from death later on."[15]

Though it is difficult for new parents to see anything malicious in the precious new life of a newborn, Proverbs begs all of us to

15. 23:14.

look beyond those incredibly cute first years of life to the consequences of lifelong patterns that can develop during that time. We must force ourselves to see beyond the "snitching" of gum from a classmate to the consequences of shoplifting or car theft. We must abandon our kids-will-be-kids response to a childish scuffle and consider the adult consequences of assault or attempted murder. Though not all adult criminal behavior begins in childhood, much of it does, and Proverbs tells us it is not an irreversible process. But parents must be willing to look at their children's behavior not through rose-colored glasses, but through the reality-colored lenses of God's Word. The truth is that because we are born in sin with a sinful nature that is alive and well from our first moments of life, "foolishness is bound up in the heart of a child." It is as much a sure thing as dirty diapers and 2:00 A.M. feedings![16]

What is the answer? The answer, when necessary, is loving discipline, or (in the words of that culture) the "rod of correction." As we will see, this does not condone hateful brutality; but it does command parental spanking.[17]

The next point that we need to consider is that physical discipline must be administered in love. How do we know? Because the opposite of discipline is *hate*. Only those parents who refuse to consider the consequences their children will suffer if they don't receive correction would refuse them the correction necessary to train them. That is not to say that all children require the same amount of correction. Some children might require only one act of discipline in a year, while others might require one a month, or one a week. Children are just as different from one another as horses and donkeys, but they all need to be trained. Just as a godly horse trainer or a farmer would train his charges with loving care, so parents should do the same, but even more so![18]

As we have already said, love requires discipline, just as discipline requires love. This twofold principle—with an emphasis on loving care—is reiterated in the New Testament: "And you, father, do not provoke your children to wrath, but bring them up in the *training* [discipline] and *admonition* [loving instruction] of the Lord."[19]

A third instruction we find in Proverbs concerns who should

16. 22:15a.
17. 22:15b.
18. 13:24; 26:3.
19. Eph. 6:4.

administer corporal discipline. The primary person is, of course, the parent. While it would be going too far to suggest that corporal punishment administered outside of the home is unscriptural, the great bulk of the responsibility for correction and discipline rests on the parents' shoulders. And as most teachers and school administrators will attest, if it is not taking place in the home, it will do pitifully little good when administered elsewhere.

Proverbs 19:18 admonishes, "Chasten your son while there is hope." This clearly addresses a parent or future parent who, by obeying this command, will help his or her child avoid "destruction," again referring to the eventual consequences of an undisciplined upbringing. By contrast we have already seen that the father who withholds discipline hates his son and, as sociologists are finally admitting, sets him on a course that almost always guarantees trouble. No amount of school detentions, daycare notes, or teachers' referral slips can ever take the place of discipline administered by a loving parent.

How should a parent discipline? Proverbs clearly teaches us the right method. When we read about a "rod for his back," unfortunately a difference in language and culture causes some of us to recoil in horror. In order to understand what the "rod" refers to, however, we need to understand that the Hebrew word for *rod* is the same as the word for the *scepter* which signified the rule of a king and the *staff* with which a shepherd kept his lambs under control. Not only is this a beautiful parallel of the way our Shepherd/King Jesus Christ cares for and disciplines us, it provides us with a vivid picture of our responsibility to "rule" our offspring righteously, and to use the *rod,* or shepherd's staff, only as much as it is necessary to keep our sheep moving in the right direction.

Obviously, in that culture not everyone was a king or a shepherd. Therefore, not everyone actually possessed a rod. It's likely, then, that the rod employed by most parents was appropriated from the nearest bush or small tree. In our parents' day, this little instrument was not too affectionately referred to as a "switch." In the ancient Near East, long before paddles, hairbrushes, or "spanking spoons," it was the "rod," the most readily available—and mercifully flexible—item available.

As for applying it to the *back* of the child in need of discipline, the Hebrew word *gav* referred specifically to the backside of a human being. Most scholars agree that in this context, it undoubtedly refers to that part of the anatomy parents instinctively swat with a switch, the child's "backside," or "seat." The pre-scribed method of discipline, then, is a brief (but effective) spanking on the bottom with nothing more harmful than a switch. That's it, that's all, and no more. It is quite clear there is to be no backhand to the face, no belt across the thighs, no fists, no verbal abuse, and certainly no brutality! Anymore than a sting across the child's bottom, and it will be the parent—not the child—suddenly in a position to experience the discipline of the Lord! *It cannot be overly emphasized that the Bible's instructions concerning physical discipline should not—and cannot—be misconstrued as justification for a parent's physical abuse of a child!*

By the same token, abuses in this area by ungodly parents—and our culture's overreaction against *any* type of physical discipline—should not deter the Christian parent from loving, controlled, level-headed discipline.

Proverbs also is reasonably clear about the types of offenses that might require physical discipline. We have already seen that Proverbs always speaks in terms of wisdom and folly, and that those two categories can be equated with willfully obeying God's standards or openly rebelling against them.

Might it be, then, that physical correction should be based on the spirit of the offense rather than on the letter of it? Perhaps parents should reserve physical correction for those offenses that are based on an active decision to disobey what the child knows is right (such as lying, stealing, disobedience, etc.), rather than involuntary or accidental offenses (like spilling milk, tracking mud on the carpet, etc.). Again, the point of discipline is loving instruction, not retribution.

Finally the book of Proverbs tells us that physical discipline is not the *only* way to correct a child, and that it can never solve problems by itself. "The rod *and reproof* give wisdom" indicates that physical correction without instruction—ideally, from God's Word—will be a waste of time, and that many times reproof alone will do the job of correcting a child.[20]

The point of God's Word is that it is incumbent on parents to correct and discipline their children. In spite of our country's acceptance of "latchkey" parenthood and the television as a babysitter, there is no such thing as putting children on auto-pilot. Even in the earliest year, "a child is known by his deeds, by

20. Prov. 29:15.

whether what he does is pure and right." That means that the behavior a child displays around others (at school, at the neighbors', at daycare) really is the best indication of where he or she is at spiritually, morally, and socially—no matter what we are sure he is really like on the inside. As almost any elementary school teacher can tell us, that is the time it all starts, and that is the time to act.[21]

The sage wrote that "a child left to himself brings shame to his mother." "Correct your son," however, "and he will give you rest; yes he will give delight to your soul."[22]

The principle of training

Though the principles we are looking at are not necessarily meant to be a chronological progression, the concept of training as Proverbs presents it might well be the next logical step in a youth's life following an infancy of instruction and correction and a childhood that includes godly discipline.

If the purpose of a family is to know Him and make Him known, if it has committed itself to perpetuating that legacy in its children, and if it has ordered its priorities accordingly, the results of that hard work and faithful love will begin to show dramatically as a child moves from the spanking stage to the training stage.

What age is that? It differs from family to family and from culture to culture. If our culture is guilty of anything, it is guilty of prolonging childhood. In schools as well as at church and at home, we are so fearful of our children becoming adults who might be different from us that we deny them adulthood well beyond an age when most cultures would consider them grown. Rather than helping them make the transition into adulthood alongside us, we force them to rebel and to assert their adulthood somewhere other than at home—and sometimes under less than wise circumstances.

This process of continuing to treat youth as children well beyond the point at which they are capable of thinking adult thoughts and making adult decisions, very often has an effect quite the opposite of what was intended. In some Christian high schools and even colleges, for example, students are loaded down with rules, rarely (if ever) listened to seriously by teachers and administrators, and generally treated by adults with far less

21. 20:11.
22. 29:15; 29:17.

respect than even adult strangers would receive. Then no one can understand why the same students rebel against the entire Christian structure as soon as they are out from under it, such as a graduation night drinking binge or choosing unsavory friends at college! Unfortunately, the same kind of treatment at home often produces the same results.

By contrast in cultures where youths the same age are *expected* to begin making adult decisions, to accept adult responsibilities, to command the respect worthy of an adult, and in general to *be* an adult, the rate of maturation is much more rapid. Again this same process can be seen in some homes with similar results.

Without doubt, the transitional period from childhood to adulthood—when the child is becoming a thinking adult in the home—is the critical period of time when a son or daughter really begins to acquire understanding based on the years of knowledge they have already received through their parents' instruction. It is the period of time when the lessons of childhood become the habits of life that will stay with them wherever they go. And it is the period of time during which the "training up" process is actually being completed.[23]

This brings up the problem of how to interpret Proverbs 22:6, which reads: "Train up a child in the way he should go, and when he is old he will not depart from it."

A problem arises in relation to this verse because of the many children who, when they were young, genuinely were "trained up" by their parents in Christian belief and behavior. They were in church every Sunday, they professed faith in Christ, and they appeared to be well on their way to full-blown Christian adulthood. Then the teen years set in and all you-know-what broke loose! They openly rebelled, and they chose their own way rather than God's. It is at this point that several explanations are offered in order to try and save face for God's Word.

The first explanation is that someday, when they are old, wayward adult children will return to the way they were trained. In some cases that may be true, but it is untrue in enough cases to still require some kind of explanation for the assurance of Proverbs 22:6.

A second explanation is that this is not a *promise* of God's Word, but a *principle*. In other words, it is generally true, but not always. The problem with this explanation is that Scripture does not really define for us which of God's statements we are to

23. 4:3–5; 6:20–22; 22:6.

understand as promises that are always true and which we are to understand as principles that are true only part of the time. In fact, often there seems to be no distinction between the two. For example, most would agree that Exodus 20:12 gives a general principle that will not always hold true: "Honor your father and your mother, that your days may be long." In Ephesians 6:2, however, we read, " 'Honor your father and mother,' " which is the first commandment *with* a *promise.*" So which is it—a principle, or a promise? The point is that all of God's Word is true, and we begin to tread on thin ice when we try to soften it or qualify it to suit our experience.

But there is a third explanation, one that the book of Proverbs provides for us. The Hebrew phrase "train up" in this passage was agrarian terminology used in reference to training a tree or vine to grow in a particular shape or direction. It was a process that began when the tree was a seedling, and was not completed until the tree was *unchangeably mature.* From that point of maturity onward, no matter what happened, the tree would continue to grow in the shape into which it was trained.

Anyone who has enjoyed a day at one of the Disney theme parks has seen the many fascinating shrubs shaped like animals and fantasy characters. Obviously, these bushes don't just happen. They are the product of years of shaping, trimming, pruning, and training in the way they should go. That process includes taking note of the natural bent of the branches, helping them along by adjusting their growth in various directions, carefully removing some parts while cultivating and nourishing the plant as a whole, and continually trimming away what is unnecessary and nonbeneficial. This is a beautiful picture of the care and cultivation parents can invest in their children's lives. And, like the role of parents, it never really ends.

One problem we've run into in understanding Proverbs 22:6 is putting too low an upper-age limit on the definition of "child." In other words, when an offspring starts driving, or shaving, or dating, we think they are beyond the Proverbs definition of a child, and beyond the process of "training up." But that's not what the context shows us. A careful reading of Proverbs reveals that the training-up process begins at birth and continues until a mature, adult human being leaves the home to live a life of his or her own.

For example, the "son" the sage is still "training up" in Proverbs is old enough to join street robbers, to be tempted by sexual sin, to patronize prostitutes, to get into debt, and to go out drinking. This is no sixth grader! He apparently was still living at home, and his training was not spoken of in the past tense ("I have taught you") until he was at least old enough to need to know how to avoid adultery.[24]

In other words, just about the time many parents think they are beyond the training-up portion of this verse and into the departing portion, they actually are in the toughest part of it— helping that emerging adult make it all the way through the training-up process to maturity. Essentially what this verse is saying is that *if* you succeed in shaping the direction of a child's life from the cradle to mature adulthood—to that point at which he is a self-determining person who chooses the narrow path of righteousness—*then* it will stay with him for the rest of his life.

More than a promise or a principle, Proverbs 22:6 is a *precept.* It is intended to give direction, vision, motivation, and encouragement to parents who are facing that process. The truly wise parent will not see it as a failed promise at the time it is needed most! And most importantly, the wise parent will recognize that all thinking adults have the freedom to choose which way they will go once they reach the final years of the training-up process.

The principle of counsel and its lasting results

One of the beautiful things about a parent/child relationship that has matured is that even after the child has become an adult, the role of wisdom and counsel never ends. What's more, if the training portion of the child's life has been well-engineered, if the child knows the parents really trust and respect his ideas and viewpoints, the role of counsel is assumed by the adult child as well as the parent.

In adulthood as well as in youth, "A wise son *heeds* his father's instruction," but "a fool *despises* his father's instruction." Because of this reciprocal relationship of love and godly respect, "Children's children are the crown of old men, and the glory of children is their father." There is mutual admiration, mutual trust, and mutual appreciation for the godly influence of both father and mother, so that it is not an unrealistic scene when a godly mother's adult children "rise up and call her blessed." For

24. 1:10–19; 2:16–22; 6:1–5, 6–10; 23:29–35; 6:22; 4:11; 5:3.

father and son, "as iron sharpens iron," so one will sharpen the countenance of the other. And even in their old age, parents will be listened to with the respect and dignity due them.[25]

In tragic contrast, the adult child who chooses to turn his or her back on the Lord and on the influence of godly parents will have a life of pain and grief. As we have already discussed, that person will bring dishonor on his entire family, and may even cause his own life to be cut short.[26]

How much better for a family to continually cultivate and nourish a mutual commitment to know the Lord and to make Him known. Beginning with a wholesale commitment to the Lord by both parents, manifested in God's wisdom taught to children in the laboratory of life, and culminating in mature, respectful, adult relationships that continue throughout a lifetime, it is by far a better alternative than what the sitcoms portray!

The fact is that Proverbs offers great optimism and assurance for those who will diligently pursue the Lord and His wisdom. God is capable of great things, but we must follow His instructions, not the least of which is to honor our commitment to Him, overcome our natural shortcomings in family life, and continue the legacy of faith and obedience in our families. In the context of Hebrew culture, *this* is the inheritance that a good man leaves "to his children's children."[27]

Wonderfully, the sage penned three verses that extend this commitment of a godly family toward each generation:

> The father of the righteous will greatly rejoice,
> And he who begets a wise child will delight in him.
> Let your father and your mother be glad,
> And let her who bore you rejoice.
> My son, give me your heart,
> And let your eyes observe my ways.[28]

---

25. 13:1; 15:5; 17:6; 31:28; 27:17; 23:22.
26. 19:26; 20:20.
27. 13:22.
28. 23:24–26.

CHAPTER 4

Marital Wisdom

THE COUPLE WAS on the verge of another spat, and the husband's exasperation was growing. Finally he blurted, "I can't understand why God made you so pretty but so stupid." The wife replied, "That's simple. He made me so pretty so you would marry me. And he made me so stupid so I would marry you."

Civilization has changed greatly over time, but amazingly marriage really hasn't changed at all. It is still a contractual relationship in which two people—of different sexes, from different families, with different backgrounds, tastes, and desires—commit themselves to a lifetime of common experience. It has been called a union that defies management, the world's most expensive way of discovering your faults, and a school of experience in which husband and wife are *clash*mates.

In reality, however, it is potentially the most fulfilling, rewarding, exhilarating, binding, spiritually satisfying of all relationships. The great tragedy in many instances is that wonderful potential is never realized. Even in the best marriages, differences and conflicts threaten the relationship from within, while temptations and distractions threaten from without.

There has been only one ideal marriage, and that was the relationship between Adam and Eve before the Fall. Robert Orben has quipped that Adam and Eve's marriage was ideal because he didn't have to hear about all the men she could have married, and she didn't have to hear about the way his mother cooked! But obviously the truth is far deeper than that. Their marriage was ideal before the Fall because both people were rightly related to God; thus they were rightly related to each other. Because they belonged together by divine design, living and abiding in an ideal relationship with the Designer produced an ideal relationship with each other. Significantly, that divinely appointed relationship did not dissolve when sin entered the picture. The nature of the marriage relationship—one man and one woman—did not change. And the sanctity of an exclusive, covenant relationship between two people did not change.

What did change was the internal factor of a fallen human nature, and the external factor of a cursed, fallen world. These elements would have a profound effect on the marriage relationship—but they would not nullify its design or its sanctity. Most importantly, these changes would make it critically necessary for each partner in a marriage to maintain a right relationship with God in order to experience a right relationship with each other.

Thus we see that once again the wisdom, or knowledge, that leads to skillful and righteous living is vital to human experience at its most basic level and, as Proverbs 1:7 reminds us, "the fear of the LORD is the beginning of knowledge." Apart from a conscious effort to continually choose the way of wisdom over the way of foolishness, a marriage partner can easily doom his or her marital relationship. Just as every other area of life demands meticulous attention to divine instruction, so marriage requires unceasing attention to God's instruction book.

The Bible's instructions concerning marriage certainly are not limited to the book of Proverbs—but in light of that book's intense practicality and pragmatic bent, it is extremely interesting to see what it includes. To be sure, it does not read like most marriage manuals on today's market. There are no references to "codependency," "dysfunctional homes," or "emotional abuse." There are no temperament questionnaires, personality inventories, or six-week pre-engagement counseling courses.

Why not? Because the vast majority of marriages in ancient Israel were *arranged* marriages. They were marriages set by the parents (ideally, with the children's best interests in mind, though not always), recognized by the community, and committed to the common moral standards of the Hebrew community.

When we understand this, we begin to understand that the real nuts and bolts of making a marriage work go far beyond the "moonlight and roses" of romance. According to God's Word, to be righteously married is to dance with the one who brought you, whether you arrived there through pre-arrangement or through romance. It has been said that in Japan, a man's wife is chosen for him, and he doesn't know who she is until after the marriage—and though the custom in the U.S. is completely different, the end result is often the same! No matter who we *think* we are marrying based on dating and courtship, the person we marry is the person we must live with in harmony—if we intend to honor the covenant we have taken with God as our witness. This is a matter of commitment, not compatibility.

Along with matters of conventional wisdom that are dealt with elsewhere in this book—matters which can have profound effects on a marriage relationship—Proverbs offers some direct wisdom to men (husbands), to women (wives), as well as to couples. Let's consider each of these areas.

WISDOM FOR MEN

By way of review, we need to remember that much of Proverbs was written as a father's advice to his son. It was "man to man," if you will, not in a macho, insensitive sense, but in the sense of a male who understands the male nature advising another male who faces the world. The phrase "My son" appears in Proverbs no fewer than twenty-two times, indicating parental advice to a young man who was likely facing, among other challenges, the beginning of his own family unity in marriage.

As we have already seen, the sage's advice for his son is to seek wisdom far more fervently than he might ever seek anything else. Wisdom, in fact, is personified as the ideal companion. At a time in life when a young man naturally craves the companionship of a woman, whether for friendship or for romance, the sage advises that he apply that drive toward seeking God's wisdom.

> Say to wisdom, "You are my sister,"
> And call understanding your nearest of kin,
> That they may keep you from the immoral woman,
> From the seductress who flatters with her words.[1]

Throughout Proverbs, the immoral woman, the harlot, the seductress, or the adulteress is presented in stark contrast to the personification of wisdom. The harlot of Proverbs 7, in fact, is the only other personification of significant length in the entire collection of Proverbs, except for the virtuous wife of Proverbs 31. The personification of wisdom and the immoral woman stand at opposite ends of the volitional spectrum, offering a man the best of choices and the worst of choices.

The problems and temptations associated with the immoral

1. Prov. 8:4–36; 7:4–5.

woman are equally troublesome for a bachelor as for a married man. Whether or not a man is married has little to do with his potential for sexual temptation! One seminary professor likes to tell about the time he and the seminary's late founder—then well up in years—were walking down the street. As they talked, they were passed by an extremely voluptuous woman walking in the other direction. Embarrassed by the total disruption of his thoughts, the younger man remarked, "I can't wait until I'm too old for that to affect me."

"Neither can I," said the elder.

In specific reference to marriage as an institution and a solemn covenant between two people, there is no greater threat from the outside than infidelity. And there is probably no greater area of weakness for men than the allurement of a beautiful woman. That no doubt is why the book of Proverbs devotes the greatest percentage of its advice to men to discussions of the temptations of the immoral woman.

Some of the advice is brief, simple, to the point. For example, wisdom, knowledge, discretion, and understanding will "deliver you from the immoral woman, from the seductress who flatters with her words, who forsakes the companion of her youth, and forgets the covenant of her God." But even this brief description of the immoral woman provides some points of recognition.[2]

She is the woman who will pursue a man with flattering words—praise, admiration, respect, a reply that sooths his frustrations and worries. She knows the way to a man's heart is through his ego. She has already forsaken the husband to whom she pledged herself in her youth—or is ready to at the first opportunity. There is no marital faithfulness in her heart, no matter what her living arrangements might be. She is the "happy divorcée," the liberated woman, the strong and independent wife who believes in open marriage or an occasional "little" affair. And she is a woman who "forgets the covenant of her God." This may refer to the covenant vows taken at the time of marriage, or it may refer to God's covenant promises made to the nation of Israel, upon which all of Jewish society and morality was built. In either case, this woman has a short memory when it comes to the Word of God. Spiritually, she is an opportunist. She will be "holy" when it suits her purpose, and when it doesn't, she will conveniently turn her back on God's moral standards.

2. 2:16–17.

This description is expanded elsewhere in Proverbs, as we discover her traits of being loud and rebellious, extremely persuasive, and self-righteous. She is euphemistically described as a "deep pit" or "narrow well" that will swallow up the victim who goes in to her, and steadily increases the number of men who become unfaithful because of her. She is the predatory female from whom wisdom and discretion will deliver a man.[3]

It is important to notice, however, that the proverbs never give the impression that a man is not responsible for his actions if he chooses to involve himself in infidelity. To the contrary, the decision a man makes concerning the immoral woman is a choice between wisdom and folly, between the wide way and the narrow, between life and death, just like every other decision Proverbs addresses. This is made abundantly clear in Proverbs 5 where the temptation to immorality is vividly portrayed: "For the lips of an immoral woman drip honey, and her mouth is smoother than oil" (v. 3). The temptation is real!

But should a man choose to yield to that temptation, verses 4–14 leave no doubt that he is the one responsible for the unsavory consequences that follow. There's no room here for the excuse, "I just couldn't help myself." The effects of an extramarital affair can be as far-reaching as loss of reputation and career (v. 9), liability to those who have been wronged (v. 10), even lifelong guilt and loss of health (v. 11). And the responsibility for them falls to no one but the man himself.

It is not because his wife doesn't understand him, nor because he has "fallen in love" with another woman, nor because he needs some excitement in his life. The one who ventures to the edge of ruin in extramarital sexual involvement is there because he has "hated instruction" (v. 12), "despised reproof" (v. 12), "not obeyed the voice of my teachers" (v. 13), nor "inclined my ear to those who instructed me" (v. 13). Not even being surrounded by the "congregation and assembly" can excuse him from the consequences of his foolish decision.

But how does a man get himself into this predicament in the first place? The process is not as obvious as we might expect. As we have mentioned already, the "flattering tongue" of a woman can get things started. But so can a man's ability to "lust after her beauty" in his heart. After all, this was David's downfall in his unfortunate affair with Bathsheba. And there is also the opportu-

3. 7:11; 14–21; 30:20; 23:27–28.

nity of eye contact that communicates far more than words. Notice that none of these elements includes physical contact![4]

There is also the foolishness of flirting with temptation by coming as close as possible without actually stepping over the line—until it's too late! Consider the young man "devoid of understanding" who decides to just pass along the street "near her corner," to stroll down the "path to her house." He doesn't overtly intend to sin, but he is putting himself in a position to fall simply because of his proximity to the temptation. He knows it's wrong to even be there, so he chooses the cover of "twilight," "evening," and "the black and dark night." In spite of his intentions, he is swept away by the moment, by the persuasiveness of temptation, and by his own libido.[5]

In every case, of course, a man must cross the line of physical contact in order to commit adultery. But even that can be subtle and insidiously persuasive. It may be a sudden kiss, a warm embrace, or the prospect of "secret sex." However it happens, once it happens, it can only lead to disaster—even death.[6]

Before we move on to the better alternative, how might we picture this in today's terms? Might a relationship between a man and a female coworker become treacherously similar to the intimacy of a fool and an adulterous woman? Would the temptations presented by a business trip or a late-night meeting be better avoided than met head-on? Is it possible that the "flattering words" of a woman whose home life is already unhappy could lead to an adulterous relationship?

One recent murder in a central U.S. community revealed just how strong—and entirely distorting—"casual" relationships can become. What began as a casual acquaintance turned into an intimate friendship, then a physical tryst, then a consuming love affair, then the murder of the man's wife—by the adulterous woman! Perhaps the most bizarre (and disgusting) twist to the entire incident was that both the lovers professed to be born-again Christians.

For the man who willfully pursues an extramarital affair, today's consequences are just as disastrous as those experienced in the ancient Near East—perhaps worse! Though our society feigns liberality in regard to marriage fidelity, nothing can ruin a reputation faster than marital unfaithfulness. Families can be

4. 6:24; 6:25a; 6:25b.
5. 7:7; 7:8; 7:9.
6. 5:20; 7:16–20; 7:23.

shattered, children shamed, security destroyed, friendships split, lives burdened with guilt, all because of a night or two of physical gratification. And of course, the prospect of fatal disease is always present. Proverbs 6:32–35 provides a timeless scenario:

> Whoever commits adultery with a woman lacks understanding;
> He who does so destroys his own soul.
> Wounds and dishonor he will get,
> And his reproach will not be wiped away.

Fortunately, Proverbs also provides a wonderful alternative—righteous marriage! True love between a man and a woman is a miraculous thing, as incomprehensible as "the way of an eagle in the air" (what holds it up?), "the way of a serpent on a rock" (what moves it along?), and "the way of a ship in the midst of the sea" (what guides it on its way?). A virtuous wife is a rare commodity, worth far more than rubies! The man who finds a wife (in contrast to finding an immoral woman) finds a good thing and is the beneficiary of the Lord's favor because of her.[7]

In a passage loaded with euphemistic language, a husband's best alternative to seeking an adulterous woman is described:

> Drink water from your own cistern,
> And running water from your own well.
> Should your fountains be dispersed abroad,
> Streams of water in the streets?
> Let them be only your own,
> And not for strangers with you.
> Let your fountain be blessed,
> And rejoice with the wife of your youth.
> As a loving deer and a graceful doe,
> Let her breasts satisfy you at all times;
> And always be enraptured with her love.[8]

The most sinister threats to a man's marriage relationship will be in situations outside his home life, for that is where the opportunities will be. God's solution is to apply His wisdom and knowledge to the sanctity of the marriage bond and forsake any thought of infidelity. "Marriage is honorable among all, and the bed undefiled; but fornicators and adulterers God will judge."[9]

7. 30:18–19; 31:10; 18:22.
8. 5:15–19.
9. Heb. 13:4.

WISDOM FOR WOMEN

If a man's greatest problem is dealing with temptation from without, a woman's is dealing with words from within. While a man might keep silent and yet be unfaithful in his heart, a woman might just as easily be essentially faithful in her commitment, yet erode a marriage through unthinking speech or imprudent actions. This is the picture in Proverbs.

We already know what the blatantly adulterous woman is like. She has no faithfulness in her heart to her marriage vows. She is openly seductive, loud, and rebellious. She is an "open pit" and a "narrow well" with no moral conscience or commitment to marriage.

But what about the woman who is committed to her marriage, to her home, and to her family? What pitfalls await her as she strives to fulfill her vows? The twofold answer from Proverbs is "words" and "works."

No one knows about the value of words like a woman, especially a married woman. Anyone who has carried on a breakfast conversation from the backside of the morning newspaper knows that, generally speaking, women are by far the best communicators in a marriage. They know the value of words, that "pleasant words are like a honeycomb, sweetness to the soul and health to the bones." That's the good news.[10]

The bad news is that a woman can wield the weapon of words to the point of harming rather than helping the marriage. Whether or not her words are the most forceful, they often can be the most plentiful, and the most harmful. This characteristic, of course, is not limited to women! But it is one aspect of a wife's role in marriage that Proverbs plainly addresses.

When it comes to quarrels, men generally have a knack for clamming up, or blowing up, and then forgetting the whole thing. Women, on the other hand, have better memories. They can keep track of individual statements and catalog them for future references. They can follow the most illogical arguments of their husbands and then repeat them in a request for explanation. They don't overlook the little things that clutter up a good quarrel—like truth, logic, and accuracy. And, if they choose, they can keep a contention fresh in their minds for continuation until it is resolved.

The problem with these wonderful attributes is that they are

10. 16:24.

not always good for a marriage. The ideal, as we will see later, is for love to "cover all sins." When this does not happen, quarrels and strife result. And "the beginning of strife is like releasing water" (17:14). More accurately, the beginning of some couples' fights is like punching a hole in Hoover Dam![11]

No matter who begins the argument, who is "in the right," or where the argument goes, there is a sense in which the peace-making is within the power of the woman. Why?

First and foremost, because the prerogative of the "last word" has been given to the husband. "Whoa!" you might say, "that doesn't fit into my idea of marriage!" While that's not surprising in our culture, the fact remains that God did assign to a man authority over his wife (not over all women), as evidenced in Adam's authority to name Eve. Notice—the function is *authority,* not *superiority.* That authority was the reason Satan had to go through Eve (by deception) in order to cause the fall of Adam (by willful sin), and it is also the model for the basic order of pastoral authority in the church. Whether we like it or not, God has established an order of authority within marriage.[12]

Along with the husband's authority also comes responsibility and accountability to God for his wife's well-being. This explains why, along with the New Testament's repeated mandate for wives to be submissive to their husbands, we also find the equally urgent command for husbands to love their wives. It also explains why marriage is a living model of our relationship with Jesus Christ. It is His responsibility to love us and provide for us; it is our responsibility to respond to Him in submissiveness and obedience.[13]

In Proverbs, then, what we find is the strong admonition to each marriage partner to avoid those things that would violate this model relationship. For a man, the most likely violation of his responsibility to love his wife would be infidelity. For a woman, the greatest violation of her responsibility to submit to her husband would be rebellion, or contentiousness, in her words as well as in her works.

Though it might seem like a small matter compared to a husband's sin of adultery, a wife's sin of rebellion against her husband is just as devastating. That's why it would be better for a husband to dwell in a corner of the rooftop, exposed to the

11. 10:12.
12. 1 Tim. 2:12–14.
13. Eph. 5:22; Col. 3:18; 1 Peter 3:1; Eph. 5:25; Col. 3:19; Eph. 5:31–32.

elements, than to have to live under that roof with a contentious, rebellious wife. Stated a little differently, it would be better for a man to live in the land of the desert, where his life would be in danger, than with a contentious and angry woman.[14]

Why? Because the contentious wife never lets a matter drop until she has had her final say—and then some. She keeps long accounts, bringing up old arguments and showing off old battle scars. She won't let a matter drop, and she certainly won't submit to her husband's leadership. Rather than leaving matters in God's hand and trusting Him to deal with her husband, she wants to take things into her own hands and straighten him out here and now.

If these statements seem uncomplimentary, remember that an unfaithful husband is described in terms ranging from a dumb ox on his way to the slaughter, to an ignorant baby bird that can't find its way back to the nest. And just as the presence of an unfaithful husband in a home would be torture for his wife, the presence of a contentious, angry, unhappy wife is something like "Chinese water torture," as one writer has paraphrased it.[15]

"A continual dripping on a very rainy day and a contentious woman are alike," Proverbs 27:15–16 tells us. "Whoever restrains her restrains the wind, and grasps oil with his right hand." In other words, if you can get a rebellious, contentious wife under control, you qualify for wind-restraining and oil-grasping status!

Just as foolish as contentious words in the home, indiscriminate works shame the rebellious wife and continue to tear down her husband and home. The wife who, out of resentment and anger against her spouse, carries out shameful behavior (whether slandering him to her friends or leaving and filing for divorce) is like a bad case of bone cancer eating away at him. This woman pulls down her house "with her own hands," and stands in direct contrast to the wise woman who builds hers. And no matter how much she dresses up on the outside, her inward disposition and lack of discretion make her adornment look as appropriate as a gold ring in a pig's nose![16]

If this were Proverbs' only picture of married womanhood, it would be pretty discouraging indeed! Fortunately the sage has provided us with the Bible's most comprehensive description of

14. Prov. 21:9, 25:24; 21:19.
15. 19:13b.
16. 14:1; 11:22.

a godly woman—far more treatment than the ideal husband ever gets!

This description, of course, is found in Proverbs 31. Here we discover that the godly wife is one in whom her husband can safely trust (v. 11); who does him good and not evil all the days of her life (v. 12); who considers care and provision for her family a fulfilling career in itself (vv. 13–15); who is a teammate in securing and handling the family's resources (v. 16); who is resourceful and industrious (vv. 17–19); who is caring and compassionate toward those in need (v. 20); who is confident and constructive (vv. 21–24); and whose words as well as works reflect wisdom and godliness (vv. 25–27).

What is her reward? Is it the drudgery of homemaking, so often disparaged by the media? Is it the horrors of motherhood, cursed and ridiculed by the feminists? Is it the insensitivity of an ungrateful husband, or the woeful anonymity of laboring over a hot stove and a cold washing machine? According to God's Word, the reward for the woman of faith is the honor of her children, and the unflagging admiration of her husband (vv. 28–29). In the final analysis, who could ask for more?

As Bishop Taylor once wrote:

> If you are for pleasure, marry; if you prize rosy health, marry. A good wife is heaven's last best gift to man; his angel of mercy; minister of graces innumerable; his gem of many virtues; his box of jewels; her voice, his sweetest music; her smiles, his brightest day; her kiss, the guardian of innocence; her arms, the pale of his safety; the balm of his health; the balsam of his life; her industry, his surest wealth; her economy, his safest steward; her lips, his faithful counsellors; her bosom, the softest pillow of his cares; and her prayers, the ablest advocates of heaven's blessing on his head.

Or, in the words of the sage,

> Charm is deceitful and beauty is vain,
> But a woman who fears the LORD, she shall be praised.
> Give her of the fruit of her hands,
> And let her own works praise her in the gates.[17]

WISDOM FOR HUSBANDS AND WIVES

Above all else, marriage is meant to be a partnership—not 50/50 but 100/100! Remember that when God created Eve for

17. 31:30–31.

Adam, He filled a void that could not be satisfied by any other created thing. She was the only one who truly corresponded to him, who was genuinely bone of his bone, and flesh of his flesh. Together they made a unit. The math was not "one plus one equals two," but "one plus one equals one." Their physical union not only symbolized that oneness, it also galvanized it. That is still God's design for marriage, just as marriage is designed to accurately represent our oneness with Him.

What a tragedy it is, then, when married couples fall into the syndrome of "joint apartness." Too often a marriage becomes the meaningless charade of two adults living separate lives under a single roof. Their communication, what little of it there is, also degenerates to a point of ongoing quarrels punctuated by slightly civil small talk.

Arthur J. Snider has made this observation:

> Some arguing occurs in every marriage, usually about money, sex, or children. But in "fighting families," everything is the subject of a struggle. Bickering is their way of life. Quarreling couples actually follow some rules without realizing it: (1) Look upon each comment as unfriendly or having an ulterior motive. (2) Rebut it by criticism in return. (3) Recall all past criticisms. (4) Recite a litany of sacrifices made for the other. (5) Press on for control of the other, never relenting, for honor is at stake. (6) If hard-pressed, storm out (he) or cry (she). (7) Resume the squabble at the earliest possible time.[18]

Anyone who has visited a home like this—or worse yet, lived in one—recognizes the wisdom of Proverbs when it declares, "Better is a dinner of herbs where love is, than a fatted calf with hatred," and, "Better is a dry morsel with quietness, than a house full of feasting with strife." For the couple who would be wise—who would choose the narrow path of God's design over the broad avenue of the world's low standards—there is a better way. All that is required to enjoy that better way is restraint of one's temper and tongue.[19]

We all know what it is like to "lose our cool." So does the Word of God. A fool's wrath, we are told, is known *at once!* The alternative for the prudent person, however, is to "cover shame"; that is, to care more about covering shame than placing blame. It is "he who covers a transgression" that "seeks love,"

18. Cory.
19. Prov. 15:17; 17:1.

not he who keeps a running list of offenses and revels in running through it one more time! Rather than being a fool who "vents all his feelings," the wise marriage partner "holds them back." Do you see a person—perhaps yourself—who is "hasty in his words"? The sage tells us "there is more hope for a fool than for him." The marriage partner who cannot control his or her temper or tongue is, quite frankly, hopeless.[20]

But because "the beginning of strife is like releasing water" which can never be retrieved, God's advice is to "stop contention before a quarrel starts." Undoubtedly that will mean leaving an accusation undefended, an argument unrebutted, a barb unretaliated, or a "last word" unresponded to. It means that rather than "fighting the good fight," one takes it upon himself to stop the fight dead in its tracks.[21]

It also means that if words are absolutely necessary, they should be "pleasant words," which "are like a honeycomb, sweetness to the soul and health to the bones." Imagine what kind of turn a quarrel might take if a compliment, humor, or other pleasant words were suddenly interjected![22]

Most importantly, the orientation of marriage partners needs to be in the direction of covering sins rather than charting them; of nourishing each other's hearts rather than starving them; of honoring the Lord in the marriage relationship, rather than resenting Him for it.

Hatred in any home is sure to stir up strife; but love really does cover all sins, and a merry heart makes for a cheerful countenance.[23]

Everywhere we look, the permanence of marriage is assumed. It is never questioned, even in the case of a husband's adultery or a wife's contentiousness. Why? Because, as we observed at the beginning of this chapter, marriage in God's eyes is built on two individuals' commitment to vows taken before Him and human witnesses—not on romance or compatibility.

That means that even if one's marriage partner fails in every point to which Proverbs addresses itself, even if he or she goes zero-for-everything in terms of godliness, wisdom, purity, faithfulness, compassion, and love—there simply is no divine license in Proverbs for throwing in the towel and forsaking one's vows.

20. 12:16; 17:9; 29:11; 29:20.
21. 17:14.
22. 16:24.
23. 10:12; 15:13.

Marriage, above all else, is a divine institution based on a covenant relationship. Because of that, one's view of marriage is a direct reflection of one's view of God.

To turn one's back on the sanctity of marriage is to turn one's back on God's perfect design. To forsake the vows of marriage is to forsake one's trust in the promises of God (see Prov. 2:17)! This is strong language for our morally lax culture, but it is the same language God has chosen to use in Proverbs.

To honor God, on the other hand, is to honor marriage. To fear the Lord is to experience deep satisfaction and to be spared the tumultuous trouble that a low view of marriage brings with it. As the sage has written: "The fear of the LORD leads to life, and he who has it will abide in satisfaction."[24]

24. 19:23.

CHAPTER 5

Moral Wisdom

COMPATIBILITY OR COMMITMENT?

LIFE IS FULL of choices with many roads to follow. Some choices are minimal like what to eat for lunch. Some are strategic like which college to attend. Still others are mundane like whether to sleep late in the morning. A few choices are of utmost importance like choosing your mate for life. All of us must make choices. Letting your hair grow after choosing the wrong barber is an easy way to correct a mistake, but other choices have permanent consequences like experimenting with an addictive substance.

As we have seen, much of God's Word deals with choices. Joshua challenged his listeners, "Choose this day whom you will serve" (Josh. 24:15 RSV). Elijah admonished the Israelites, "If the LORD is God, follow Him; but if Baal, then follow him" (1 Kings 18:21). Jesus spoke of those who follow the broad way that leads to destruction, a decision which the majority make, and He said that few travel the narrow way. The book of Proverbs places two paths before believers. We must decide whether to follow God or the world. The consequences of following God or the world are major themes in Proverbs. Moreover, this book of wisdom clearly teaches that choosing the way of life and righteousness over the way of folly and destruction is pivotal to living a meaningful, moral life before God.

THE CALL TO A MORAL LIFE

The book of Proverbs allows us to view two diverging avenues, righteousness and wickedness. All of us stand daily at the fork between these roads. Unfortunately, few choose the way of righteousness. It remains the road less traveled. Consider Robert Frost's thoughts about these choices in his poem *The Road Not Taken*.

> Two roads diverged in a yellow wood,
> And sorry I could not travel both
> And be one traveler, long I stood
> And looked down one as far as I could
> To where it bent in the undergrowth;
>
> Then took the other, as just as fair,
> And having perhaps the better claim,
> Because it was grassy and wanted wear;
> Though as for that the passing there
> Had worn them really about the same,
>
> And both that morning equally lay
> In leaves no step had trodden black.
> Oh, I kept the first for another day!
> Yet knowing how way leads on to way,
> I doubted if I should ever come back.
>
> I shall be telling this with a sigh
> Somewhere ages and ages hence:
> Two roads diverged in a wood, and I—
> I took the one less traveled by,
> And that has made all the difference.

In Proverbs the path of the righteous is described as a highway, and the route of the wicked is described as blocked by thorns (see 15:19; 22:5). Thorns block the way of the one who is unwilling to clear them. This image also portrays the sluggard who is too lazy to remove the thorns (see 15:19) and to show how the goals of the wicked are thwarted by a hedge from God (see 22:5). The righteous labor to maintain a clear path. The image is that of building a highway by raising a grade and removing many rocks and obstacles.[1]

High in the Rocky Mountains of Colorado and New Mexico a few sections of the old Denver and Rio Grande Western narrow-gauge railroads still remain. Now operated as historic attractions, these steam engine lines testify to the construction abilities of the western pioneers. Through careful surveying and tedious planning, the builders of these railroad sections managed to lay track through impassable canyons and gorges, up seemingly

---

1. Woodcock, 124.

insurmountable mountain ranges, and down unthinkable grades. They carefully sought the wisest way to navigate changes in elevation, raised grades over arroyos and gulleys, and cleared paths through solid rock and fields of boulders. Because of that kind of applied knowledge and diligent execution, these lines are still operating over one hundred years later.

In Proverbs, we might consider the righteous path as a well-surveyed railroad track. The wise look ahead and consider their next moves so they will not wander onto the path of disaster (see 4:25–27). The upright are faced with tempting exits that divert them and decide ahead of time how they will respond.

The path of righteousness is bathed in light, while the wicked stagger in darkness.

> But the path of the just is like the shining sun,
> That shines ever brighter unto the perfect day.
> The way of the wicked is like darkness;
> They do not know what makes them stumble. (4:18–19)

Just as our highway departments construct adequate lighting on highways and freeways helping us avoid disaster as we drive, so God lights the path for the righteous helping us see our way through life (see 13:9). As one writer has noted, "Figuratively, light pictures the Lord's presence, wisdom, life, blessing, happiness, and prosperity—reasons for rejoicing."[2]

The righteous can count on ultimate vindication from God. "Though they join forces, the wicked will not go unpunished; but the posterity of the righteous will be delivered" (see 11:21). "Though they join forces" (literally "hand in hand") means that, though the wicked convenant together, they will not be able to stand against God's judgment. The term "hand in hand" can also be understood to describe the covenant God makes to assure the punishment of the wicked. The righteous walk a path that promises the deliverance of God, while the wicked pursue a path leading to retribution.[3]

In our society we are faced with innumerable coalitions and alliances of those who have chosen wickedness over righteousness. United by legal protection and media approval, groups of homosexuals, drug users, prostitutes, and anti-God hatemongers seem to be getting the upper hand in our courts and legislative

2. Woodcock, 126.
3. Woodcock, 76–77.

assemblies. Yet God's Word promises that ultimate vindication will come for those who go against the odds and choose the narrow path of righteousness over the broad avenue of wickedness.

While the two paths have very different destinations, choosing the right road requires skill. Even the wicked route often appears good. "There is a way that seems right to a man, but its end is the way of death" (see 14:12). The wise ponder their actions and possible consequences before pursuing a path that may lead to evil. The wise make proper choices while the wicked may falter in their decisions. Those who do not make choices but drift through life are called simple and usually wander onto the trail of wickedness (see 14:18).

More than once during the Civil War, the great Confederate general Robert E. Lee used inferior forces to outmaneuver and outfight superior Federal forces by moving the battle into territory his forces had already scouted. Because Lee's troops knew which paths to choose, while the Northern forces had to move blindly into unmapped territory, the advantage went to those who knew which path to choose at every fork in the road.

According to Proverbs, that is what life will be like for those who choose to live according to God's revealed wisdom. The decision of which path to take is clear. All that is required is a commitment to go where God wants us to go.

Alice, in *Alice in Wonderland,* stood at the crossroads and pondered which road to take. "Where do you want to go?" she was asked.

"I don't know," she said.

Therefore she was told, "If you don't know where you're going, then it doesn't matter which road you take."

The wise in Proverbs know they are going toward righteousness and carefully choose roads to arrive there.

In some passages, like Proverbs 12:13–23, God's Word makes contrasts between the righteous and the wicked:[4]

Righteous	Wicked
12:13 Escapes trouble	Is ensnared by transgressing lips
12:14 Satisfied by good words, deeds	Pays for misdeeds

4. Adapted from I. Jensen, p. 75.

Righteous		Wicked
12:15	Heeds advice	Refuses counsel
12:16	Overlooks insults, shame	Easily angered
12:17	Speaks truth	Deceives
12:18	Speaks healing words	Speaks rashly
12:19	Established by truthful speaking	Is destroyed by his lies
12:20	Finds joy in counseling peace	Devises evil from a heart of deceit
12:21	Is protected	Is filled with evil
12:22	Delights the Lord with truth	Is an abomination because of his lies
12:23	Conceals his knowledge	Proclaims his foolishness

HUMILITY VERSUS PRIDE

The Bible teaches that pride is at the core of all sin. In fact, pride was the first sin. If we understand Ezekiel 28:11–17 as referring to Satan, we see this was the first moral evil to enter the world. We read:

Moreover the word of the LORD came to me, saying, "Son of man, take up a lamentation for the king of Tyre and say to him, 'Thus says the Lord GOD:

"You were the seal of perfection,
Full of wisdom and perfect in beauty.
You were in Eden, the garden of God;
Every precious stone was your covering. . . .
The workmanship of your timbrels and pipes
Was prepared for you on the day you were created.

"You were the anointed cherub who covers;
I established you;
You were on the holy mountain of God;
You walked back and forth in the midst of fiery stones.
You were perfect in your ways from the day you were created,
Till iniquity was found in you.

"By the abundance of your trading
You became filled with violence within,
And you sinned;
Therefore I cast you as a profane thing
Out of the mountain of God;
And I destroyed you, O covering cherub,
From the midst of the fiery stones.

"Your heart was lifted up [proud] because of your beauty;
You corrupted your wisdom for the sake of your splendor;
I cast you to the ground,
I laid you before kings,
That they might gaze at you." ' "

The pride expressed by this angel of God has been the curse of the world. The prince of Tyre is mentioned in Ezekiel 28:1–10, as well as the king of Babylon in Isaiah 14:13–14:

For you have said in your heart:
"I will ascend into heaven,
I will exalt my throne above the stars of God;
I will also sit on the mount of the congregation
On the farthest sides of the north;
I will ascend above the heights of the clouds,
I will be like the Most High."

Assuming these verses refer to the pride that arose in Satan's heart at the beginning of the universe, we clearly see that pride is the root of all sin. Pride is sin that begets more sin. Therefore, God looks for humility in his creatures and exalts them only when they manifest humility.

In the ancient world, however, humility was *not* popular. A modest, self-effacing attitude was equated with subservience or slavery. Today, we don't appear to have made much progress in moving away from that incorrect perspective. Humble people are not likely to climb the corporate ladder. They are not the ones who "think and grow rich." They are not those people who watch out for number one. Our culture claims humble people are pushed around, used, and abused. Fortunately, this equation of humility with timidity or softness is not the biblical view. In the Bible, humility is directly connected with grace as a direct outgrowth of our relationship with God. Humility is a matter of recognizing our position before God and under God and living life in constant awareness of His superiority over every thing, every person, and every circumstance.

Proverbs shows us how humility may be expressed. These verses help us avoid severe embarrassment when we heed wisdom's teaching.

Do not exalt yourself in the presence of the king,
And do not stand in the place of great men;

For it is better that he say to you,
"Come up here,"
Than that you should be put lower in the presence of the
    prince,
Whom your eyes have seen.

It is not good to eat much honey;
So to seek one's own glory is not glory. (25:6–7, 27)

PRIDE AND HUMILITY

Pride will thrive as long as men live. No nation, family, or church is immune. It you want proof of how susceptible we all are to pride, compare the number of people who volunteer to serve on a prestigious church committee with the number who ask to work in the nursery. Or take an inventory of your church's governing board and compare the number of white collar executives to those who work with their hands for a living. Or look on a Christian music album to see how self-effacing the artist really is. Sadly, humbling ourselves is a rare expression of living wisely. Fortunately, God's Word has much to say about the issues of pride and humility for those who care to listen.

Consider the example of the proud man and contrast him with the humble man.

The Proud Man

The banquet room of the Pharisees' house buzzed with the activities of the feast. Each Pharisee wore a pious mask that camouflaged the struggle for the highest seat at dinner. Only a veneer of politeness kept them from a mad scramble for the chair next to the host, the place of honor. Jesus exhorted them not to strive for the highest place, but to take a lower seat, explaining, "For whoever exalts himself will be abased, and he who humbles himself will be exalted." All through Scripture the contrast between the proud and the humble stands out in stark distinction.[5]

Like the Pharisee who schemed for the highest seat, the proud man of Proverbs attempts to exalt himself in another's presence. He aspires to the Hall of Fame, to see his name chiseled into a monument. But the sage warns of the danger of high places. He says pride marks a man as a fool. "In the mouth of a fool is a rod of pride, but the lips of the wise will preserve them." The fool

5. Luke 14:7–11.

boasts of himself and reduces the stature of others to reach the advantage he lusts after. His pride leads him to lying, slander, and accusations against others. Overestimating his own wisdom causes him to speak without thinking and give false or faulty counsel. No wonder the wise man finds protection in his humble speech.[6]

On May 1, 1991, two significant milestones in baseball were reached almost simultaneously. The way the two athletes responded brought comment from scores of sportswriters, and provided a lesson on both ends of the humility spectrum. The first was Ricky Henderson's shattering of Lou Brock's record for stealing bases. When Henderson passed the long-standing mark of 939 by stealing third base, he immediately pulled the base up from its anchor and held it over his head like a hero's booty. Brock had traveled across the country so he could be there when his record was broken. He congratulated Henderson, who proclaimed, "Lou Brock was a great base-stealer, but today I am the greatest of all time." One major league player commented, "It made me want to puke."

Half a continent away, forty-four-year-old Nolan Ryan of the Texas Rangers spent the evening pitching a no-hitter—the *seventh* of his amazing career. When the last fastball was thrown and the final batter went down swinging, Ryan simply smiled and began making his way toward his catcher to congratulate him on a game well played. As his fellow players mobbed him and the crowd cheered, Ryan looked almost embarrassed by all the fuss. He then said he was most happy for his hometown fans and for his team. It is arguable whether one athletic feat can overshadow another. What is certain, however, is that humility always upstages pride.

Not only do pride's insidious germs infect a person's relationship with others, they ultimately infect one's relationship with God. Proverbs introduces us to the absurdity of a tiny man with titan pride shaking his puny fist in the face of the Almighty. "A proud and haughty man—'Scoffer' is his name; he acts with arrogant pride." What the proud think, say, and do show blatant disregard for God and His Law. In the mind of the arrogant, pride swells into a tumor so large it blocks their vision of the sovereign God. The world of the proud is so small, and the

6. Prov. 25:6–7; 14:3; Alden, 110.

proud themselves loom so large, that God is pushed out. God hates this kind of pride.[7]

"These six things God hates, yes seven are an abomination to Him: A proud look. . . ." God's powerful feelings concerning pride emerge in two other passages in Proverbs. The attitude that ignores God's will and purposes is an abomination, detested and hated by the Lord. Seeing the Sovereign's view of pride, the wise easily understand pride's grievous consequences.[8]

The proud saunter through life's field sowing seeds of conceit. But in God's eyes, even haughty plowing is sin and the proud harvest bitter fruit indeed. One fruit of pride is strife. "By pride comes only contention, but with the well-advised is wisdom." The proud approach relationships with a closed mind and an open mouth, two essential ingredients for a fight. Instead of healthy business and personal relationships, contention surrounds proud people. Their egotism breeds "clashes of competing and unyielding personalities."[9]

Pride yields more than just conflict, it also brings a harvest of shame. Ironically, while the proud work and wait for a harvest of self-exaltation, they reap shame. "When pride comes, then comes shame." God rewards the arrogant with what they fear most—humiliation. They swagger down the road of self-promotion that ends in disgrace. All their efforts focus on building an edifice for themselves, but "the LORD will destroy the house of the proud." When the wise peer down the path of the proud they wisely turn from apparent prosperity and advise traveling the rewarding way of the humble. "Better to be of a humble spirit with the lowly, than to divide the spoil with the proud."[10]

Now let us consider the humble man. Humility quietly delivers what pride vainly promises. "By humility and the fear of the LORD are riches and honor and life." The proud crave riches, honor, and life but arrogance has convinced them they must acquire those things on their own terms. The proud believe God's way inferior, and their own ways superior. But the humble simply walk in God's way and find abundance.[11]

Imagine two men. One pours his energy into work. He takes

7. Prov. 21:24.
8. 6:16–17a; 8:13, 16:5.
9. 21:4; 13:10; Kidner, 102.
10. Prov. 11:2; 15:25; 16:19.
11. 22:4.

great pains to polish his image, to meet all the right people and say all the right things to each one of them. He worries. He hurts a friend in order to obtain a promotion. "That's just the way it works out there," he explains to himself, "besides he probably would have done the same thing to me." He has money, but not enough. He has gained prominence, but a higher position lies just ahead out of reach. Another day, another dollar, another rung on the ladder. He desires everything, but as yet nothing has satisfied.

Now consider the other man. He does his work well, but he does not need it to make him important. Compliments and honors come as sweet surprises. Because he does not expect them, they are genuinely appreciated. He has time to cultivate a loving, faithful family which crowns him in his old age. He smiles as he sees character flourish in his children. His friendships are deep fountains that refresh him often. He may not have much money, but he is rich in contentment. His place of honor rests not in his own mind, but in the minds of others. He has mined the golden vein of humility.

Look again at these two men. One feeds an insatiable pride. The other man lives satisfied in humility that gives contentment. Humility brings honor. It is also a prerequisite to wisdom. "When pride comes, then comes shame; but with the humble is wisdom." Pride starts a series of events that lead to shame. Humility begins the process of acquiring wisdom. The humble listen and learn. Because they are not focused on themselves they remain open to counsel.[12]

Twice in Proverbs humility is linked to the fear of the Lord. These two characteristics form the foundation of a wise person's house. Both humility and the fear of the Lord are attributes of a proper perspective. Those who fear the Lord see themselves in proper relationship to the sovereign God. Those who are humble see themselves in proper relationship to others around them. The man or woman who has this perspective has indeed found considerable wisdom.[13]

Humility not only leads to wisdom, it also brings grace from God. "Surely He scorns the scornful, but He gives grace to the humble." This essential truth, originated here in Proverbs, echoes twice in the New Testament. James and Peter both quote

12. 11:2.
13. 15:33; 20:4.

from here and remind the reader that God grants bountiful grace to the lowly while He resists the proud. The proud scoff at God's help and receive none. But the humble man petitions for God's aid and obtains it in abundance. "Better to be of a humble spirit with the lowly, than to divide the spoil with the proud."[14]

DILIGENCE VERSUS LAZINESS

Laziness

Let's spend a day with the sluggard. The sun rises to shine on the many who head toward the fields to work. Morning finds the sluggard moaning sleepily in bed. "A little sleep a little slumber, a little folding of the hands," he says, which means, "Just five more minutes." Today he would not even consider an alarm clock without a snooze button that could be pushed at least ten times. The sage picturesquely describes him as a door turning on its hinges. He does not need rest from a long day previously. Instead he is armed with thick comfortable covers to battle the prospect of labor. He rises slowly.[15]

At the table he toils. For the sluggard even lifting his hand from the plate to his mouth is a wearisome job. "The slothful man buries his hand in the bowl; it wearies him to bring it back to his mouth." He fondly remembers the days when he was an infant fed by his mother. Life was so much easier then.[16]

The burden of responsibility pulls him grudgingly to his door where he comes face to face with his lifelong nemesis—work. It stares him coldly in the face so he quickly retreats, "There is a lion in the road! A fierce lion in the streets!" How ridiculous he sounds. Even in Old Testament times, a lion would not venture into town. They lived far up in the mountains away from the city.[17]

When all excuses have failed, the sluggard begins his work. Many around him enjoy the satisfaction of productivity and appreciate activity, but not the sluggard. "The way of the lazy man is like a hedge of thorns." Because his ultimate aspiration is idleness, every undertaking he approaches looms like a hedge of

14. 3:34; James 4:6, 1 Peter 5:5; Prov. 16:19.
15. 24:33; 26:14.
16. 26:15.
17. 26:13; Draper, 60.

thorns. Every task brings too much strain for too little progress. The sluggard never gains enough momentum to move on. He does not work his fields. They deteriorate. If he ever expends the energy to hunt for food and finds game, he cannot bring himself to do the chore of dressing and cleaning it. The thought of savory venison roast quickly spoils with the prospect of sweat.

The end of his day comes early. Later he watches the sun set in the west while laborers return tired but satisfied. The sluggard has expended himself far more than he had planned yet senses no reward. "The soul of the lazy man desires, and has nothing." He craves prosperity but his loathing of labor denies him success. "Tomorrow I will set out with new resolve, new plans, and renewed effort," he thinks, "tomorrow I'll have success without work."

Springtime, summer, harvest, and winter pass and still the sluggard waits for success without effort. Today his plans for the future hang on lottery tickets, sweepstakes entries, and get-rich-quick schemes. Idly waiting for a nonexistent ship to come in, the sluggard's days pass slowly and sadly empty. What happens to the sluggard? Poverty:

> I went by the field of the slothful,
> And by the vineyard of the man devoid of understanding;
> And there it was, all overgrown with thorns;
> Its surface was covered with nettles;
> Its stone wall was broken down.
> When I saw it, I considered it well;
> I looked on it and received instruction:
> A little sleep, a little slumber,
> A little folding of the hands to rest;
> So your poverty will come like a prowler,
> And your want like an armed man. (Prov. 24:30–34)

The Proverbs portray the ultimate sluggard. Few people can relate to this kind of sloth. The value of this portrait is that close observers see stark colors of laziness which they recognize in the muted hues in their own lives. Each ought to examine the painting closely and carefully compare likenesses. Sometimes, even while at work, our hearts prefer indolence. "Our desperate and eager work is not for work's sake, but in order to get rich; our ambition is to be idle rather than to be employed, to be raised above the necessity of labor which is our health by the possession of wealth which is our ruin." Sluggishness, inertia, and procrastination are obstacles to be overcome in all of our lives.

Diligence

Proverbs praises the dignity of hard labor. Weary bones and
calloused hands signify satisfaction. The diligent man first plans.
"The plans of the diligent lead surely to plenty" (21:5). Unlike
the sluggard who schemes to avoid labor, the diligent man looks
for work. As the old saying goes, he plans his work and works
his plan.

The industrious man has the same human needs as the sluggard, but his needs move him to do something about it. "The
person who labors, labors for himself, for his hungry mouth
drives him on" (16:26). The need to provide for himself and his
family motivates the worker. He does not come home empty.
"He who tills his land will have plenty of bread" (28:19). In fact
the diligent man harvests in abundance from his labor. "He who
deals with a slack hand becomes poor, but the hand of the
diligent makes one rich" (10:4).

The working man enjoys his endeavors. His labors bring him
many benefits. He fulfills his desires by striving to achieve them.
He profits from work. He advances in status to rule rather than
being forced to labor. His path through life is not filled with
thorns like that of the sluggard. The industrious man's way is a
highway allowing progress. A working man also earns honor.
"Do you see a man who excels in his work? He will stand before
kings" (22:29). A working man realizes a multitude of benefits.
His toil earns him possessions as well as honor. His work also
gives him character. "Diligence is man's precious possession"
(12:27).

One cannot examine the issue of diligence in Proverbs without
giving special place to the woman of chapter 31. She is the
virtuous wife who labors before dawn through the day and into the
night taking care of her family. She bears a lot of responsibility.
She is a businesswoman. Her life exemplifies the reward of
those who labor diligently. From the field of toil they reap a
bountiful harvest of honor, satisfaction, and joy. The people
around them rise up to praise them. What a glorious benediction
for those who labor.

Anyone seeking a wise man sitting on a mountaintop should

tell him to descend to the fields below to discover wisdom. The wise man works.

CHOOSING FRIENDS AND FRIENDSHIPS

The sage shows much interest in friendship. The proverbs finally collected in the book of Proverbs were gathered by wise friends comparing their reflections on life. Several types of friendships surface in Proverbs.

The first kind of friend is the neighbor. The word is taken from a root that means a good or bad inhabitant. The neighbor lives nearby. The sage advises befriending those close by for "better is a neighbor nearby than a brother far away" (27:10b).

Another type of friendship is rooted in a different word translated as "neighbor." This person is more involved in one's life than merely living next door. This term commonly describes friends or neighbors in the Old Testament and occurs thirty times in Proverbs.

A close friend in Proverbs is the companion, who is a respected advisor, or even one's best man. The companion in Proverbs is chosen carefully because of his great influence.

The intimate friend is rarely described in Proverbs. Psalms depicts him splendidly:

> But it was you, a man my equal,
> My companion and my acquaintance.
> We took sweet counsel together,
> And walked to the house of God in the throng. (55:13–14)

The word for *intimate* friend appears three times in Proverbs. Each time it denotes a close bond which one can only break by engaging in immorality or gossip.

Finally, the closest kind of friend in Proverbs is the one who loves. This one "sticks closer than a brother" (18:24). Even when it seems the loved one brings pain, he still seeks the best for his friend. This is the one of whom it is said, "Faithful are the wounds of a friend" (27:6).

The characteristics of friendship

Friendship is necessary. If we aspire to live skillfully, we cannot isolate ourselves from those around us. The portrait of the wise guru sitting atop the desolate mountain falls woefully short of true wisdom. The skills necessary for wise living are honed by friends. "As iron sharpens iron, so a man sharpens the countenance of his friend." "A man who isolates himself seeks his own desire." Not only do the unsociable ignore opportunity to acquire important skills, they are also exposed as selfish. To be in contact with others might impinge on precious time. The second half of this proverb states that the unfriendly person is a fool. "He rages against all wise judgment." The one who separates from people "breaks out against the community and good common sense."[18]

Dr. Jimmy Draper tells of a photo that illustrates the necessity of friendships. "The other day someone brought me a newspaper clipping, picturing a man sitting forlorn and alone on a park bench. A caption simply read 'solitude.' Underneath the picture the text said, 'Solitude can be a blessed relief from a hectic day, or endless hours of agony for those who find themselves constantly alone. There are times when being alone is a comfort, but loneliness is never comforting.'"[19]

Friendship is steadfast. The sage warns of the many pseudo-friends that abound during prosperous times and then vanish. The rich have many friends. A man once remarked, "Being rich is relative. The richer you are, the more relatives you have." Multitudes flock to the celebrities of today, but the person who can claim a faithful friend is blessed indeed. The wise not only seek out "a friend who sticks closer than a brother" and "loves at all times," strong loyalty to friends is also cultivated. A wise person does not forsake friends. In fact, a wise person maintains and develops the relationships his father endears. Acquaintances who provide upward mobility seem productive for the time being, but a staunch companion is a legacy.[20]

Friendship is honesty. "Faithful are the wounds of a friend, but the kisses of an enemy are deceitful." If you have a friend who willingly tests the relationship by lovingly speaking the truth, you have a worthy friend. Empty flattery is deceitful and dangerous. "A man who flatters his neighbor spreads a net for his feet." Empty praise is a hunter's snare waiting to snatch prey. Derek Kidner notes the grievous consequences of not confronting

18. Prov. 27:17; 18:12; 18:16; Johnson, 179.
19. Draper, 132.
20. Prov. 19:4, 14:20; 18:24; 17:17; 27:10.

wrong: "David shirked his duty to Adonijah his son ('He had not displeased him at any time in saying, "Why hast thou done so?"' 1 Kings 1:6), and it cost that son his life."[21]

Friendship is loving. Nowhere does the love of a friendship have a more beautiful portrait than that found in David and Jonathan. Jonathan loved David "as he loved his own soul." The commitment sealed between two young men stood the test of trouble times. David deeply lamented his friend's death:

> I am distressed for you, my brother Jonathan;
> You have been very pleasant to me;
> Your love to me was wonderful,
> Surpassing the love of women.

Love's mighty cord in friendship went beyond Jonathan's life. David sought one of Jonathan's family to whom he could show kindness. Kindness in Hebrew means covenant faithfulness. David's love for his friend bound him to Jonathan and to generations beyond.[22]

David's son, Solomon, wrote of the friend who loves at all times. Love in a friendship means forgiveness and tolerance. "He who covers a transgression seeks love, but he who repeats a matter separates the best of friends." A true friend overlooks the shortcomings of the friendship and quickly forgives wrongs. The one who forgets no wrongs, but rather rehearses them will soon drive a wedge into the strongest friendship.[23]

Friendship is selective. One can have a multitude of acquaintances, but the intimacy of true friendship requires selectivity. The reason the sage exhorts his students not to forsake their fathers' friends is because a friendship of the highest quality occurs so rarely. Like a priceless heirloom passed from generation to generation, a friend is unique to the possessor. In Proverbs 1, godly parents warn their child to avoid making friends with those who seek evil. Because peer pressure from such friends can force a young person to sin, they should be avoided. "My son, do not walk in the way with them, keep your foot from their path." The exhortation extends to all to select companions with care.

21. 27:6; Eph. 4:15; Prov. 29:5; Kidner, 45.
22. 1 Sam. 18:1,3; 20:17; 2 Sam. 1:26; Prov. 9:1.
23. 17:17; 17:9.

> Make no friendship with an angry man,
> And with a furious man do not go,
> Lest you learn his ways
> And set a snare for your soul.[24]

Friends exert incredible influence, for bad or for good.

"The righteous should choose his friends carefully, for the way of the wicked leads them astray." This proverb could be translated, "The righteous searches out his friend, for the way of the wicked causes them to wander." The word "choose" or "search out" (Hebrew *tur*) is used most often of a man searching out land. In Ecclesiastes it describes Solomon searching out wisdom under the heavens three times. The wise man explores and evaluates prospective friendships and selects prudently. The fool wanders blindly into bad relationships and suffers for it.[25]

SPEECH

"There is nothing which seems more insubstantial than speech, a mere vibration in the atmosphere which touches the nerves of hearing and then dies away. There is no organ which seems smaller and less considerable than the tongue; a little member which is not even seen, and physically speaking, soft and weak. But the word which issues out of the lips is the greatest power in human life." "Death and life are in the power of the tongue." Words powerfully affect others and define the character of the speaker.[26]

Derek Kidner defines the powerful effect of words on others in two ways—penetration and spread. Words can penetrate past the physical realm into the spirit of a person. "There is one who speaks like the piercings of a sword." That speech may bring an overwhelming broken spirit or it may bring health and joy to a troubled heart. Speech that strengthens not only soothes the spirit, but aids physical well-being also. "Pleasant words are like a honeycomb, sweetness to the soul and health to the bones."[27]

Words not only affect our spirits, they also change our view of our fellows. Gossip sounds intriguing every time. "The words of a talebearer are like tasty trifles, and they go down into the inmost body." Once digested, those tasty morsels sour the hearer's image of the one slandered. How many words of gossip uttered when praying aloud have devastated helpless believers? Words penetrate.[28]

Words also spread their seeds over a broad field. "An ungodly man digs up evil, and it is on his lips like a burning fire." The sage uses two metaphors to communicate the healthy scattering of godly words. "The mouth of the righteous is a well of life." This "is a metaphor picturing a refreshing source of vitality from which a high quality of life flows. Those who drink from that fountain will be refreshed and experience health and vitality." Godly speech also is a tree of life. "In the book of Proverbs, 'tree of life' refers to God's sources of renewal and vitality apart from any cosmic or eschatological significance." Proper words give life to the speaker and it spreads to his hearers. Both the metaphors picture the healthy use of speech that refreshes those who receive wise words.[29]

Words also reflect the character of the speaker. "The words of a man's mouth are deep waters." " 'Deep waters' pictures the total range of thoughts, attitudes, feelings, plans and decisions that combine in many complex ways to characterize the ordinary mind." Happiness, encouragement, cunning, discouragement, anger, sex, terror, and a broad range of emotions are reflected in the metaphor of deep waters. All that comprises the inner recesses of a person is expressed in words. Thus, words reflect deep waters because they represent the real person behind them. If that person has wise counsel within, the understanding listener will attempt to draw out that godly advice.[30]

Wise speech displays skill for living. Mouths of the wise bring forth wisdom that flows from a godly heart. They do not speak without thinking. The sage says, "The heart of the wise teaches his mouth, and adds learning to his lips." But the fool is not so. "He who answers a matter before he hears it, it is folly and shame to him." "It is foolish and shameful to answer without listening. Your irrelevant reply will make clear your inattention, which displays your apathetic, impolite, and insulting manner." The deep waters of fools contain neither wisdom nor concern, so their natural reaction is to spout their folly. "The mouth of fools pours forth foolishness." The term translated here as "pours

28. 18:8.
29. 16:27; 10:11; Woodcock, 95; Prov. 15:4; Woodcock, 183.
30. Prov. 18:4; Woodcock, 183; Prov. 20:5.

forth" refers to "an uncontrolled pouring or flooding, here a torrent of words either from a fool who lacks the sense to remain silent when he has nothing to contribute, or from a wicked person who refuses to shut up even when his comments are vicious and offensive."[31]

The sage extols the value of wise words. "A man has joy by the answer of his mouth, and a word spoken in due season, how good it is!" A good word must be more than beneficial, it must also be timely. If the hearer cannot assimilate counsel, even great wisdom becomes useless. But "a word fitly spoken is like apples of gold in settings of silver."[32]

Godly speech first comes from a prepared heart. "The heart of the righteous studies how to answer." He ponders how to employ his knowledge to the fullest benefit of others. "The tongue of the wise uses knowledge rightly." He also recognizes the true source of knowledge for wise words is God Himself. "For the Lord gives wisdom; from his mouth come knowledge and understanding."[33]

Godly speech soothes anger. "A soft answer turns away wrath." R. F. Horton comments, "If in the tumult of passion, when fiery charges are made and grievous provocations are uttered, the tongue can be held in firm restraint, and made to give a soft answer, the storm will subside, the angry assailant will retire abashed, and the flaming arrows will be quenched in the buckler of meekness which opposes them." Choice words can heal the wounds of strife and rage. "Pleasant words are like a honeycomb, sweetness to the soul and health to the bones." To those bruised by hostility, kind words salve their anguish and restore lost joy. "Anxiety in the heart of man causes depression, but a good word makes it glad."[34]

Wise words are honest. "Righteous lips are the delight of kings, and they love him who speaks what is right." The prized possession of honesty is appreciated by all, but vigorously guarded by few. The truthful man lives in blessing.

> He who says to the wicked, "You are righteous,"
> Him the people will curse;

31. 10:31, 15:3, 7; 16:23; 18:13; Woodcock, 185; Prov. 15:2; Woodcock, 185.
32. Prov. 15:23; 25:11.
33. 15:28; 15:2; 2:6.
34. 15:2; Horton, 172; Prov. 16:24; 12:25.

> Nations will abhor him.
> But those who rebuke the wicked will have delight,
> And a good blessing will come upon them.
> He who gives a right answer kisses the lips.

The just recognize evil and confront it and bring joy to those around them. The just "gives a right answer." "Right" means "straight" or "straightforward." Candid honesty characterizes righteous speech. The one who speaks rightly "kisses the lips." The kiss pictured "affection, friendship, trust and commitment." Like a kiss from a faithful companion, honest words richly bless the receiver.[35]

Proper speech brings bounty. "From the fruit of his lips a man is filled with good things as surely as the work of his hands reward him." Three times Proverbs instructs that wise speech benefits the speaker. Here the proverb uses a farming analogy to illustrate the truism, good speech produces good things. Another proverb contrasts the wise one who enjoys the fruit of beneficial speech with the wicked one who feeds on strife. Still another precept uses repetition: "A man's stomach shall be satisfied from the fruit of his mouth, and from the produce of his lips he shall be filled." The wise investor of words enjoys maximum capital gains.[36]

Wise voices also rebuke. Flattery may seem enjoyable at the moment, but timely rebuke is better. "He who rebukes a man will find more favor afterward than he who flatters with the tongue." "Open rebuke is better than love carefully concealed." A wise person rebuking a ready listener builds character. "Like an earring of gold and ornament of fine gold is a wise rebuker to an obedient ear."[37]

The one skillful in the use of words possesses the power to evade traps and snares. While the hypocrite's mouth destroys, the righteous speak with knowledge and are rescued. The wise saves many who would be crushed by lies. "A true witness delivers souls, but a deceitful witness speaks lies."[38]

For all the good found in words the sage still warns his students to use them sparingly. "In the multitude of words sin is

35. 16:13; 24:24–26; 24:26; Kidner, 48; Prov. 24:26; Alden, 177.
36. Prov. 12:14 (NIV); 13:2; 18:20.
37. 28:23; 27:5; 25:12.
38. 11:9, 12:6, 14:3; 14:25.

not lacking, but he who restrains his lips is wise." Since wise speech is thoughtful and timely, the one who constantly babbles will certainly blunder. Taking the time to speak well prevents too much talking. A man of few words is knowledgeable, understanding, and in control. "He who has knowledge spares his words, and a man of understanding is of a calm spirit." Proverbs uses three terms to show how the wise man spares his words. First, he restrains his lips. This means he holds his tongue. Another term rendered "holds his peace" can be translated "to say nothing" or "to keep silent." A third phrase is he "shuts up." The power of silence can even mask a fool. "Even a fool is counted wise when he holds his peace; when he shuts his lips, he is considered perceptive." The blabbermouth reveals how little he values his own drivel by strewing it far and wide. "When your money is all in copper, you may afford to throw it about, but when it is all in gold you have to be cautious."[39]

If the tongue wields such power, for both good and evil, how can we control it? God, the giver of all wisdom, also grants us the ability to craft virtuous words. "The preparations of the heart belong to man, but the answer of the tongue is from the LORD."[40]

COMPASSION

When we look closely at wise people, we find them cautious in business, skillful in relationships, and profound in thought. But the description is incomplete without the virtue of compassion toward the poor.

The poor and needy encompasses a surprisingly large group in Proverbs. Four Hebrew terms are used to describe the needy. The first word depicts one who "is weak and uninfluential, but not necessarily destitute or even in want." The vast majority of ordinary people fit under this umbrella. They have no special power or position. You don't see them in the headlines you see them in the front yard.[41]

The second word defines those in physical need. Due to sickness or misfortune they can no longer adequately provide for their basic needs.

39. 10:19; 17:27; Woodcock, 184–85; Prov. 10:19; 17:28; Ibid.; Horton, 171–72.
40. Prov. 16:1.
41. Adapted from Horton, 288–89; Horton, 188.

The third term describes the distressed. Their sadness and
helplessness move them to depend on God for all they cannot do
for themselves.

The fourth expression pictures the truly destitute, the man or
woman with more than need. All they own is need. These people
wait outside a union gospel mission in hopes of a meal and a bed.
Sometimes they get food and shelter. More often they shiver
under a bridge on a cold night. With garbage for food, discarded
pennies for pay, and a back alley for a bedroom, they are the
poorest. The poor of Proverbs range from the destitute to the
faceless masses that comprise most of our society. The wise
show compassion on them.

While many ignore the poor as inconsequential, God does not.
In the eyes of the Lord, rich and poor remain the same. "The rich
and the poor have this in common, the LORD is the maker of
them all." "The poor man and the oppressor have this in common: The LORD gives light to the eyes of both." When all the
temporal tinsel is stripped away, everyone is equally dependent
on the sovereign Creator for life and health. In fact, the special
needs of the poor incline God's heart toward them.[42]

According to the Bible, one who oppresses the poor is opposed
to God. "He who oppresses the poor reproaches his Maker."
While the needy seem defenseless, God will not be suppressed
or silenced.

> Do not remove the ancient landmark,
> Nor enter the field of the fatherless;
> For their Redeemer is mighty;
> He will plead their cause against you.

The word rendered "redeemer" (*goel*) means the avenger of
blood who had the right and responsibility to avenge the death of
one who had been murdered. Even the poor are warned not to
abuse their fellows. "A poor man who oppresses the poor is like
a driving rain which leaves no food." In the end gain turns to
loss. "One who increases his possessions by usury and extortion
gathers it for him who will pity the poor." God makes the
oppressive rich poor. The cries of those who ignore the poor are
unheeded.[43]

42. Prov. 22:2; 29:13.
43. 14:31, 17:5; 23:10–11, 22:22–23; see Josh. 20; Prov. 28:3; 28:8; 22:16; 21:13.

While God despises those who despise the needy, He heaps blessings on those who pity the poor. "He who has mercy on the poor, happy is he." The righteous are compassionate because they understand God's inclination to the poor. God faithfully rewards the merciful. "He who has pity on the poor lends to the LORD, and he will pay back what he has given." "He who has a bountiful eye will be blessed, for he gives of his bread to the poor." "He who gives to the poor will not lack." What a joyous opportunity when we invest our resources with those who cannot repay! The co-signer of our account is God, who never ceases to repay.[44]

ALCOHOLISM

During 1990, 22,470 people died in automobile crashes involving alcohol—nearly half of all automobile deaths. Every day 62 people die in alcohol-related accidents. Annually an estimated $11 to $24 billion is lost because of the effects of alcoholism. To combat this colossal crisis, federal and state governments have enacted over a thousand laws since 1980. America reels from the blows of alcohol abuse.[45]

Old Testament Israel also had those in its midst who abused alcohol. The sage saw alcoholism and instructed his students to apply their wisdom to the use of wine. In Old Testament times, people often relied on wine. To say that Scripture always casts a negative light on alcoholic beverages is to overstate the case. The typical meal of that day included wine as a beverage. Wine was also used in the sacrificial offerings to God. The Psalms say wine has benefits for the temperate: "Wine . . . makes glad the heart of man." The sage of Proverbs wrote wine was a sign of a prosperous man. "So your barns will be filled with plenty, and your vats will overflow with new wine." Wine was considered a useful drink that would not carry water-borne diseases. But its abuse receives considerable scorn in the Bible, especially in Proverbs. In fact, Proverbs contains the longest biblical passage concerning alcohol abuse.[46]

Proverbs 23:29–35 graphically portrays the man brutalized by his lust for wine.

44. 14:21; 29:7; 19:17; 22:9; 28:27.
45. Mothers Against Drunk Driving.
46. See Gen. 14:18, 27:27, Judg. 19:19, 1 Sam. 16:20; Ex. 29:40, Lev. 23:13; Ps. 104:15; Prov. 3:10.

Who has woe?
Who has sorrow?
Who has contentions?
Who has complaints?
Who has wounds without cause?
Who has redness of eyes?

The sage answers, "Those who linger long at the wine, those who go in search of mixed wine." His heart is heavy with woe. His mouth spouts strife. His eyes fracture into bloodshot patterns. His body suffers gashes and bruises from falling down in unknown places. He had longed for the sparkling red wine swirling invitingly in the glass. Too late did he realize that the swirl was the poison of a viper and the sparkle the glint of his fang. Too much wine causes the drunk to slur words and imagine strange things. The phrase "strange things" can be rendered "strange women" as it is in Proverbs 22:14. The man captured by alcohol has his judgment impaired. Not only can he not control his physical abilities, he cannot control his latent lusts. He seeks to satisfy his desires without restraint. Alcohol puts him into a rudderless drift on a raging sea. The sage pictures the alcoholic as one floundering in the sea, rocking like a mast in a storm. As the stupor eases its cruel grip, the drunk awakes bruised, battered, and confused. One would expect him to realize his condition and promise never again to fall for the seductions of alcohol. Does he have any regrets? No. "When shall I awake, that I may seek another drink?" he asks. In the Old Testament culture wine was enjoyed or disastrously abused. He whose passion for wine controls him will soon come to poverty.[47]

Those in Christian circles today who argue for free consumption of alcoholic drink accept no substitutes. Though nonalcoholic wine and beer are available in quantity, they continue to argue for the intoxicating variety. They continue to promote drinking alcohol as an activity that is directly and indirectly responsible for far more deaths and disabilities each year than any disease. Drinking in our society goes far beyond recreational drunkenness. Much of the Christian realm has ignored the Bible's warnings concerning wisdom in this area. We are now suffering the consequences.

This is the way of moral wisdom, or the lack of it. God's Word does not bother to present lengthy treatises, columns of

---

47. 23:29; 23:30; cf. 23:31–32; 23:33; 23:34; Ibid.; 23:35b; 21:17.

statistics, or philosophical arguments concerning moral choices. It simply presents life as it really is, and gives the reader credit for having enough brains to figure it out.

And to live it.

CHAPTER 6

Sexual Wisdom

Today we are confronted by sexual temptations nearly as old as the human race. Ever since the Fall we have been tempted to follow the lusts of our eyes. We are faced with countless images of sexually explicit scenes on television, at the theater, and in advertising. Just as some earlier civilizations were so degenerate they condoned homosexuality, our contemporary culture is leaning toward that same irreversible decision.

Some of history's greatest spiritual leaders, like King David, for instance, were brought down by their attraction to beautiful women. And some of our spiritual leaders today are succumbing to the lust of the flesh. Ancient times were no different. Illicit sex was available to men of means and influence; even Solomon fell prey to immorality, adultery, and polygamy. Eventually, in fact, he became so mired in sexual sin that "his heart was not loyal to the LORD his God." If Solomon did so poorly in this area, then, what gives him the right to warn us against sexual immorality?[1]

There are two reasons. Solomon spoke from experience. He knew the ill effects of immorality. And he was writing under the inspiration of the Holy Spirit. Just like all the heroes and human authors of Scripture (except Christ), Solomon was a sinner God used to transmit His Word. That makes the wisdom of Proverbs as relevant to our society today as when it was written! Solomon warned of the dangers of prostitutes and adulteresses who seek to entice men. Although Solomon's instruction was directed toward his sons, the same principles apply equally to women.

When experienced properly, sex is the pinnacle of intimate human experience. But practiced immorally, it becomes a destructive weapon of Satan. The most fulfilling physical interac-

---

1. 1 Kings 11:4; For a description of Solomon's sin of polygamy, see 1 Kings 11:1–13.

tion between husband and wife can also be the most destructive influence in the life of a fool. Because sexual experience reaches far into the depths of human emotion, it can become the most dominating, life-controlling power in a person's life. It is like the power of electricity—it has the power to benefit us or the power to harm us. The power of sexual experience can either profit or pervert, build up or tear down, fulfill or frustrate.

With immensely practical wisdom, Proverbs describes both aspects of God's great wedding gift. For those who seek wisdom, the instructions Proverbs offers is as clear as any found in Scripture. But for those looking for moral loopholes or sexual license, the advice of Proverbs seems archaic and prudish. Even so, the truth of Scripture is not dependent on our willingness to accept it. And as we approach Proverbs, we find plain talk on both the negative aspects as well as the positive attributes of sex.

THE ILLEGITIMATE USE OF SEX

True to the spirit of the sexual revolution of the 1960s, the media today promote sex as a cheap commodity, something to be bartered, borrowed, and bandied about. The sanctity of sexual experience is ignored, and its purity defiled by crass innuendo and shameless display. The terms "promiscuous" and "illegitimate" regarding sex have all but disappeared from our popular vocabulary. And with widespread sanction of sexual permissiveness has come a new terminology—the word "immoral" has been replaced with the phrase "sexually active"; "homosexual" with "gay"; "adultery" with "affair"; and "pornography" with "mature entertainment." But if God's Word is truth, no amount of happy talk and media hype will change the reality behind the facade. According to Proverbs, illegitimate sex is a dead-end street. It devastates emotions, destroys marriages, decimates human bodies. Ultimately, it kills.

Proverbs warns against the illegitimate use of sex with a portrait of a naive man's encounter with an immoral woman (7:6–23). This man lacked the information or understanding of God's law. He lacked thoughtful interaction with God's Word and willingness to be warned by its truth. Because he lacked sense (v. 7), he placed himself in a position to encounter temptation. He chose to be in that part of town "near her corner" (v. 8). Many men today think they can handle going to lunch with an attractive secretary, or being alone with an attractive counselee, or having dinner with a casual acquaintance on a business trip. Like them, this senseless youth believed he could turn back any tug at his libido.

What the young man in Proverbs hadn't counted on, however, was this woman's ability to appeal to his ego as well as his senses. With passionate kisses (v. 13), flattering words (v. 15), a little spiritual lingo (v. 14), and fantasy (vv. 16–20), she hooks him, plays him, and reels him in. He suddenly follows her, in the same way an ox blindly follows its master into the slaughterhouse (v. 22). Ultimately it cost him his life (vv. 23, 26).

The example of the naive man shows we need to remember three things. First, this is a scenario typical of the sage's day. Obviously it is not the only way sexual promiscuity or adultery can occur! We must be careful not to shrug this off as just another Bible story. Make no mistake—the enemy can offer your favorite allurement anytime you're ready! A couch can be a waterbed. Linens can be furs. Spices can be champagne and soft music. And a husband's business can be business of another kind! The point is anyone lacking a commitment to God's Word is not far from a fatal fall.

Second, we need to remember that the genders presented here are immaterial. Because the writer was warning his son, his example is a man being tempted by a woman. Had he wanted to warn a daughter, the genders may well have been reversed. Our society glorifies aggressive women and cultivates passive men. So reversing gender is not altogether unrealistic. It could easily be a case of the man seducing the woman. Or, in the most perverted scenario, a man or woman could be seducing someone of the same sex. But regardless of the form of perversity, the outcome is the same—disaster.

Third, just because a youth is the example, we cannot assume age disqualifies us from the temptations described. Lust has no age limits. Paul warned Timothy to "flee...youthful lusts" (2 Tim. 2:22). Fleshly desires come upon us at puberty and stay around to dog, distract, and pester us until the day we die. These desires find their greatest outlet among the young, but they are by no means limited to those under thirty!

Proverbs shows how difficult it is to envision the consequences of our actions. This shortsightedness is aggravated by a culture that has drummed into a philosophy of instant gratification. Therefore we don't look far enough ahead to see what it will be like when, as one says, "the fun turns to ugly."

For the lips of an immoral woman drip honey,
And her mouth is smoother than oil;
But in the end she is bitter as wormwood,
Sharp as a two-edged sword.
Her feet go down to death,
Her steps lay hold of hell.[2]

The consequences of immorality are inevitable and unavoidable. It doesn't matter if you are a backstreet bum, a senator, a professional athlete, or a minister. When it comes to sexual sin, it's payday someday. People talk. Husbands find out. Reporters snoop. Pregnancies happen. Diseases spread. Guilt builds. God works. It is true that God offers forgiveness to those who repent and agree with Him concerning their sin (1 John 1:9). But the law of cause and effect is never suspended. Often sexual sin irreversibly damages the lives of repentant Christians.

To draw the shortest line of application between Proverbs and our lives today, the immoral woman is *anyone* who would encourage us to have sex outside of marriage. What can we learn about those who tempt us *before* the encounter? Among other things, they stimulate our imagination, promise us forbidden pleasures, appeal to our eyes, meet our needs, understand our hurts. They offer secrecy and promise safety. And they won't stop tempting us until they have prevailed.

The sage was so graphic and adamant in his warnings about temptation because when we are in the midst of the temptation it is difficult to see and understand the consequences. A blindness sets in, we are told, and it is a dumb ignorance that leads to actions that would seem unthinkable at any other time.

Not long ago, a man, whose wife was ill with a debilitating disease, and a woman who was estranged from her own husband, met at a health club. Before long, the two were meeting secretly and became sexually involved. Eventually the man persuaded his lover to pose as a robber and murder his wife—a crime the lover committed and later confessed. Amazingly, both professed to be Christians!

Though murder may not always be the outcome, Proverbs tells us the person who participates in the deeds of the adulteress will be led into degradation. We learn that one who succumbs to the wiles and flattering tongue of adultery will be "reduced to a crust of bread; and an adulteress will prey upon his precious life."

2. Prov. 5:3–5.

An adulterous relationship drains a person's energy for living. Life becomes worthless. Those things God ordained as most important (marriage vows, parental responsibility, and moral purity) take a back seat to living for the moment, maintaining emotional intensity, and protecting reputations.[3]

This is *not* the picture our culture paints for us. Soap operas and novels try to convince us that changing sex partners has no more consequence than changing our socks. The media's features on celebrities and many successful people suggest sexual allegiance is as non-binding as preference for a certain make of car or brand of cereal. We are urged to live for the passion of the moment, to let our glands be our guide, and to give no thought to the outcome. The attitude of society today is that we can engage in sex and not experience any consequences. But Scripture proves that wrong:

> Can a man take fire to his bosom,
> And his clothes not be burned?
> Can one walk on hot coals,
> And his feet not be seared?
> So is he who goes in to his neighbor's wife;
> Whoever touches her shall not be innocent.[4]

This is also true of the woman who goes to her neighbor's husband. The law of cause and effect is never suspended for the sake of sexual gratification. Among the consequences of adultery are "wounds and dishonor," "reproach," a spouse's fury, even the destruction of one's own soul. In regard to the latter consequence, it is no mystery that the hearts of hundreds of thousands have been hardened to the gospel because of the guilt and shame associated with adultery and immorality. Today we see the physical maladies that come from wide disregard for chastity, including sexually transmitted diseases like herpes, syphilis, gonorrhea, and the deadly HIV virus.[5]

When sexual passion reaches pathological dimensions in someone's life, the person becomes trapped in an addiction to sexual sensations. The addiction demands greater and greater risks in order to achieve the same level of sexual intensity until the entire day's activities are spent trying to satisfy desires. The addicted

3. 6:26.
4. Prov. 6:27–29.
5. 6:33a; 6:33b; 6:34; 6:32.

person begins to hate the very thing he spends his time trying to satiate. He tries to stop, but it is too late. The cravings control him, and he is filled with self-hate for falling into the temptation.

In recent years numerous sex offenders have testified that their criminal behavior began with exposure to some type of sexual indulgence, such as pornography or unrestrained illicit sex.

In Proverbs' example, the temptress beckons, "Come, let us take our fill of love until morning; let us delight ourselves with love." But it was deception. It wasn't love. It was a cheap imitation, at triple the price. The sage goes on to warn, "He did not know it would take his life." No matter how we try to rationalize, minimize, or spiritualize the gross error of adultery, death is written all over it. Sexual non-restraint kills. It kills the body, it kills marriages, it kills friendships, it kills relationships with one's children, it kills fellowship, it kills spiritual vitality, it kills sensitivity to God. It is the ultimate dead-end.[6]

PROPER ENJOYMENT OF SEX

Along with serious warnings, Proverbs provides positive instruction for those seeking a wise sexual life. Solomon wrote,

> Drink water from your own cistern,
> And running water from your own well.
> Should your fountains be dispersed abroad,
> Streams of water in the streets?
> Let them be only your own,
> And not for strangers with you.
> Let your fountain be blessed,
> And rejoice with the wife of your youth.[7]

Proverbs teaches that God's plan for sexual enjoyment prescribes exclusive love of a husband for his wife. In God's design for sexual fulfillment, a husband receives the pleasure of love from his wife alone. He shares her with no one else. He sees that her needs are met so that she is not tempted to tell some other man "my husband is not home; he has gone on a long journey." In the same way, a wife should view her relationship to her husband as exclusive and precious. He is hers alone. She, too,

6. 7:18; 7:23.
7. 5:15–18.

wishes to share him with no one else, nor to give her affections to any other man.[8]

Some people seem to believe that the Bible allows sex only for procreation. The Bible clearly teaches otherwise. While one of the purposes of sex *is* procreation, God also gave sex for a man and his wife to enjoy. "As a loving deer and a graceful doe, let her breasts satisfy you at all times; and always be enraptured with her love."[9]

It's not enough simply to stay away from other men and women. Anyone who seeks to be wise sexually must delight in his or her mate. Each must study the other and learn what makes him or her feel special, motivates each other to do good, and encourages each other to worship and glorify God. The man who does this has a wife who cannot wait for him to come home from work. She throws her arms around him, admires him, and fulfills his needs. The woman who does this has a husband who cannot wait to meet her at home, treasure her, treat her with loving respect, and fulfill her deepest desires.

There's no one more beautiful than a woman who is loved by her husband. While the adulteress dresses seductively and adorns herself with jewelry and fashionable hairstyles, the virtuous woman adorns herself with Christ. She displays the joyous knowledge that God produces faithfulness in her husband. She is a showcase for true love, the love which is from above, not a cheap imitation. "Charm is deceitful and beauty is vain," we read, "but a woman who fears the LORD, she shall be praised."[10]

Proverbs admonishes the wise to teach these biblical principles to others. The sage taught his sons:

> Therefore hear me now, my children,
> And do not depart from the words of my mouth.
> Remove your way far from her,
> And do not go near the door of her house,
> Lest you give your honor to others,
> And your ears to the cruel one.[11]

In our degenerate culture, our sons and daughters desperately need to be educated in this area as soon as possible, so that when they are confronted with sexual temptation, they will

8. 7:19.
9. 5:19.
10. 1 Peter 3:3–6; Prov. 31:30.
11. 5:7–9

know the right thing to do. They also need examples of parents who are deeply in love. Such examples provide children with security, significance, and esteem. It helps children exemplify the principles in Proverbs when they grow up and love and cherish their spouses the way God intended.

GUIDELINES FOR SEXUAL SURVIVAL

The book of Proverbs is not preoccupied with sex. It does, however, provide us with a number of insights so completely contrary to the constant programming we receive every day, we would do well to note them and apply them.

Let's consider a few of these as guidelines for sexual survival.

Don't fall for the world's public relations job. One of Satan's most effective weapons against the purity of believers is the public relations job he performs regarding sexual promiscuity. In advertising, television, magazines, movies, and other forms of entertainment, he paints a picture of blissful indulgence. The playboy lifestyle is one of soft flesh and a liberated conscience. The objective, of course, is to tempt our flesh to follow our base desires.

However, Proverbs warns, "Do not let your heart envy sinners, but in the fear of the LORD continue all day long; for surely there is a hereafter." No matter how the media makes life appear, our actions are not without consequences. As one radio Bible teacher likes to phrase it, "Nobody is getting away with anything." A lifestyle without consequences simply *does not exist!* To fall for that deceit is naive.[12]

Unfettered pleasure is not the ultimate experience in life. Ours is one of the most self-indulgent, self-oriented cultures that has ever existed on earth. We are a society preoccupied with personal rights we love to define according to our own standards. Among these standards is the belief that pleasure is a deity. Our society claims the highest achievement in life is personal pleasure.

Without even looking into God's Word we can see the emptiness of pleasure for pleasure's sake. Whether it is a professional baseball player now addicted to the pleasure of gambling, a promising young race driver dead from the consequences of unfettered sexual pleasure, or a self-made millionaire bankrupt

12. 23:17–18a.

from the pleasure of high-stakes speculation, we see that pleasure is a cruel and uncompassionate god.

God's wisdom, however, warns that "he who loves pleasure [pleasure for pleasure's sake] will be a poor man." In more illustrative language, Proverbs warns, "Have you found honey? Eat only as much as you need, lest you be filled with it and vomit." Though many things, including sexual enjoyment within the boundaries established by God, bring us momentary pleasure, living for pleasure alone is following a sure path to personal destruction.[13]

The senses can never be satisfied. The quest for sexual gratification is grounded in the senses. And, according to Proverbs, the wise recognize the senses can never be satisfied. Almost any man will tell you, for example, the eyes are never satisfied. That is why the lust to see more and more is never satiated. As Proverbs warns, "Hell and Destruction are never full; so the eyes of man are never satisfied." Living solely to satisfy the senses only leads to a life of vanity or emptiness. Though the hucksters of our age appeal to our senses at every turn, the wisdom of God admonishes us to seek wisdom, and let her satisfy our needs.[14]

Happiness has nothing to do with fun, and fun has nothing to do with happiness. In our society fun is presented as the key to happiness. If you're having fun, you're happy. If, on the other hand, you are not having the rip-roaring fun of a beer commercial or dancing a tango in the tropics, our culture claims happiness will escape you. And, of course, we are taught that the quickest avenue to fun is the broad way of sex.

In Proverbs are many glimpses of people having fun. There are violent youths who lie in wait for someone to mug. There is the naive youth who finds his way into a beautiful woman's bed. There are those who linger long over fine wine. And the list goes on. These are not the same people Proverbs pictures as truly happy, satisfied, or content. These fun lovers, in fact, experience the opposite. They have nothing left when the fun has ended. They are the ones whose end is destruction, whose reward is the grave, whose appetite brings them to a hasty conclusion.[15]

It is not that the wise have no appreciation for life, sense of

13. 21:17; 25:16.
14. 27:20; Eccl. 1:8; Prov. 4:8.
15. Prov. 1:11; 7:6–27; 23:29–35.

humor, taste for godly revelry, or appetite for wholesome fun. But, as one writer puts it, "Happiness is what you have left when the fun is over." God desires that all His children find sexual happiness, just as He desires that we find true meaning and happiness in every area in life. The only catch is that happiness in this area comes only by following God's path to wisdom.

It is not any easier, nor it is any more difficult, than following the simple percepts of God's Word. All that is required is submission to the truth, power, and authority of His perfect Word.

CHAPTER 7

Religious Wisdom

PROVERBS WAS WRITTEN to teach us how to live wisely. It was written to be understood by everyone who has to face daily life. While Proverbs deals with the religious affections of man, it leaves deeper study of religion to the priestly writers. Proverbs provides wisdom, however, when religion touches daily life. While the sayings of Proverbs do not dwell on the temple of God, they show how worship casts its shadow over daily life before God.

THE RELIGIOUS LIFE

Though the book of Proverbs does not present a detailed treatment of religion, it contains many instructions for the righteous man. As we have already seen, concepts of righteousness and wisdom are inseparable in Proverbs. Fearing God is equated with wisdom. There is no wisdom apart from knowing Him. "The fear of the LORD is the beginning of wisdom, and knowledge of the Holy One is understanding." Knowing God and fearing Him provide the only real basis for the kind of wisdom on which an upright life can be built. Proverbs bluntly concludes that a man's daily life reflects his inner devotion (a concept echoed by James in the New Testament). "He who walks in his uprightness fears the LORD, but he who is perverse in his ways despises Him." The righteous obey the revealed Word of God. "Where there is no revelation, the people cast off restraint; but happy is he who keeps the law." Law refers to Torah (meaning instruction), the Word God gave His people to guide them in all aspects of their lives. Because it was incumbent on every Hebrew family to perpetuate faith in the true God, the wise father exhorted his son to remain faithful to God's instruction: "My son, do not forget my law, but let your heart keep my commands."[1]

What a contrast to our contemporary curricula for Christian instruction. Too often it softens the revelatory aspects of God's law and ignores the Word of God altogether. Most of the references to God's Word found in Proverbs describe the Pentateuch. We must understand the importance of a *balanced* presentation of the full scope of Revelation in teaching our children. God's law is without fault. We read, "Every word of God is pure and he is a shield to those who put their trust in Him." Proverbs shows that God blesses the obedient with protection. Heeding God's instruction also leads to long life and reward. Therefore, "He who heeds the word wisely will find good, and whoever trusts in the Lord, happy is he."[2]

THE SPIRITUAL IMPERATIVE

Proverbs 3:1–10 is a detailed exhortation to a young son concerning his religious affections. In it the father employed sixteen imperative ("must do") verbs in his zeal to charge his son to be faithful. First, the father urged his son not to forsake instruction (or Torah). To that he adds, "Let not mercy and truth forsake you." Mercy is used here to mean kindness and love shown to other people. When mercy is used in reference to God, it means God freely gives His love and obligates Himself by covenant to His people. The righteous man follows this example set by God, and binds mercy and truth to his inmost being.[3]

The command is also given to seek God's favor as well as man's. Though Proverbs 3:4 is usually translated "and so find favor and high esteem in the sight of God and man," this imperative may also read "*seek* favor and high esteem in the sight of God and man." This means that a righteous man seeks the commendation of God upon his life and knows a wise and righteous life results in a character esteemed by all men.

The father continued instructing his son

> Trust in the LORD with all your heart,
> And lean not on your own understanding;
> In all your ways acknowledge Him,
> And He shall direct your paths.

1. Prov. 9:10; 14:2; 29:18; Hartley, 404; Prov. 3:1.
2. 30:5; 3:2, 13:13; 16:20.
3. 3:1–2; 3:3; Harris, 305; Prov. 3:3.

The Hebrew word for *trust* was very similar to an Arabic word that meant "to throw one down upon his face" or to "lie extended on the ground." The idea, therefore, was to find security in submission to something or someone who gives confidence. Other Hebrew words related to trust show that confidence is confidence in God. The picture, then, is one of placing all of our concerns on God, and wholly relying on His faithfulness.[4]

As the stories of soldiers' escapes and rescues during the Vietnam War began to surface, almost every one of them had one thing in common. Regardless of the perilous routes and uncertain circumstances that led to rescue by helicopter or airplane, virtually every soldier spoke of a feeling of absolute release and trust when they knew they were in an American aircraft flying away from enemy-occupied territory. Often, they threw themselves headlong into the aircraft putting their confidence in the crew to take over. This is the kind of trust in God written of in Proverbs. We throw ourselves into God's care, and we have absolute confidence He can do it.

Parallel to trusting in the Lord is the command not to trust in ourselves: "Lean not on your own understanding." The picture here is of using a staff or rod for support, applied figuratively to trusting. In Ezekiel 29:6–7 the Lord says Israel had leaned (trusted) on Egypt like a staff, and Egypt broke. So too, the one who trusts his own discernment leans on a rod that will quickly splinter.[5]

The righteous man acknowledges God in everything he does. The son received the command to *know God* in all his ways. Some kinds of knowledge can be acquired through contemplation, but often it is experience that produces knowledge. Therefore Proverbs exhorts us to *contemplate* the knowledge of good and evil so that we may avoid sin. But if we want to be truly righteous, we will know God in our meditations and in our *experience*. By fearing the Lord rather than leaning on our own abilities, we receive health and strength from Him.[6]

Proverbs 3:9–10 also urges the son to "honor the LORD with your possessions, and with the firstfruits of all your increase." To honor means "to make weighty or heavy." Therefore we conclude that upright people recognize God as weighty and give

4. 3:5–6; Brown, Driver, Briggs, 105; Oswalt, 101; Ibid.
5. Prov. 3:5; Austel, 945.
6. Prov. 3:6; Lewis, 3; It is knowledge and discretion that keep one from adultery in 5:1–3; 2:1–5; 3:6; 3:7–8.

him the honor He deserves. How do we honor God? The context clearly indicates God is honored by generous giving. In Hebrew worship the firstfruits were given as a sacrifice in the worship of God. Today we give the first and the best, rather than the rejects and the leftovers. The worshiper who reveres God's lofty position gladly brings offerings *in abundance*. This is the person who ultimately experiences overflowing prosperity from the hand of God: "So your barns will be filled with plenty, and your vats will overflow with new wine." This verse demonstrates fulfillment of any basic needs—*not* necessarily the satisfaction of every 20th-century want![7]

Proverbs shows us true worship of God penetrates into life's every detail. And for those who heed the advice of Proverbs, diligence in righteousness reaps an abundant blessing from the Lord.

WORSHIP IN PROVERBS

Proverbs does not entirely ignore formal worship in the believer's life. Limited though it may be, Proverbs does make other specific references to the worship of God. One writer described worship this way: "References to worship in Proverbs are rare; but what is taken for granted does not require frequent mention." The sage did not refer to the Sabbath or to circumcision and he rarely mentions sacrifice. The sage did not oppose Israel's worship but knew, "It was the duty of the priestly teachers to give instructions about it; it did not come within the scope of what the sages taught."[8]

When sacrifice does appear in Proverbs, it challenges the reader's attitude toward worship. For example, "The sacrifice of the wicked is an abomination to the LORD, but the prayer of the upright is His delight." To bring a sacrifice to God empty of essential reverence mocked the meaning of the sacrificial system. God desired a worshipful heart or no worship at all. Sacrifice had meaning when worshippers understood the significance of the sacrificial ritual in the worship of God. Empty ritual performed by the wicked induced God's wrath. "The sacrifice of the wicked is an abomination; how much more when he brings it with wicked intent." A sacrifice presented by a wicked person did not

7. Brown, Driver, Briggs, 457; Ex. 22:29; Prov. 3:10.
8. Oesterley, 67; Ibid.

atone for wicked acts. Instead, hypocritical sacrifice stoked the anger already burning in God's heart.[9]

We must beware if we are attending services in our church for the business contacts we make, or because there are a lot of singles there, or even because we get a lot out of it. We must also guard against sitting in church while harboring hate in our hearts toward a brother or sister in Christ.

The sage observed that God desires heart worship over material presence and personal holiness over public ritual. "To do righteousness and justice is more acceptable to the LORD than sacrifice," says God's Word.[10]

GOD IN PROVERBS

Of the 93 times God is mentioned in Proverbs, 85 of those instances use His covenant name, Yahweh, which God gave to His people through Moses. The God who keeps covenants, who promises to bless those who obey Him, and discipline those who disobey Him, is always in view. Proverbs guided the covenant people in their daily lives as the Psalms led them in praise. And both books can do the same for us.[11]

Proverbs discloses several characteristics of Yahweh. Let's examine some of them.

The Sovereignty of Yahweh

The God of Proverbs is absolutely sovereign. "The LORD works out everything for his own ends—even the wicked for a day of disaster." All that occurs happens with God's recognition and permission. Human beings plan and strive, but God still is the one who fulfills His purpose. He directs everything according to His desire, and nothing He does requires an explanation. Wisdom, therefore, requires that we recognize "a man's heart plans his way, but the LORD directs his steps."[12]

God rules all rulers. "The king's heart is in the hand of the LORD, like the rivers of water, he turns it wherever He wishes." And religious wisdom indicates that we understand that those who devise against the Lord ultimately will fail, for "there is no wisdom or understanding or counsel against the LORD."[13]

9. Prov. 15:8; 21:27.
10. 21:3.
11. Ex. 3:1–22.
12. Prov. 16:4 (NIV); 16:9, 19:21.
13. 21:1; 21:30.

Israel relied on God's sovereignty by casting lots to settle various matters. "One method may have been to place two distinguishable stones into a fold or pocket in the priest's garment. Whichever stone was chosen would provide the answer. They believed that by controlling which stone was chosen, God would reveal His will concerning the decision to be made." Thus the proverb, "The lot is cast into the lap, but its every decision is from the LORD." Israel knew that God's sovereignty extended to selecting a stone in casting lots.[14]

The Holiness of Yahweh

Inherent in God's name and majesty is His holy character. Sin does not warp His attributes. He is the righteous God who considers and overthrows the house of the wicked. He alone holds and dispenses true justice. "Many seek the ruler's favor, but justice for man comes from the LORD." The pure holiness of God stands in contrast to the confession of the sage, "Who can say, 'I have made my heart clean, I am pure from my sin'?"[15]

The Providence of Yahweh

God meets the needs of His people. God laid the foundations of the earth and set His creation in motion. Even now He sustains it. He gives to His people. Life and health flow from God. "The hearing ear and the seeing eye, the LORD has made both of them." The eyes and ears provide man two reliable ways to gain knowledge and wisdom.[16]

Twice Proverbs notes that a godly wife is a gift of God's provision. "He who finds a good wife finds a good thing, and obtains favor from the LORD." "Houses and riches are an inheritance from fathers, but a prudent wife is from the LORD." A man may obtain riches through labor or birthright. The comfort, joy, and blessing of a good wife, though, is a gift from God.[17]

The Protection of Yahweh

Another characteristic of God revealed in Proverbs is the protection of His people. "The name of the LORD is a strong tower;

14. Woodcock, 62; Prov. 16:33.
15. 21:12; 29:26.
16. 3:19–20; 20:12; Woodcock, 62.
17. Prov. 18:22; 19:14.

the righteous run to it and are safe." The image of a tower represents this truism. In Old Testament times, people built tall towers where they could run and hide from the arrows of their enemies. The Lord is that tower for His people. The righteous find refuge from distress by trusting in God.

> Do not be afraid of sudden terror,
> Nor of trouble from the wicked when it comes;
> For the LORD will be your confidence,
> And will keep your foot from being caught.[18]

The Omniscience of Yahweh

The sage reveals God's omniscience, His knowledge of all the ways of humanity. "For the ways of man are before the eyes of the LORD, and He ponders all his paths." "The eyes of the LORD are in every place, keeping watch on the evil and the good." Not only does God see everything people do, He also delves into their hearts to judge their motives. As a smith tests the purity of gold or silver in the flames of a crucible, God tests everyone's motives.[19]

The Wisdom of Yahweh

Wisdom flows from the fountain of God. Our wisdom is acquired, but God's is infinite and eternal. Agur, himself one of the wise men, counted himself ignorant in comparison to the all-wise God:

> Surely I am more stupid than any man,
> And do not have the understanding of a man.
> I never learned wisdom
> Nor have knowledge of the Holy One.[20]

God's wisdom contains no impurity. While He tries with fire our impure motives and plans, God's wisdom is already refined. The image of the crucible again is used, but to show the purity of God's wisdom.[21]

God's wisdom extends to His works. "The LORD by wisdom founded the earth; by understanding He established the heavens." One of the first of God's works was the creation of wisdom.

18. 18:10; 3:25–26.
19. 5:21; 15:3; 16:2, 20:27; 17:3.
20. 30:2–3.
21. 30:5.

"I have been established from everlasting, from the beginning, before there was ever an earth. When there were no depths I was brought forth."[22]

We must remember this aspect of God's character when we encounter circumstances we feel require an explanation. Because God is perfectly wise, and because His wisdom far exceeds ours, we are foolish to try to explain the inexplicable from the divine viewpoint. Saying to a bereaved parent, "God must have something to teach you," or telling a terminally ill patient, "You must not have enough faith," only does damage and reveals the speaker's ignorance.

CONCLUSION

The traits of God's character are revealed by Proverbs in order to establish His rightful place as the focus of every person's adoration. As we have seen, God deserves our reverence. The wonderful truth about worshipping Him is that those who fear the Lord meet the one who introduces us to true wisdom. In Proverbs, righteousness and wisdom are inseparable. In order to be wise, we must be righteous, and in order to live righteously, we must be wise.[23]

---

22. 3:19; 8:23–24a.
23. See section on "Fear of the Lord", p. 22–24; Kidner., 31–32.

CHAPTER **8**

Educational Wisdom

"EDUCATION," HENRY WARD Beecher once
observed, "is the knowledge of how to use the whole
of oneself. Many men use but one or two faculties out of the
score with which they are endowed. A man is educated who
knows how to make a tool of every faculty—how to open it,
how to keep it sharp, and how to apply it to all practical
purposes."

While today's public educators might agree with this statement, few would argue that the spiritual side of every person is
as much a faculty to be trained as any other part of the human
personality and makeup.

Pick up any newspaper and you'll probably find a lawsuit, an
injunction, a controversy having to do with our society's insist-
ence that education be separated from spirituality. In the same
paper you'll likely find page after page of troubling news items
outlining the consequences of that kind of education. For example, what was lacking in the education of a 19-year-old honors
graduate who shot himself while playing Russian roulette? What
is missing from the curriculum of a school where four students
commit suicide in one year? And what was left out of the
academic track of college graduates who by the thousands have
broken marriages, abused children, alcohol or drug dependencies, and shattered lives?

THE NATURE OF EDUCATION

"America's founding fathers did not intend to take religion out
of education," says Billy Graham. "Many of the nation's greatest
universities were founded by religious leaders; but many of these
have lost the founders' concept and become secular institutions.

Because of this attitude, secular education is stumbling and floundering."

Most Christians recognize there is more to education than what we pick up in the classroom. God has been saying it for several thousand years. In Proverbs, in fact, His Word provides several concepts of education, all of them necessary if we want to live life skillfully. The most natural way to find out what education is in the mind of God is to look at the specific words used to describe it.

Discipline—*Musar.* The idea behind this biblical word focuses on the discipline (translated: *hard work*) it takes to acquire wisdom. It is "a far from static term . . . giving notice at once that wisdom will be hard-won, a quality of character as much as of mind." The person who seeks understanding—and education that really *works*—will discipline himself to know it. And, as we have already seen, self-discipline begins with a reverence for God, for "the fear of the LORD is the instruction of wisdom." God gives wisdom to the seeker who fears Him and gives himself to understanding God's ways. This means there are no shortcuts to true life education from the perspective of God's Word. There's no such thing as "instant maturity." The person who wishes to be wise from God's Word sets himself to study it and applies himself to learn it.[1]

Musar also carries with it the idea of correction. In some passages of Proverbs, it is used synonymously with God's discipline. Verse 3:11 says, "My son, do not despise the chastening (*musar*) of the LORD, nor detest His correction." Though this discipline usually refers to verbal persuasion rather than physical punishment, it means that the person who learns God's Word not only works hard to know it, he works just as diligently to apply it as a cleansing, purging, and correcting agent in his life.[2]

How many times have we watched as supposed "spiritual giants"—men or women who know their Bibles front to back—fall flat on their spiritual faces? For that matter, how many times have we sat through Bible study or listened to a powerful sermon and then almost immediately succumbed to temptation, fear, anger, or some other sin? Proverbs makes it clear that there is a vast difference between mastering the Word of God and letting it master us! If we want to gain wisdom, we will learn it through

1. Kidner, 36; Prov. 23:12; 15:33.
2. Kidner, 36.

discipline and we will be careful and open to correct ourselves or to be corrected by our Lord.

Understanding—*Bin*. In Old Testament Hebrew, this word communicates the ideas of discernment, perception, and insight. Behind this word stands the concept of an ability to perceive what is right and what is wrong in a given situation. Solomon, for example, used this word in his prayer for wisdom to rule Israel. He asks for understanding "that I may discern (*bin*) between good and evil."[3]

What a contrast to our wishy-washy ideas of morality, values, and ethics today! Though the 60s battle cry "everything is relative" is not parroted much in classrooms today, it has become the insidious premise behind our society's sliding scale of "right" and "wrong." We live in an age of adjustable morality, and Christians are not exempt! Consider, as just one example, how many small adjustments we have made in our ideas of right and wrong in order to reach the point where we can watch news reports of widespread abortion, so-called "homosexual rights," and the murder of handicapped newborns with little or no righteous indignation.

Tragically a majority of Christians today have reached the point of ignorance, indifference, or intimidation that has rendered them deaf, dumb, blind, and mute when it comes to matters of what is right and what is wrong. God's standards are *not* adjustable. His truth does not change. And the person who has gained God's brand of understanding in the process of life education will not compromise what he or she knows to be right or wrong.

The message of Proverbs is clear: understanding and wisdom go hand in hand. Wise people possess visible understanding, and people of understanding live lives of wisdom.[4]

Good Sense—*Sekel*. When it is translated into English, the Hebrew word *sekel* is often rendered as *wisdom, understanding, knowledge,* or *discretion.* When it is used as a verb, it means to be successful at something. If you have *sekel*, for example, you have the ability to skillfully handle practical affairs. We might call it "common sense" or "level headed" today.[5]

Common sense doesn't just happen, of course, as anyone who has ever raised a teenager knows! It has to have an objective

3. Woodcock, 35; Kidner, 36; 1 Kings 3:9.
4. Woodcock, 36; Prov. 16:21; 14:33.
5. Kidner, 36–37.

basis. It has to come from somewhere. In a biblical context, and in the context of real life, good sense receives its guidance from the teachings of the Word of God. It can keep us from losing our heads in difficult circumstances. It alone can give us a consistent, unwavering foundation for exercising good sense. And, according to Proverbs, when we have God's brand of good sense, we will be rewarded by gaining authority and honor among those around us.[6]

Discretion—*Mezimma*. This word is particularly interesting because it communicates the idea of planning or devising. Everyone makes plans in life, whether the plans concern what to buy at the grocery store or what direction to go in college or career. From "to do" lists to five-year business scenarios, we all have plans. And, as the careful record-keeping of drug dealers, prostitutes, and burglars proves, planning is not limited to the righteous!

Perhaps the most uncomfortable thought many people face is the truth that God not only weighs actions, He weighs motives and plans as well. After all, once we get past the Santa Claus stage of life, when we believe he sees us when we're sleeping and knows when we're awake, we like to think that our plans and motives are our own and that we are accountable only for the visible results. The Bible, however, paints a different picture.

God's Word tells us that His evaluation of our actions begins with our plans and that nothing escapes His notice. If a person's plans are evil, then the schemer—sooner or later—will suffer God's judgment. By contrast, the righteous person who plans justly or righteously will keep himself from evil. This means that if we truly desire to live a godly life, we'll learn how to look past the ends of our noses and understand the consequences we face if we intentionally disobey God.[7]

It also lets us know that those who obviously have planned evil and seemingly have gotten away with it—the "Christian" businessman who cheats his associates, the deceitful wife who plans and carries out an adulterous affair, the scheming gossip who destroys innocent Christians' reputations—actually are not getting away with anything. God simply has His own timing and His own ways of dealing with people.

However, those who seek to live life with righteous intentions

6. Prov. 3:1–4; 19:11, 10:19; 16:20; 17:2; 14:35.
7. 12:2, 14:17; 2:11–12.

and prayerful forethought can expect success in the eyes of God. The idea is that in forethought and discernment *that have been trained by the Word of God*, we can envision potential traps and avoid sin. The wicked, however, will continue to stumble along like unsuspecting prey about to be caught in a snare.[8]

"The godly man is in the best sense a man of affairs, who takes the trouble to know his way about, and plans his course realistically." A closely related term for discretion presents the image of a ship pilot skillfully using steering ropes to follow a safe course. As one writer has aptly put it, "He knows the ropes."[9]

It doesn't take much imagination to figure out what happens when we try to "steer" our lives without that ability.

Knowing—*Yada*. This was a very common Hebrew word that conveyed several ideas. Most of them, however, related to knowledge gained by "experience and through physical senses." This is the kind of knowledge which can be gained by few shortcuts but many detours are possible. As elder generations have long warned their successors, experience is a hard teacher— but it's the only way for some fools to learn![10]

In one Latin American city, the spread of the gospel and the response of thousands created a leadership crisis as the need for shepherds outstripped the Christian community's ability to train them. Therefore, several leaders got together to figure out how more pastors could be trained from the crop of new converts. They looked at the need for mature pastors, the average age of the new believers, and the time available to train them and announced their conclusion. They said, "To turn an immature, twenty-five-year-old seminary student into a mature, thirty-five-year-old pastor will take about ten years."

Knowledge is important, but it is no replacement for experience and application. Wisdom, in fact, often has been defined as "righteously applied knowledge." Appropriately knowledge and wisdom are intertwined throughout the fabric of Proverbs. In the balanced life of righteousness, they are entirely interdependent. Knowledge provides the foundation of wisdom and the wise person seeks to increase knowledge.[11]

The Proverbs never disconnect knowledge from wise living or

8. 22:3.
9. Kidner, 37; Brown, 286–87; Kidner, 37.
10. See section on "Religious Life", p. 120–122; Woodcock, 36.
11. Prov. 1:2; 15:14.

wise living from the increase of knowledge gained from the Word of God.

Instructions—*Tora*. This crucial Hebrew term refers specifically to teaching. In its historical context, it represented the Pentateuch, God's revealed teaching to guide His covenant people. In Proverbs, it refers to the wise instruction of the person who teaches God's Law. With that in mind, the communication of God's Word is pictured as both *a light* and *a fountain of life*. In other words, *tora* is what we need to see and what we need for an abundant life. We need constant, consistent, faithful instruction from the Word of God.[12]

What a tragedy it is that in our generation so many contemporary churches have replaced teaching with entertainment in order to attract an entertainment-oriented society. While the ploy perhaps has worked in terms of crowded pews and bulging church rosters, we are witnessing a generation of biblical illiteracy unprecedented in modern church history. Even more tragic, we are suffering the consequences of our failure to tap into the source of light and life—the life-changing Word of God.

The effects in our culture are increasingly evident. Though statistics say there is an amazingly high percentage of "bornagain believers" in our society, the moral decline we see around us is even more amazing. Why? Because teaching—along with evangelism—has been woefully neglected. But the problems around us go deeper than that.

Not only are thousands of people simply ignorant of God's teaching, ours is a generation that exalts rebellion against God's standards of godliness and mocks those who teach it. When was the last time, for instance, you saw a movie or television portrayal of an evangelical Christian that was not demeaning and derogatory? In a classical reversal of truth, the media today portray those who teach God's Word as wicked, while portraying the wicked as heroes.

Of course, this is nothing new. According to Proverbs, people who forsake teaching (the teaching of God's Word) will always exalt wickedness. And though they may feign religiosity when it suits their purposes, in reality God abhors their prayers. Because those who follow righteous teaching shame the lawless and

12. In 29:18 in the original, *tora* may refer to the Pentateuch. Elsewhere *tora* points to wisdom teachings; 6:23, 13:14, 7:2.

display a discerning spirit, they will receive animosity and insults from the wicked—but rewards from the Lord.[13]

Though the sage drew primarily upon the Law to form the crucial foundation of his instruction, we need to remember that God has not changed. Though the *regulatory* nature of the Law has ended, its *revelatory* purpose—that which it reveals about God's nature and character—continues. Just as Proverbs distills practical truths from the Law and serves them in zesty tidbits, so we receive the full counsel of God from His Word today.

And when we follow the counsel of godly teachers, we will live out the Word of God and be blessed for it.[14]

THE PURPOSE OF EDUCATION

According to Proverbs, the purpose of education is twofold: To cultivate a heart for God and to develop singleness of purpose.

> My son, give attention to my words;
> Incline your ear to my sayings.
> Do not let them depart from your eyes;
> Keep them in the midst of your heart;
> For they are life to those who find them
> And health to all their flesh.
> Keep your heart with all diligence,
> For out of it spring the issues of life.[15]

The picture presented in this passage might best be understood through a negative illustration. In recent months several parts of the world have been faced with terrible outbreaks of cholera. Cholera by nature is communicable only through the ingestion of unsanitary food or water. Usually it spreads fastest wherever ground water has been tainted by waste water. By contrast, where the water supply can be purified, spread of the disease can be arrested. Why? Because out of the water supply springs the issues of health. Pure water supply, pure water. Tainted water supply, tainted water.

The same is true of the human heart. Proverbs makes it clear that wisdom springs only from a wise heart. The heart warehouses the purity—or pollution—of our every action. "The heart," as it is translated in our English Bibles, refers to our inner being.

13. 28:4; 28:9; 28:4; 28:7.
14. 29:18.
15. Horton, 56–64; Prov. 4:20–23.

Because our inner person fears the Lord, we begin the acquisition of wisdom. And this hidden cache must be constantly guarded with the sentinel of obedience. By heeding God's instructions, we keep our inner wisdom—and our outer issues—pure.[16]

The second objective, vitally related to the first, is to develop singleness of purpose. In the New Testament, James wrote that a double-minded man is unstable in all his ways. Throughout history people have poured their lives into the achievement of a single goal. The athlete who has lived his childhood dream of playing in a world championship, or an author who holds the finished copy of his life's endeavor, knows the rewards of a single-minded purpose of a single heart.[17]

In the same way, wisdom calls the hearer away from superficial pursuits and beckons him to fix his purpose on skillful, godly living:

> Let your eyes look straight ahead
> And your eyelids look right before you.
> Ponder the path of your feet,
> And let all your ways be established.
> Do not turn to the right or to the left;
> Remove your foot from evil.[18]

The teaching of wisdom seeks to produce a heart set on God and a purpose focused on prudent living.

THE NEED FOR EDUCATION

Though we might balk at the notion that we are all fools at heart, Proverbs makes it clear that, just as we are all sinners by nature, we are all fools by practice, beginning in our earliest childhood years: "Foolishness is bound up in the heart of a child, but the rod of correction will drive it far from him." That's why the need for education, especially at an early age, is stressed so strongly in Proverbs. Can there be any question that our society's notion that the best education is a total lack of restraint has failed miserably? Seldom before has it been so evident that a different idea of education—God's concept of education—is in order.[19]

16. 4:23; 4:23, 4:20–21.
17. James 1:8.
18. Prov. 4:25–27.
19. 22:15.

It is important to understand at this point that foolishness in a child is not necessarily the same as the acts of folly we see in adults. Rather, it is an *absence of wisdom* which eventually can and will lead to folly. How many of us will climb into a car, start it, and then mash on the gas pedal without even touching the steering wheel, expecting it to take us where we want to go? How many people will hire a new employee and expect him or her to do a good job without being trained and instructed?[20]

These examples are no more ridiculous than parents who think they can put their children on "autopilot" and expect them to know how to live their lives wisely. Our nation's juvenile detention centers, jails, and prisons are filled with people who were never instructed in biblical wisdom. Granted a small minority of life's failures received godly instruction and then chose to reject it, but that fact is a pitifully sorry excuse for failing to provide the guidance God has deemed necessary for every child!

Proverbs teaches that a child left entirely unguided will take the downward path to folly and evil. Why? Because "they are not wise enough to avoid their sinful and foolish inclinations." They don't have good information—or a good example—to operate on.[21]

Of course, the fall of mankind (Gen. 3) is the fountainhead of the foolishness in all children. Adam's sin cursed the race to the point that all human offspring enter the world with a natural propensity for evil. "As is the root, so are the branches. As is the fountain, so are the waters." Therefore, parents who recognize this fact will act quickly and deliberately to change the child's natural bent toward foolishness. Likewise, parents who ignore it will suffer. "To leave a child to himself is to manifest a cruel indifference to the fate of one committed to our care."[22]

The Word of God does not leave parents without a remedy: "The rod of correction will drive it far from him." "Folly is such a serious flaw that serious steps must be taken to drive it far from children's hearts." It doesn't take a genius to look back over the past fifty years of our culture's history and see that as laxity and tolerance have increased in regard to hands-off parenting, rebellion, wickedness, and moral decline have increased.[23]

This is serious business.

20. Thomas, 554.
21. Woodcock, 174.
22. Bridges, 414; Ironside, 251.
23. 22:15b; Alden, 162.

> Do not withhold correction from a child,
> For if you beat him with a rod, he will not die.
> You shall beat him with a rod,
> And deliver his soul from hell.
>
> Chasten your son while there is hope,
> And do not set your heart on his destruction.
>
> Correct your son and he will give you rest;
> Yes, he will give delight to your soul.[24]

As the chapter "Family Wisdom" points out, the rod was an instrument of authority, correction, and guidance. It was *not* an instrument of hate, vengeance, or abuse. Therefore, we must never forget that the love of a parent is inseparable from the administration of the rod. Correction cannot be correction if it is motivated by anger. That is abuse. On the other hand, discipline which comes from a loving parent's heart recognizes that for the child's benefit and lifelong well-being, foolishness must be driven away.

Throughout life, there is a need for ongoing education because of the evil that can flow from ignorance. "Also it is not good for a soul to be without knowledge, and he sins who hastens with his feet." This poetic parallelism equates a lack of knowledge with a tendency to rush into sin. Like children who have not been taught the dangers of playing in the street, we often will walk blindly into temptation and sin because of our ignorance of God's Word.[25]

Though we might jokingly say "ignorance is bliss," Proverbs teaches it is not good to be ignorant. A mind without knowledge is a mind that lacks the tools to live skillfully. Imagine taking your ailing automobile to a mechanic and then noticing, as he prepares to work on it, that his toolbox is empty or filled with children's toys! What quality of work would you expect him to do? A life without knowledge—without education in the things of God—is no different. We can expect disaster.

As we've already seen, wisdom builds on knowledge, and a lack of knowledge reveals a mind that has flabby mental physique. Exercise in the pursuit of knowledge tones the faculties and quickens the reflexes. If we do not seek a broad range of

24. Prov. 23:13–14; 19:18; 19:2.
25. 19:2.

biblical knowledge and do not train our minds to apply it to life's many situations, our future will look very bleak indeed!

No matter how we might otherwise fill up our busy Christian schedules with activities, hobbies, meetings, groups, and get-togethers, Proverbs is adamant that ignorance in the things of God is a peril to the soul. Ignorance paves the way to evil. The ignorant person is prone to sin that comes from haste; he does not possess the skill of forethought and so hurtles blindly toward the cliffs carved by evil. Conversely, if we will faithfully seek the knowledge of God, He will replace evil impulsiveness with prudent, godly, mature contemplation.[26]

THE METHODS OF EDUCATION

"Inherent in the idea of wisdom," one teacher has written, "was that it could be taught, whether as a technical craft, as rules for the good life, or as profound understanding of the meaning of human existence." In other words, the first and most crucial link in the chain of solid teaching is the person who teaches.[27]

In Old Testament Israel, there were three types of teachers. First and foremost, parents were under the divine command to instruct their children. Second, the religious teacher, the priest, passed on Israel's worship rites. Third, the sage, or tutor, taught students the practical wisdom of life. Ideally, all three types of teachers meshed and coordinated their instruction to produce a model citizen and worshiper.

The guidance of the wisdom teacher or sage was contained and communicated in pithy sayings called proverbs. They were different from authoritative commands in that they were observations on how life actually works. "Proverbs were rules in another sense," writes one authority, "generalizations from experience about how 'the world wags' and men behave, with the good or bad consequences that have been observed to follow." They did not try to pass on imperatives of the Decalogue, but desired to stir the minds of students. "Their purpose is not indoctrination," we discover, "but illumination and education." Today we might say that the Law was lecture, while the advice of the sage was lab work. Together they cover the theoretical as well as the practical.[28]

26. Thomas, 413.
27. Scott, 48.
28. Scott, 52; Ibid.

Besides the use of pithy statements to open the hearer's mind, the sage often spoke about the necessity of receptivity, or a willingness to learn and change, in education. No matter how carefully crafted a key might be, it can't unlock a sealed door. If we hope to acquire wisdom, we must be willing to receive God's teaching.

Lady Wisdom cries out to the listener:

> Now therefore, listen to me, my children,
> For blessed are those who keep my ways.
> Hear instruction and be wise,
> And do not disdain it.
> Blessed is the man who listens to me,
> Watching daily at my gates,
> Waiting at the posts of my doors.
> For whoever finds me finds life,
> And obtains favor from the LORD.[29]

The Lady Wisdom reminds that richest blessings await the hearing ear.

The believer who is receptive is always open to wise instruction. He's also ready to obey the Lord's commands, as well as his correction or chastening. He searches out wisdom and willingly pays the price to acquire truth, wisdom, and understanding, for "wisdom is for the humbly eager."[30]

THE ROLE OF PARENTS IN EDUCATION

The sage brings to the forefront the responsibility of parents in influencing their children toward wisdom. One scholar, John E. Johnson, has written at length about the parental responsibility found in Proverbs, and he observes, "The primary responsibility of a parent is to maintain a sense of order, both in his personal life and in the life of his home. This order manifests itself in a righteous character."[31]

Though the traditional family is under attack today in the media and among such groups as homosexuals and militant feminists, sociological experts keep returning to the stability and guidance that seemingly can be obtained nowhere else but from parents. We are told—even by secular authorities—that youth

29. Prov. 8:32–35.
30. 9:9; 10:8; 3:11, 17:10; 23:23; Kidner, 38.
31. Johnson, 121–26; Johnson, 121.

who lack parental guidance of any kind already have two strikes against them.

Let's consider, then, how the proverbs stress the impact parents' instruction and example have on their children. "The righteous man walks in his integrity; his children are blessed after him," makes the point that a righteous man's sons have the benefit of an excellent role model who sets a standard for them to live by. Daily they see the fruits of righteousness, and they acquire a taste for them. They also gain a good name in the community—a desirable reputation—from their father. A good name is a blessing in itself, but it also provides a positive challenge for the sons to maintain that reputation. And even when they fail, that good name becomes a tool God uses to return them to wisdom.[32]

Proverbs 14:26, "In the fear of the LORD there is strong confidence, and his children will have a place of refuge," also shows the benefits of righteous parents. Regardless of what our caustic, pessimistic society may say, the Bible tells us that parents' fear of the Lord will allow their children to grow up in an atmosphere of confidence and security. They will observe a parent or parents whose reverence of God has provided the observable benefits of wisdom. Because God-fearing parents grow in security as they grow in the knowledge of the Lord, their children also acquire a sense of security and stability. This environment in turn encourages children toward healthy self-images, a balanced concept of the world around them, and solid, consistent values.[33]

The image the Bible presents is that the confidence of a righteous parent builds a refuge for his children. McKane calls that refuge "a stronghold surrounded by God's protection, a place of safety." The same refuge an upright parent has found in the name of the Lord then becomes the tower where his children can also find sanctuary in the midst of a tumultuous world.[34]

Throughout Proverbs, God's design for the parental relationship is emphasized as one of the most valuable and rewarding of life's realities, as in "Children's children are the crown of old men, and the glory of children is their father." The ideal family is one where children grow up with respect for their righteous parents and then mature into glorious "crowns" that adorn their parents' later years. In this context, "glory" is related to joy and

---

32. Prov. 20:7.
33. Johnson, 122.
34. 14:26b; McKane, quoted in Johnson, 122; Prov. 18:10.

rejoicing, just as it is used in Proverbs 28:12 to refer to the rejoicing of the righteous.[35]

In startling contrast to today's concept that raising children is toil and drudgery, the Bible teaches that homes that aggressively produce godly offspring will enjoy multiplied blessings. The home that produces foolish children, on the other hand, will suffer greatly.

> He who begets a scoffer does so to his sorrow,
> And the father of a fool has no joy.
>
> A foolish son is a grief to his father,
> And bitterness to her who bore him.
>
> A foolish son is the ruin of his father.[36]

Failing to educate a child in wisdom is a sure recipe for sorrow and bitterness when that child matures in his folly. When we consider the rich rewards for the faithful parent—as well as the disappointment for the father of a fool—we should be amply motivated to carefully educate our children in the things of God. When we do, "The father of the righteous will greatly rejoice, and he who begets a wise child will delight in him."[37]

35. 17:6.
36. 17:21; 17:25; 19:13a.
37. 23:24.

CHAPTER 9

Political Wisdom

WHY POLITICS?

THE BIBLE HAS a lot to say about the institution of human government and our relationship to it as believers. In God's Word, the state is not automatically viewed with suspicion, nor is the state an agent of evil or Satan. Rather, the Bible indicates God has established human government as one way to exercise His rule in the lives of people, and to express His common grace. And the book of Proverbs is consistent with God's desire to set forth principles of governmental rule.

As we have already seen, Proverbs is a book of Solomon the king, and it is directed toward the princes of Israel. It was an instruction manual for the rulers and future rulers of Israel, teaching them how to exercise their duty justly and in a responsible manner.

The Bible does not promote any one system of government over another, such as a monarchy over a democracy. Rather, it prescribes the proper characteristics and behavior for any leader or head of state, regardless of the political system. Of course, this may automatically condemn some types of harsh, brutal, totalitarian rule, while allowing for some types of rule other than ones to which we are accustomed.

Proverbs goes beyond the methods of political administration and addresses motives and morals as well. It sets forth the nature of moral government and its benefits, but it also presents the characteristics of evil government and its consequences. In its pages we see God intends for leaders of local, state, or national government to follow the precepts of Proverbs for righteous rule within sinful society. This does not advocate a state ruled by a church. It does, however, teach us that a leader who submits

himself to God and the principles He lays down is simply following the guidelines God Himself gave for good government.

The teachings of Proverbs not only relate to political government, they also apply to other forms of rule we deal with on a
daily basis, including the laboratory of self-rule, the home. These
wise sayings may be applied to self, home, business, church, or
any other context of authority in which rule or authority is
exercised.

Let's take a closer look at some of the specifics.

THE QUALITIES OF A GOOD LEADER

Anyone who leads a people or nation must have certain qualities of leadership in order for the nation to prosper. As goes the
leader, so goes the nation.

This was easily seen in the 1990–1991 Persian Gulf crisis. As
President of the United States, George Bush was well trained for
the international incident. He had previously served as a military
man, as director of the Central Intelligence Agency, as ambassador
for the United States on two occasions, and as Vice President for
two terms. His skill in diplomacy and knowledge of how to
properly wage warfare when necessary combined to bring the
conflict to a rapid resolution.

In the same way, any ruler or leader must possess experience
and training for his job. But he must always be open to new
avenues of thought and new types of solutions. A nation that
seeks righteousness must pursue men for its administration who
exemplify righteousness. A nation that seeks peace must find
peacemakers to lead it. A nation that seeks prosperity must be
committed to raising up rulers obsessed with obtaining wisdom.
These are the kinds of attributes the book of Proverbs advocates
for anyone with political authority.

Let's consider a biblical illustration of this principle. During
the reign of the king Hezekiah, Judah's capital city, Jerusalem,
was besieged by the Assyrian army. King Sennacherib of Assyria
initiated this siege because the Jews had refused to pay the annual
tribute he demanded. The Assyrian army was the most powerful
army of its day. Hezekiah and his people found themselves
standing alone against this great army.[1]

In the midst of these difficult times, Hezekiah seemingly had

1. 2 Kings 18:9–19:37.

nowhere to turn for advice. Whatever confidence he placed in Egypt came to nothing. His country had no other allies who could help. The outlook was bleak at best, desperate at worst.

At this point of despair, Hezekiah put his trust in God. And through this episode's outcome, the Bible provides us with a wonderful picture of how God comes to the aid of those who trust in Him for deliverance.

Though we don't know when the following portion of Proverbs was copied by Hezekiah's men, chapters 25–29 (especially 25:1–5) provide us with qualities essential to a good leader and good leadership, just as they guided many generations of the people of God in ages past.

> These also are proverbs of Solomon which the men of Hezekiah
>   king of Judah copied:
> It is the glory of God to conceal a matter,
> But the glory of kings to search out a matter.
> As the heavens for height and the earth for depth,
> So the heart of kings is unsearchable.
> Take away the dross from silver,
> And it will go to the silversmith for jewelry.
> Take away the wicked from before the king,
> And his throne will be established in righteousness.[2]

Let's take a closer look at the various aspects of godly leadership revealed in this passage and elsewhere in Proverbs.

Leaders search out the facts.

According to God's Word, anyone who makes rash decisions without diligently searching out the facts surrounding the case is a fool. By contrast, the wise ruler will search out a matter before acting on it. "It is the glory of God to conceal a matter, but the glory of kings to search out a matter."[3]

This verse draws a striking contrast between God's infinite wisdom and humanity's limited knowledge. God knows every fact and every possibility. He knows all hypothetical situations. He knows everything that is, was, and is to come. Yet He chooses to reveal only a portion of that information to us. Paul said, "Oh, the depth of the riches both of the wisdom and knowledge of God! How unsearchable are His judgments and His ways past finding out!" When we contemplate God's attri-

2. 25:1–5.
3. 25:2.

bute of omniscience, we stand in awe of God's greatness and glorify Him.[4]

God in His perfect wisdom knows precisely when and to whom to impart knowledge. He is not a twenty-four hour cosmic news station, letting everyone know everything He knows. Rather, God dispenses knowledge according to His timing and purposes.

The Scriptures tell us that "the secret things belong to the LORD our God, but those things which are revealed belong to us and to our children forever, that we may do all the words of this law." God gives revelation so that we will be careful to obey Him. Even so, He does not reveal everything that can possibly be known. Therefore we must trust Him with unknown matters.[5]

No matter what their position, all rulers are humans just like us. No matter what their prestige, title, or privileges on earth, they do not have access to infinite knowledge. Therefore it is to a wise leader's credit that he seek as much knowledge as possible before making decisions. Further, he needs to be continually aware of all that is happening within the areas for which he is responsible.

At one time or another, nearly everyone has fallen victim to a ruler, someone in a position of authority, who has leveled accusations or criticisms based on wrong information. Maybe it was secondhand (or thirdhand, or fourthhand) gossip; maybe it was a jealous coworker's fabrication; maybe it was a case of mistaken actions or words. If that ruler sought out accurate information based on two or three *eyewitness* observations, brought everything out in the open, and reserved judgment until the matter was clearly established, he showed signs of good leadership, according to Proverbs. If, however, that leader trafficked in anonymous gossip, trusted in his own fallible discernment, and passed judgment as though he himself were not accountable to God, he acted as a fool, according to God's standard of wisdom.

Our generation—and countless generations before us—fosters the notion that a position of leadership automatically endows a person with insight or maturity superior to those under him. Tragically, the entire sphere of Christian ministry has fallen victim to this unbiblical misconception. Ministries have been ruined, willing servants have been spiritually mauled, and fami-

4. Rom. 11:33.
5. Deut. 29:29.

lies have even been broken apart by abuses inflicted by Christian leaders whose concept of leadership was far removed from the one we find in Proverbs.

Of course, the consequences of poor leadership are even more devastating when God's standards are ignored at a national or international level. Good leadership is critical in our era of representative government. In order for a senator, congressman, supervisor, or mayor to adequately represent his or her constituents, they must seek out accurate information. They must know where their constituents stand on various issues, rather than caving in to the whims of vitriolic special interest groups. They must know their constituents' needs, wants, and dreams, rather than following trends the media promotes through biased coverage. And, they must have the ability to establish sound priorities, since all issues cannot be equally or immediately addressed.

In international affairs, it is absolutely crucial for leaders to have excellent and accurate intelligence information. Again looking to the Persian Gulf War for an illustration, the inability of Iraq's leadership to monitor the movements of the Allied troops proved to be fatal for their army once the battle began. Conversely, the high-tech satellites, reconnaissance flights, and the presence of special forces deep in enemy territory provided the Allied generals with valuable information that enabled them not only to achieve a quick, decisive victory, but also to keep the loss of Allied lives to a minimum.

Anyone who is in a position of leadership and desires to execute his or her office in a wise and godly way must have thorough, accurate information. And a leader will operate in perpetual humility, knowing only God possesses all knowledge.

Leaders choose wise and righteous advisors.

Since leaders have neither infinite knowledge nor time to research every issue and the possible effects of each decision, they must rely on the knowledge of others. This means the people with whom they surround themselves will influence them through information and advice they provide at critical decision making times. Whether these counselors are good or bad often determines in which direction the leadership goes, just as the quality of the leader often determines the quality of the advisors. The sage recognized this problem and said,

> Take away the dross from silver,
> And it will go to the silversmith for jewelry.
> Take away the wicked from before the king,
> And his throne will be established in righteousness.[6]

What does this mean? Dross is the slag or waste material that develops on the surface of molten metal. It consists of impurities and scum that are part of the metal before the refining process begins. Because jewelry made from unrefined metal falls apart and becomes worthless, precious metals must be refined before they can be used and considered of great value.

In government, the dross are those people who live wicked and immoral lifestyles. Their god is their own personal desire. They do not have the common good as their top priority. Their measure of success is prestige, power, or the size of their paycheck. People like these, says Proverbs, need to be removed from the presence of the leader like slag skimmed from silver. "Blessed is the man who walks not in the counsel of the ungodly," wrote the psalmist, "nor stands in the path of sinners, nor sits in the seat of the scornful." Taking the advice of the wicked will only achieve wicked results. The leader needs to rely on skilled advisors who exhibit righteousness.[7]

"Where there is no counsel, the people fall; but in the multitude of counselors there is safety." "A wise king sifts out the wicked, and brings the threshing wheel over them." The leader who wishes to establish his domain in righteousness weeds out wicked advisors because, "by the blessing of the upright the city is exalted, but it is overthrown by the mouth of the wicked."[8]

"An evil man seeks only rebellion..."[9]

"A wicked messenger falls into trouble, but a faithful ambassador brings health."[10]

Fortunately, in our day it is relatively easy to remove from office corrupt leaders who are appointed. But it is far more difficult for a wise, righteous leader to winnow out those evil representatives who hold elected office. For this reason it is extremely important for all Christians of voting age to monitor their officials and make sure they work hard to preserve biblical

6. 25:4–5.
7. Ps. 1:1.
8. Prov. 11:14; 20:26, 11:11.
9. 17:11.
10. 13:17.

values. If the godly do not take an interest in who holds offices of privilege and influence, leaders will become more and more evil.

Elsewhere in Proverbs we can find other valuable characteristics of leadership.

Leaders are dependent on people.

A wise leader recognizes that he needs people as much as, if not more than, they need him. In Proverbs we read, "In a multitude of people is a king's honor, but in the lack of people is the downfall of a prince."[11]

History is replete with examples of rulers who were out of step with the general wishes of their subjects. While there is sometimes room for legitimate disagreement between leaders and people, a wise leader keeps a finger on the pulse of his city, state, or nation. If there is too much disparity between a leader and the people, then he needs to either convince the people to change their minds or step down and allow someone else to lead.

A king who rules well over many obviously receives great honor. But when a leader finds no one is following him (at least not willingly), then "his solitary splendor," says one writer, "is self extinguishing."[12]

Though many people in positions of leadership today have learned the craft of wielding employee evaluations, critiques, and performance appraisals to secure obeyance from their staff, real Proverbs-style leaders are woefully rare. You recognize good leaders, though, by the heartfelt loyalty they enjoy from those who follow them.

A story is told of a gentle old pastor who, day after day, watched a young boy pass his house dragging a struggling, scraggly, mixed breed puppy behind him. Because of the collar and leash that kept him attached to the boy, the puppy had no choice in the matter.

One day the pastor stopped the boy and questioned him about the dog. He learned that the puppy was a stray the boy had found, and when it was not under the boy's control at the end of the leash, it was locked in a dark corner of the boy's barn. The boy was sincere enough, he just didn't want the dog to have a chance to turn tail and run away.

11. 14:28.
12. Kidner, 101.

The wise pastor gave the boy some advice. He advised the lad to spend an hour every day just talking to the puppy, petting it, and paying attention to it. Make sure it has three meals and a full water dish every day. If his parents would allow it, let the puppy share a room inside the house. And if a leash remained necessary, let the dog take the lead until he is used to it.

Within a few weeks, of course, the scene in front of the pastor's house was quite different. Though the boy was undoubtedly the master and the puppy was the pet, the two would pass by side-by-side—with no leash.

This is the kind of leadership Proverbs pictures for us.

Leaders administer justice based on God's standards, not their own.

Despite secular voices crying out that morality is relative and cannot be legislated, God's Word still tells us that certain standards are absolute. God's Word teaches that justice does not come from any one person's sense of right and wrong. Rather, it comes straight from God. According to Romans 1, God has placed a basic sense of morality (though now fallen and perverted) in every person's heart. Moreover, He has given the written Word to us and as long as we understand it correctly we cannot go wrong in determining what God requires. Both our basic need for moral guidance and God's special revelation which provides that guidance are necessary in order to administrate justice on the human level.

If God left us alone to determine what is just and right, then those in charge would be given a green light to dole out justice to whoever makes the most noise, because "many seek the ruler's favor." This is as true today in all levels of government as it was in Solomon's day. Our leaders are approached by everyone from the far right to the militant left for favors as well as legitimate needs. And all insist that they alone are right. Yet Proverbs tells us that all leaders have a responsibility to look to God's standards of righteousness rather than doing things the way everybody else does them. We learn, in fact, that if an official trusts the Lord to give him a just heart, and diligently studies God's Word to obtain it, he will have the wisdom to determine the merit of each request.[13]

Interestingly, when the mother of James and John requested

---

13. Prov. 29:26.

seats of power and prominence for her sons in the coming
kingdom of God, Jesus relied on the wisdom and justice of God
when He said, "It is for those for whom it is prepared by My
Father." The king—or any other leader—with a just heart will
not grant special favors based on anything other than God's
requirements. "The king establishes the land by justice, but he
who receives bribes overthrows it."[14]

A leader's office is a gift from God.

On this earth are many different forms of government—
democracies, totalitarian systems, socialistic societies, monarch-
ies, and even governments consisting of religious rule. We may
look on some forms of government as ungodly or unbiblical,
because the people do not have the privilege of determining their
own rulers, or because rule is passed down from generation to
generation, or because we were raised under a particular kind of
government.

Though democratic and representative forms of government
have certain advantages, the Bible has a different perspective.
Solomon affirms in Proverbs that *every* authority is instituted by
God. Nothing, not even political authority, is outside of His
control. And while many other factors, such as a country's
openness to His revelation, political history, and treatment of
His covenant people may determine what He allows, He is in
control of who rules, how much, and for how long.

Proverbs records the voice of wisdom,

> By me kings reign,
> And rulers decree justice.
> By me princes rule, and nobles,
> All the judges of the earth.[15]

All rulers, whether righteous or unrighteous, derive their authority from the supreme authority. While all authority comes
from God, not all authorities are submitted *to* God. Leaders often
abuse their power. Yet according to the Bible, they must be
obeyed. Even during the cruel reign of Rome, Paul wrote, "Let
every soul be subject to the governing authorities. For there is
no authority except from God, and the authorities that exist are
appointed by God." Likewise, Daniel told the unbelieving

14. Matt. 20:23; Prov. 29:4.
15. 8:15–16.

Nebuchadnezzar, "For the God of heaven has given you a king-dom, power, strength, and glory...."[16]

Leaders who desire godly leadership must recognize their position comes from God alone and not from merit. And anyone faced with the scriptural injunction to obey all those in authority must recognize that God is capable of raising up and putting down rulers as He chooses.

Leaders act under God's sovereignty.

The sovereign Lord who created the heavens and the earth also has a divine plan for the ages. In carrying out His plan God sovereignly guides the actions of kings and rulers in order to accomplish His purpose. Solomon described God's sovereignty when he said, "The king's heart is in the hand of the LORD, like the rivers of water; He turns it wherever He wishes." Solomon wrote, "the river of water" to illustrate the will of the king. Writing on this passage, one scholar has observed:

> Its commencement is a single spring; scarcely capable of turn-ing an handmill to grind a day's corn. But increased by the confluence of other small or great streams, it may turn hundreds of mills, and provide food for thousands. So the thoughts of the king's heart are first a single imagination for the good of his subjects; then swelled by the attendant thoughts of his mental resources, 'till what appeared desirable rises to the full power of accomplishment. But after all, the Great Sovereign turns the most despotic rule, all political projects, to His own purposes, with the same case, that the rivers of water are turned by every inflection of the channel. While this course is directed, the waters flow naturally and unforced on their own level. The king's heart He directs as a responsible agent, without interfering with the moral liberty of his will.[17]

A vivid example of the way God directs the hearts of those who rule took place in the former Soviet Union. A nation that was once closed to Christian evangelism has turned full circle. It now actively encourages Christian organizations to send representa-tives to educate their citizens about Christianity. Under God's sovereign guidance, atheist communist leaders actually helped this miracle occur.

When we look in the Scriptures, we see God influencing the

16. Rom. 13:1; Dan. 2:37.
17. 21:1; Bridges, 364.

hearts of Abimelech, Pharaoh, Nebuchadnezzar, and many others. The crescendo of the book of Esther is when King Ahasuerus could not sleep. It just so happened when the king asked for something boring read aloud to lull him to sleep, Mordecai's good deed was selected as reading material. This providential act saved the Jews from extinction. God indeed does direct the affairs of rulers! This does not imply that God is party to what the evil kings do. But He always causes the evil that is done to work toward His ultimate purposes.[18]

The sovereignty of God does not encourage us to hold a fatalistic view of rulership. A leader must not have a careless attitude that actions do not matter because God will work everything out His way. Rather, leaders should recognize the limited authority they have is always subject to the sovereignty of God. They must submit as well as they know how to God's leading.

THE MORAL RESPONSIBILITY OF GOVERNMENT

When God bestows authority as He wills, it is a great privilege to be trusted as a leader of a nation, state, or province. And with great privilege comes great responsibility. Government is not for the people to serve with blind allegiance. Rather, government is given by God to serve the populace.

Jesus told those who desired to be great in God's coming kingdom, "Whoever desires to become great among you, let him be your servant." Jesus was the supreme example of this type of leadership, "Just as the Son of Man did not come to be served, but to serve, and to give His life a ransom for many."[19]

It is the responsibility of leaders to emulate Christ's example, especially in righteousness, justice, wisdom, kindness, faithfulness, and knowledge. True leaders are servants who pursue these obligations with vigor. Let's examine each characteristic of servant leaders.

Righteousness

"It is an abomination for kings to commit wickedness, for a throne is established by righteousness."[20]

According to Proverbs, a ruler who behaves in an arbitrary

18. Gen. 20:6; 41:37–45; Dan. 1:19, 2:48.
19. Matt. 20:26; 20:28.
20. Prov. 16:12.

way is an abomination to God. A ruler is also a citizen and should be subject to the same laws as other citizens.

The result of a corrupt government is corruption throughout its administration. Wicked rulers normally surround themselves with like-minded administrators. In Solomon's time this led to abuse of the common people by government officials. Today it is widespread in Central and South America as well as communist regimes. Rejection and overthrow of many of those corrupt governments is frequently the result.

When rulers speak and behave in a righteous manner, their reputation with the people is enhanced. A righteous government must be ethical. It acknowledges correct standards of behavior and enforces them. It protects the equality of all citizens entrusted to its care. As one author wrote, "God sets the standards; it is the state's responsibility to understand and administrate them."[21]

Righteousness increases in society by ridding the population of wickedness. "When the wicked arise, men hide themselves; but when they perish, the righteous increase." This sort of "civil righteousness" is desperately needed in the inner cities of North America, where gangs fight to control drug territories. Citizens daily live in fear of being robbed or murdered. Repeat offenders flourish because they know there is little chance they will be successfully prosecuted for their crimes. This is the result of slow justice, partial law enforcement, and short prison sentences for those convicted. The government often becomes a part of the problem because of corruption. And neighborhoods continue to suffer and die slow, miserable deaths.[22]

By contrast, in communities where government officials have recognized the need for righteousness, and where citizens have cooperated to fight crime through crime watches and other neighborhood programs, drug dealers have been driven out and neighborhoods have become living communities once again. There is no substitute for God's standard of righteousness and morality in the public arena.

Justice

Leaders need to provide justice. Solomon said, "The king establishes the land by justice, but he who receives bribes overthrows it." The word "justice" in this verse means establishing the land. It is a tool for ensuring peace and stability. Leaders need

21. Johnson, 214.
22. Prov. 28:28.

to enact legislation based upon what is just. Justice requires enforcement be even-handed.[23]

God is the supreme judge and all judicial systems must pattern standards of justice after Him. Peter acknowledged that "God shows no partiality." In the same way, those who are trusted to exercise justice on the earth are expected to maintain the same spirit of impartiality. The president, monarch, prime minister, general secretary, governor, senator, or judge who violates justice shows utter contempt for the rule of law.[24]

Contempt for the law undermines society and leads to chaos as crime escalates. Colombia, after years of permitting drug lords to evade justice, now finds itself fighting a war within its borders in order to return law and order to its cities.

"The lot is cast into the lap, but its every decision is from the LORD." Wise rulers will always offer up their decisions to God. God promises to instill His sense of justice to those who submit to His sovereignty. Leaders serious about modeling God's impartiality humbly come before the throne of God and ask for divine guidance in all decision making. Such rulers receive from God wisdom and compassion and their administrations are a beacon of God's glory.[25]

Wisdom

Like righteousness and justice, wisdom is an essential foundation for good government. In an age when nations have the power to enslave less powerful neighbors with mighty weapons that can destroy entire cities, wisdom has never been in greater demand.

Counsel, understanding, strength, and sovereignty are in wisdom's possession.

> Counsel is mine, and sound wisdom;
> I am understanding, I have strength.
> By me kings reign,
> And rulers decree justice.
> By me princes rule, and nobles,
> All the judges of the earth.[26]

Wisdom in government includes knowledge, aptitude, talent, and discernment in its leaders. It also includes an ethical dimen-

23. 29:4.
24. Acts 10:34 (See also Rom. 2:11, Eph. 6:9, Col. 3:25).
25. Prov. 16:33.
26. 8:14–16.

sion. "A wise king sifts out the wicked, and brings the threshing wheel over them." One writer says, "the wise king protects the ethical terrain of the land." When immorality exists, ethical government roots it out before it becomes a cancer that ends righteousness in the nation.[27]

Kindness

When George Bush received the nomination as the Republican Party's candidate for the President of the United States, he said he would like the country to become a "kinder and gentler nation." This was precisely Solomon's point when he wrote, "Mercy and truth preserve the king, and by lovingkindness he upholds the throne." The wise ruler of a land was not to use his office as a platform for tyranny and oppression. Instead he was to protect the rights of everyone entrusted to his care by God.[28]

Good leaders are characterized by concern for those entrusted to their care. During the Persian Gulf War General Norman Schwarzkopf repeatedly expressed his personal concern for the welfare of his soldiers, the privates as well as officers. He was not willing to send his troops into battle until he felt sure of winning it with the lowest possible number of casualties. Further, the general's men came from a country characterized by justice and concern for the welfare of its people. The soldiers loved their nation and trusted their leaders at home as well as on the battlefield. Loyalty felt by Schwarzkopf's soldiers kept them fighting.

Iraq's leadership, however, led through fear and intimidation. Execution squads loyal to Saddam Hussein were used to keep civilians and soldiers in line. When the battle began, frightened Iraqi soldiers surrendered rather than fight. And the civilian populace rebelled. There was no loyalty to Saddam because neither kindness nor concern was shown the common people of Iraq. Kindness is preserved when the leaders constantly display mercy and diligently preserve the truth.

Knowledge

"Wise people store up knowledge, but the mouth of the foolish is near destruction."[29]

We may wonder why knowledge is included in a list of ethical characteristics for leadership. Leaders unaware of the nation's

27. 20:26; Johnson, 218.
28. Prov. 20:28.
29. 10:14.

needs serve to perpetuate a corrupt and immoral government. One writer noted, "Ignorance is a bedfellow of oppression, as well as political corruption. Citizens expect and need a government that is knowledgeable, lest errors of judgement cost a nation its power and its freedoms."[30]

"The glory of kings is to search out a matter." Good leaders investigate and get at the truth. People have less confidence in leaders with no idea of what subordinates are doing. Wise rulers do not cover up the wrongdoings of administrators. Rather, good leaders get at the heart of the matter and hold the perpetrators responsible for their actions. Richard Nixon fell from power for violating this principle in the Watergate scandal. Ronald Reagan maintained national support by instituting an investigation of the Iran–Contra affair.[31]

Wise rulers are aware of the needs, hurts, and aspirations of the people they govern.

Rulers who fashion their administrations according to the book of Proverbs are mindful of three things: Righteousness needs to be tempered with kindness. Justice needs to be balanced with mercy. Knowledge needs to be used with discretion. Just, kind, moral, righteous, and wise rulers exemplify the character of God and set the moral tone for the rest of the nation.

THE IMPACT OF ETHICAL GOVERNMENT

The Word of God is clear. Righteous, moral, just, and ethical government serves to create an environment of trust, respect, and joy among its people. The book of Proverbs lists many benefits when leaders follow the model God established for good government.

The nation stands firm.

When national leaders follow the guidelines God gives in Scripture, the people of the land experience inner stability. "The king establishes the land by justice. . . ." A country has political stability as long as the king continues to be just. The nation does not require force to hold it together because the people are content with the leadership.[32]

"The king who judges the poor with truth, his throne will be

30. Johnson, 219.
31. Prov. 25:2.
32. 29:4.

established forever." When rulers are deceptive, their people become discontented and rebel. When rulers treat the underprivileged with compassion, their nations give them allegiance.[33]

The people rejoice.

Maintaining the spirit of a nation requires consistent, righteous leadership. "When the righteous are in authority, the people rejoice, but when a wicked man rules, the people groan." As one Bible scholar has noted, "A nation's morale is strategic to its stability."[34]

When the national mood becomes depressed, productivity sinks, the defense forces grow lax, corruption becomes rampant, drug and alcohol abuse abound, and eventually the nation dies a slow death. But when the people rejoice, they bring special vigor to every area of life. Corruption is not tolerated, and the defense forces feel the nation is worth defending.

"Righteousness exalts a nation, but sin is a reproach to any people." When righteousness abounds, the joy experienced is often overwhelming. Righteousness lifts a nation and preserves it. And it prepares a nation for God to do great things in the lives of its people.[35]

Wickedness is curbed.

Righteous government must punish evildoers. By removing criminals and encouraging honesty, people follow their leaders. Good leaders remove the wicked from society.

This is what Solomon meant when he said, "A king who sits on the throne of judgment scatters evil with his eyes." And again, "A wise king sifts out the wicked, and brings the threshing wheel over them." The image is that of a man with a pitchfork throwing grain into the air so that the wind can separate the chaff and leave pure grain. The Hebrew language in the last verse is particularly vivid. To sift means the wise king sifts out the wicked with the utmost intensity and eagerly crushes evildoing.[36]

The poor receive compassion.

The poor often have no voice in government. Therefore, it is left to benevolent leadership to see the poor receive justice. Solomon addressed this issue when he said,

33. 29:14.
34. 29:2; Johnson, 223.
35. Prov. 14:34.
36. 20:8; 20:26.

> Open your mouth for the speechless,
> In the cause of all who are appointed to die.
> Open your mouth, judge righteously,
> And plead the cause of the poor and needy.[37]

Many societies exploit and oppress their poor to keep them from gaining any kind of political power. This has led to many violent revolutions throughout human history. The kind of leader described in Proverbs is one who protects the poor from exploitation.

The government receives honor.

A government that practices righteousness finds its own people and nations abroad bring the nation glory and respect. Solomon observed, "Righteousness exalts a nation, but sin is a reproach to any people." The ethical ruler is appreciated, and in a democracy, may be elected to office over and over again. People appreciate rulers who avoid "ignorant rhetoric and mindless reactions." When diligently pursuing the requirements of office, good leaders earn the respect of everyone.[38]

RESULTS OF UNETHICAL LEADERSHIP

Since the Fall, sin has pervaded every area of life. Government is no exception. No government is perfectly ethical, but perfection is a goal. When government chooses foolishness instead of righteousness there are severe consequences.

Wickedness: Americans tend to view certain forms of government as evil. In the fifties, communism was the menace to fight. In the sixties, it was imperialism. During the seventies and eighties, many considered our own bureaucracy suspect. Currently, dictatorships are resisted. But God does not judge a government by its constitution, He looks to the moral character of its leaders. As one writer put it, "governments which dishonor God are wicked."[39]

When rulers are evil, kingdoms fall. "Like a roaring lion and a charging bear is a wicked ruler over poor people." Like territorial animals who desire to guard what is theirs, evil rulers maul and eat anyone who threatens them.[40]

37. 31:8–9.
38. 14:34; Johnson, 224.
39. Johnson, 225.
40. Prov. 28:15.

Greed: Evil government completely owns its citizens and their wealth. It exacts more than what is necessary to finance government. Many countries with evil governments support rulers living in opulent luxury while their people live in squalid conditions. The late Ferdinand Marcos of the Philippines and Manuel Noriega of Panama provide excellent examples of this kind of leader. The good of the people was secondary to their personal enrichment.

Oppression: "A ruler who lacks understanding is a great oppressor." Wicked rulers do not care to learn about their people. Often, such rulers are ignorant, or even insane, violently suppressing the smallest rebellion with crushing force. Saddam Hussein rules Iraq by violence and intimidation, even so far as exterminating rebellious villages with nerve gas.[41]

Wicked rulers spend much time and money gratifying personal pleasures and cravings. King Lemuel's mother certainly had this in mind when she exhorted her son:

> Do not give your strength to women,
> Nor your ways to that which destroys kings.
> It is not for kings, O Lemuel,
> It is not for kings to drink wine,
> Nor for princes intoxicating drink;
> Lest they drink and forget the law,
> And pervert justice of all the afflicted.[42]

Increase in transgression: "When the wicked are multiplied, transgression increases." When the king participates in sin and degradation, his advisors and bureaucracy do the same. When voices rise up from righteousness and justice, they are ignored or suppressed. This often occurs in third world governments where officials are corrupt.[43]

Suffering: Suffering is always a natural outgrowth of transgression in government. "When a wicked man rules, the people groan." Joel spoke words of God to the leaders of Israel who had forsaken the Lord

> How the beasts groan!
> The herds of cattle are restless,
> Because they have no pasture;
> Even the flocks of sheep suffer your punishment.[44]

41. 28:162.
42. 31:3–5.
43. 29:16a
44. 29:2b; Joel 1:18.

The suffering was so severe than even animals experienced it. One commentator put it this way: "Foolish policies lead to foolish wars, irresponsible fiscal policies bring economic hardship, and evil ideologies leave a people in hunger for the truth."[45]

Fear: "When the wicked arise, men hide themselves." When oppression increases, so do the number of refugees. People flee totalitarian regimes at the earliest possible opportunity.[46]

Proverbs 28:12 is translated the same way as 28:28, but it uses a different word for "hide." The word used in verse 12 means to be searched out. When a climate of fear pervades a country, even the strong flee. If all the people flee, evil leaders are failures. So these leaders must keep people from exiting the country. Refugees are found and executed or sent to insane asylums. And fear increases.

National ruin: What begins as indulgence in innocent vice by unwise leaders rapidly progresses to lying to their people, over-taxation, brutality, domination, and outward oppression. Soon the nation speaks out against the government but is squelched. Emigration begins in search for freedom, in spite of sealed borders. Shops are boarded up. The army turns on its own people. Survivors must forage for food, use contaminated water, shiver in the cold. They haven't the time to worry about loved ones who have been taken away by the authorities for who knows what. Survival is their only thought.

In its weakened state, the nation is prime for an aggressor to capture and occupy. Its end may be with a bang, or it may be with a whimper; nevertheless, the nation dies.

The Scriptures tell us that when Christ returns to the earth, He will establish a government of righteousness. His administration will be characterized by justice, integrity, wisdom, prosperity, and above all, the glorification of God the Father. Until then, earthly leaders are to exemplify Christ.

The responsibility for good government lies not only with the leadership, but also with the people. It has been said that people get the kind of government that they deserve. People must insist leadership acknowledge the sovereignty of God and the rule of law. It is important for Christian citizens to pray for their leaders in four ways:

45. Johnson, 230.
46. Prov. 28:28.

Pray for their salvation.

The first priority with any individual is the state of the soul, for unbelievers can never understand, let alone apply, divine principles.

Pray for their enlightenment by God.

In order to face the inevitable crises of leadership, leaders need to be stable and mature, qualities which are nurtured by biblical doctrine.

Pray for their safety.

In twentieth century America political assassinations have become all too common.

If leaders are wicked or ungodly, pray for their removal.[47]

Prayer changes things. James tells us that "Elijah was a man with a nature like ours, and he prayed earnestly that it would not rain; and it did not rain on the land for three years and six months. He prayed again, and the heaven gave rain, and the earth produced its fruit." We have seen miracles God has done as a result of the prayers of godly people—the crumbling of the Berlin wall, the rise of God-fearing government in Poland, the opening of the old Soviet Union to Christian evangelism. During the Persian Gulf War, the President of the United States called the nation to prayer in a most trying time, resulting in such a low number of Allied deaths that General Norman Schwarzkopf called it miraculous.[48]

A people that humbles itself before God deserves and receives godly leadership. Godly leaders who are humble before God form godly nations.

47. K. Jensen, 129, 130.
48. James 5:17–18.

CHAPTER 10

Vocational Wisdom

WHAT IS WORK?

PAUL HARVEY REPORTEDLY said, "Take your hobby, make it your job, and you'll never work a day in your life."

Not a bad philosophy for those who have that option open to them. But what about countless others who work at the only careers available to them? Or those whose exciting careers have been slowly transformed into drudgery, boredom, and monotony? Or those who would be thankful to have *any* job rather than languishing in the uncertainty of unemployment or subsistence labor?

Fortunately, the Bible has much to say about work. In an earlier chapter, we learned work is *not* a part of God's curse on the earth. God created us to enjoy meaningful work. Before God joined woman to man, and before sin ever entered the earth, God gave Adam fulfilling work to do, tending the garden of God. Work was included in Adam's natural obedience to God before the Fall. Adam also worked by naming the animals. Once God brought Eve to Adam, God entrusted to them the administration of all creation under His authority, the most meaningful kind of work performed in obedience to Him.[1]

Through the Fall, however, Satan usurped mankind's rule over all creation and became the god of this age, the prince of the power of the air. Not only did Adam and Eve lose meaningful work, they also lost the ability to obey God perfectly. The

---

1. Gen. 2:15, 20; 1:28.

presence of a sinful nature perverted the experience of work. Work became burdensome and filled with toil.[2]

This presents a paradox with regard to work. Whereas the desire to experience fulfilling work is a part of our nature, sin has warped that desire, or in some cases, eliminated it altogether. No earthly job can provide perfect fulfillment. Work is now characterized by toil or hard effort. Even were we to find work that is relatively fulfilling and meaningful, the fruit of that work generally does not last.

The book of Ecclesiastes explores the troublesome aspects of work. "All the labor of man is for his mouth," wrote the preacher, "and yet the soul is not satisfied." Work is necessary and has tremendous potential for enjoyment and fulfillment— but only in its proper place. Ecclesiastes admonishes readers to seek God *first,* then put one's hands to work.[3]

> Fear God and keep His commandments,
> For this is the whole duty of man.
> For God will bring every work into judgment,
> Including every secret thing,
> Whether it is good or whether it is evil.[4]

Work is best when it begins in obedience to God. Vocational wisdom begins with obedience. Or, "The fear of the LORD is the beginning of knowledge." Our work or vocation is hollow accomplishment apart from obedience and commitment to God and His purposes. If we begin with a personal commitment to God, and continue in faith and obedience, we will experience much fulfillment in work and career.[5]

WHAT YOUR VOCATION *CANNOT* DO

Biblically speaking, there are certain things a job or career cannot do for us. In the final analysis, a job is simply a job, a career is simply a career. Our culture has cultivated the idea that a career offers the ultimate purpose and meaning to life. This is simply not true. Living life with that mistaken belief is "toil and grasping for the wind." One of the major lessons of Ecclesiastes

2. Gen. 3:17–19.
3. Eccl. 4:6; 5:10–11; 6:7.
4. Eccl. 12:13–14.
5. Prov. 1:7.

is that *career is no substitute for a relationship with God.* Work exclusively for the sake of work profits nothing. The preacher wrote concerning someone we today might call a workaholic,

> There is one alone, without companion:
> He has neither son nor brother.
> Yet there is no end to all his labors,
> Nor is his eye satisfied with riches.
> But he never asks,
> "For whom do I toil and deprive myself of good?"
> This also is vanity and a grave misfortune.[6]

Not only does this person's work dominate his life, it keeps him from thinking correctly about life in general.

By contrast, Proverbs 16:3 shows that when our work begins with commitment to the Lord, work is fulfilling and our thoughts are established by Him. "Commit your works to the LORD, and your thoughts will be established."

Some religious leaders in the ancient Jewish culture taught that material possessions were a sign of God's blessing. It was easy to become preoccupied with the kind of success that could only come from being sold out to career or profession. But that outlook was as foolish then as it is now. It is pure folly to trust a job to provide that which only God can give. Jesus put it quite plainly when He said, "No one can serve two masters; for either he will hate the one and love the other, or else he will be loyal to the one and despise the other. You cannot serve God and mammon." In this passage Jesus equated *love* and *loyalty* and He went on to equate *loyalty* with *service.* Though today we may profess to put Christ first over our careers, in reality our loyalty—measured by our commitment of time, talent, and treasure—is with our careers. For many, a promotion is more important than ministry; status symbols are more important than missions; meetings are more important than fellowship; and image is more important than evangelism. Because our work is committed to something other than the Lord, our thoughts and priorities are in error.[7]

Another crucial lesson the Bible teaches us about work is that *vocation is no substitute for home and family.* It is amazing how often in television programs, movies, and commercials, the idealized

6. Eccl. 4:6b; 4:8.
7. Matt. 6:24.

professional person is the one who stays late at the office, travels for days or weeks at a time, and places career above the seemingly trivial matters of home and family. And most corporate work environments automatically assume that family always plays second fiddle to work.

This is a tricky area for believers, since commitment to our work is necessary in order to do a good job and provide for our families. But many families have been destroyed by a career that began as a means for good provision. Work gradually becomes a distraction, then an obsession or even an idol. Many homes become war zones as one or both partners in a marriage have taken on the added pressures of work in order to improve their lot in life—and the marriage crumbles as a result.

This is nothing unique to the twentieth century! The sage saw the same thing in his day when he wrote, "Better is a little with the fear of the LORD, than great treasure with trouble." All of us must examine what a promotion, move, a different job, or a second income is going to *provide* for us in light of what it will *cost* us! There may be times when an increase in income will severely cut our spiritual profit margin, or even jeopardize the stability of our corporate union in marriage.[8]

There is another threat that an obsession with career poses to home and family—marital infidelity. How interesting is the crafty harlot's punch line as she tempts the undiscerning young man in Proverbs 7,

> Come, let us take our fill of love until morning:
> Let us delight ourselves with love.
> For my husband is not at home;
> He has gone on a long journey;
> He has taken a bag of money with him,
> And will come home on the appointed day.

Nothing like a lengthy business trip to open the door to adultery! Just about any two people can become romantically entangled if they are placed in the right (or wrong) circumstances day after day, week after week, month after month. Consider what may happen when a man and a woman work closely with each other in a typical office. They see each other at least 40 hours per week, without the interruptions of children, chores, or household cri-

8. Prov. 15:16.

ses. They look their best and are together during their most rested, productive hours of the day. They leave domestic arguments and marital squabbles at home and spend all day with someone who shares some of the same interests, skills, goals, and frustrations. He may recognize her as someone who really appreciates all the hard work he does. She may see him as someone who really admires her industry and ability. They think together, tackle projects together, maybe even go on business trips together. It is easy to see why many vocational relationships are a seedbed for adultery, immorality, and divorce. It is also easy to see why some of the apostle Paul's best vocational advice to his chief disciple, Timothy, was to "flee ... youthful lusts." When the office becomes a more enjoyable place to be than the home, it is time to get out of the office—*not* the marriage![9]

One final word is needed on the insufficiency of career to take the place of home and family. *No one* at life's end ever regretted spending more time with their family than they did with their jobs! It is a sad and hollow realization to devote far more of our time to spreadsheets and salaries than to our life's partner and children. Not even those in vocational Christian ministry are exempt. In fact, many times it is often easy to neglect home and family for God's work.

A third observation about career is that *vocation is no substitute for fellowship with God's people.* In other words, the boardroom is not the assembly of the saints! The company cafeteria does not have the same edifying, uplifting effect on a person as the worship center or fellowship hall at church. Corporate productivity is a poor replacement for corporate worship.

Ministry among God's people must take precedence over career. Any professional minister will confirm that 95 percent of the work of the ministry is being performed by 5 percent of the people. The demands of career either take away the time we need to invest in the work of ministry, or we are simply too worn out to work for the Lord. In the words of our Lord, our hearts have "laid up treasures on earth," without "laying up treasures in heaven." The really sad thing is that we are investing our lives in something woefully inferior to eternal commodities.[10]

> Do not overwork to be rich;
> Because of your own understanding, cease!

9. 7:19–20; 2 Tim. 2:22.
10. Matt. 6:19–20.

> Will you set your eyes on that which is not?
> For riches certainly make themselves wings;
> They fly away like an eagle toward heaven.[11]

Finally, *career is no substitute for faith and obedience.* Status is not the same as spiritual maturity, and affluence does not equal automatic qualification for spiritual leadership. In many Christian circles today success in the business world is taken as proof positive that a Christian also qualifies for spiritual leadership. In some cases, the two *are* coincidental. In many cases, however, there is no more correlation between secular success and spiritual maturity than there was when Jesus condemned the Pharisees for holding to the same misconception.

Too many churches, Christian organizations, governing boards, and leadership groups are overstocked with those who were chosen for their success in the world. As a result, the broad diversity of leadership God intended for His church has a vertical, repetitive sameness to it. And churches become more like corporations than families, more like businesses than the body of Christ.[12]

This is not to say that there is no room for Christian businessmen in leadership. But there is also room for Christian welders, Christian mechanics, Christian clerks, Christian salesmen, Christian accountants, and Christian schoolteachers. If God is more impressed with the discerning poor than the foolish rich, perhaps we should be too! We must not mistake success for spirituality.[13]

WHAT YOUR VOCATION *CAN* DO

As we will see, there are many ways in which God may choose to work in our lives through the work we do. First, work provides enjoyment and fulfillment in our lives. As we have already seen, apart from a priority to know and obey God, our life's work is utter futility, a grasping after wind. Why else do some of the most successful people in the world suffer depression and even suicide? With the issue of eternal priorities settled, however, our careers can give us a limited amount of enjoyment and fulfillment. That's why the preacher said in Ecclesiastes, "Whatever your hand finds to do, do it with your might; for

11. Prov. 23:4–5.
12. 10:22; 1 Cor. 12:4–11.
13. Prov. 19:1.

there is no work or device or knowledge or wisdom in the grave where you are going." This is not a statement of grim resignation to depression. Rather, it is encouragement to find something we do well, and to do it to its fullest while we can. After all, it is linked to, "Live joyfully with the wife whom you love all the days of your vain life . . . under the sun."[14]

Once the issue of seeking and serving God is settled, both family and career are potentially two of the most enjoyable avenues of expression we experience. Work brings out our strengths and provides us with the satisfaction of having employed those strengths for positive gain—"the labor of the righteous leads to life." Though work can't provide the kind of fulfillment God alone gives, Proverbs 12:11 says that "he who tills his land will be satisfied with bread." There is a certain righteous satisfaction in a job well done (see Prov. 12:14b and 13:19a). Proverbs 14:23 reminds us that "in all labor there is profit."[15]

Second, work reveals to us areas of immaturity and weakness in order to help us grow and develop. Whether it's a teenager's first summer job or an aspiring young executive's first stab at management, some job challenges, accepted with a heart open to the Lord, can develop maturity and deepen a relationship with Him. Because we spend about a third of our lives working, our jobs are an essential part of the laboratory of life in which Proverbs expects us to develop. As challenges, circumstances, situations, temptations, and frustrations arise, work is one of the best places to:

> Ponder the path of your feet,
> And let all your ways be established.
> Do not turn to the right or the left;
> Remove your foot from evil.[16]

God is concerned about how we do in all "the ways of man." There are characteristics He wants us to acquire from the work we do—diligence, integrity, honesty, humility, and godliness. More than anywhere else besides the home, our jobs will require we live out Proverbs 3:5–6:

14. Eccl. 9:10; 9:9.
15. Prov. 10:16.
16. 4:26–27.

Trust in the Lord with all your heart,
And lean not on your own understanding;
In all your ways acknowledge Him,
And He shall direct your paths.[17]

Third, work provides us with opportunities to apply what we already know about living righteously in an unrighteous world. It offers us chances to turn down invitations to join in the schemes of the wicked; apply honesty consistent with the God we know and worship; work diligently at the tasks assigned to us; or show compassion and pity to those in need. Our jobs keep us in the laboratory of life, where God uses us as His ambassadors, as light and salt, as His people in the right place at the right time. It is an opportunity to be ready and willing to witness to unbelievers about the wonderful saving grace of God.[18]

Finally, our life's work is a channel through which God rewards righteous wisdom or skillful living. The law of cause and effect never sleeps on the job! Many times it is through success at work that God rewards the righteous lifestyle of those who take His wisdom seriously and seek to apply His Word diligently. Many times even the most difficult situations at work are supernaturally smoothed out when "a man's ways please the Lord." God evaluates employees differently than their earthly employers do, weighing motives and giving rewards.[19]

This concept of divine "performance appraisals" was emphasized by Paul when he wrote

Servants, be obedient to those who are your masters according to the flesh, with fear and trembling, in sincerity of heart, as to Christ; not with eyeservice, as men-pleasers, but as servants of Christ, doing the will of God from the heart, with good will doing service, as to the Lord, and not to men, knowing that whatever good anyone does, he will receive the same from the Lord, whether he is a slave or free. And you, masters, do the same things to them, giving up threatening, knowing that your own Master also is in heaven, and there is no partiality with Him.[20]

Though God chooses to bless righteous wisdom through our life's work, this is not restricted to careers that bring home a

17. 5:21.
18. 1:10–19; 11:1; 10:4; 19:17; Acts 1:8.
19. Prov. 16:7; 21:2; 19:17.
20. Eph. 6:5–9.

paycheck. Vocational wisdom and blessing are in the life of the virtuous woman of Proverbs 31. And if the amount of space given to the Proverbs 31 woman is any indication, this calling of God's is as important as any other!

Regardless of one's calling, Proverbs is clear that righteous wisdom produces reward, and this is no less true in one's professional life than in private.

THE SPECIFICS OF VOCATIONAL WISDOM

For those who grapple daily with the ups and downs of job or career, there is no more reliable guidebook than Proverbs. Rather than educating us on how to dress for success on the outside, it reveals the essentials of inward character we need to realize success in God's eyes. Superior to any books written by humans, Proverbs teaches us business ethics, management style, employer/employee relations, motives, attitudes, and actions that will always be pleasing to God. Proverbs' wisdom never becomes outdated or archaic. If we long for the narrow path of righteous wisdom, it is the final word on how we should approach our jobs and careers.

Let's consider, then, some of the specific areas it addresses about vocation.

Motives in vocation

What do drug pushers, dropouts, and crack couriers in the inner city have in common with many gray-suited businessmen? Their motives.

For years the standard line encouraging inner city youth to avoid trouble and stay in school was, "You have to stay in school and get a good education so you can get a good job and make lots of money." Now, however, kids are faced with the option of skipping the first several steps involving education and career to make more money in one drug deal than many of us make in a month—or a year!

In other words, if the only motive for our actions is monetary gain, we're headed for big trouble. Our society is in love with big bucks and easy money. We idolize those who get rich quick, whether they are lottery winners, first-round draft choices, or the overnight successes of the business world. We want wealth, and we want it *now*. We want to think and grow rich, hit the "big one," win the publisher's sweepstakes!

According to Proverbs, this is one of the most dangerous and damaging attitudes we possess. It is the same attitude as thieves who don't want to work for their income. The desire to get rich quick is motivated by envying others who have done the same. This desire is specifically condemned by God's Word. Such greed corrupts morals and ruins entire households. It causes people to risk home and security foolishly on a slim chance of the big payoff. And it may ultimately lead to the tragedy of compulsive gambling. As Paul was quick to point out in 1 Timothy 6:10, it is an attitude from which believers are *not* immune—"For the love of money is a root of all kinds of evil, for which some have strayed from the faith in their greediness, and pierced themselves through with many sorrows."[21]

It is not hard to see that this mentality is a dead end. The same false get-rich-quick hope that motivates muggers causes the downfall of saints: "So are the ways of *everyone* who is greedy for gain; it takes away the life of its owners." It is an attitude that denies the ability of God to provide according to His will. Such an attitude brings dire consequences. As we have seen time and time again in the news, quick wealth generated by greed often disappears through scandal, criminal activity, tax evasion, indebtedness, or irresponsibility.[22]

When we realize blessings come from the hand of God as He wills, it is easy to see that setting our hopes on some fantasy of sudden wealth is an affront to His ability to provide for us. We should consider instead the perspective of Psalm 127:1–2:

> Unless the LORD builds the house,
> They labor in vain who build it;
> Unless the LORD guards the city,
> The watchman stays awake in vain.
> It is vain for you to rise up early,
> To sit up late,
> To eat the bread of sorrows;
> For so He gives His beloved sleep.[23]

Knowing that God will bless us precisely as He wills is *not* license to become lazy and slothful. Depending on God's blessing frees us to live our lives pleasing Him. This keeps us from

21. Prov. 1:13–15; 12:12; 23:17; 24:1; 28:22; 15:27.
22. 1:19; 28:20b; 28:22.
23. 10:22.

corruption and provides the best possible foundation for a lifetime of seeking and serving God. As the sage prayed,

> Two things I request of You
> (Deprive me not before I die):
> Remove falsehood and lies far from me;
> Give me neither poverty nor riches—
> Feed me with the food You prescribe for me;
> Lest I be full and deny You, and say, "Who is the LORD?"
> Or lest I be poor and steal,
> And profane the name of my God.[24]

This kind of life is well within reach of every believer today. As Paul assured the Philippian believers, "Not that I speak in regard to need, for I have learned in whatever state I am, to be content" (Phil. 4:11).

Poverty vs. vocation

The Bible has much to say about the sluggard. Though God's Word expresses much compassion toward the poor, it does not make folk heroes out of those who are poor because they are lazy, nor does it advocate handouts for those who refuse to work. Lazy people want many things, but they do nothing to earn these things for themselves. Even when they actually earn something, they do not behave responsibly and lose the benefit of what little work was invested. Lazy people always have excuses for not working.

Everything from bad weather to imaginary obstacles prevents work. Laziness is a degenerative symptom of deeper, self-perpetuated problems that prevent some people from gaining or retaining employment above the level of "forced labor."[25]

This brings up questions of caring for the homeless. How should we take care of the poor according to God's Word? Should all believers take it upon themselves to take care of the poor? Or does benevolence toward the impoverished only perpetuate the problem?

God set standards in His Law regarding care for the poor. These standards included caring for widows and orphans, providing access to food through labor (by leaving ungleaned fields),

24. 30:7–9.
25. 13:4a; 12:27; 20:4; 26:13–16; 12:24; 13:18; 19:15.

and remaining sensitive to those *within the family of faith* who were in need. The standards He set for Israel's behavior applied to everyone in the nation, including those proselytes participating by faith in the covenant community. But the spirit of the Law regarding the poor was blatantly overlooked by the religious leaders of Christ's day.

By way of application, the Church's first priority today should be the needy within its own fellowship. It is a tragedy that churches throw money at the problem of poverty in society while ignoring the needs within their own congregations! However, godly, evangelical churches in third world countries have discovered the joy of providing for the needy in their congregations through the generosity of those who have an ample supply and a heart for giving.

There is certainly nothing wrong with addressing the needs of the poor as a means of evangelism when the gospel is presented with an opportunity given for individuals to trust Christ as Savior and to grow in Him. Many of today's most effective evangelistic ministries worldwide (especially among children) operate out of Christian kitchens, schools, and medical clinics.

What is most important to realize is that God did not group all of the poor and needy into one broad category called the homeless. He clearly condemns laziness, wickedness, greed, drunkenness, dishonesty, or any other form of ungodliness that leads to poverty. However, God *never* condemns poverty accompanied by godliness and faith. Nor does He condemn the poor who are not able to change their situation. God says that "better is a little with the fear of the LORD, than great treasure with trouble."[26]

Clearly, the symptom of poverty is in an area in which those who are wise seek to please God by ministering to those in need. At the same time, however, ministry must never become an avenue for rewarding the ungodly and unresponsive poor in rebellion against God. Though our society may pressure believers to adopt a one-size-fits-all attitude toward all poor people, we would do well to apply discernment and the wisdom of Proverbs on a case by case basis.[27]

26. 13:4, 18; 10:2, 4; 20:13; 23:29–35; 26:13–16; 15:16; 19:1.
27. 19:17; 21:13; 22:16; 29:7.

Diligence in vocation

The Bible teaches that if our desire is to serve the Lord, we will apply godly diligence in all we do. Because God has created in us the capacity for meaningful work, we are most fulfilled when employed in meaningful industry, even though such work involves sweat and toil. We must beware of any attitude or philosophy that promises to provide us with sustenance apart from industry and diligence.

Proverbs warns that the person "who is slothful in his work is a brother to him who is a great destroyer," and the half-hearted worker who "deals with a slack hand becomes poor." Anyone who has ever employed an irresponsible staff person knows that "as vinegar to the teeth and smoke to the eyes, so is the sluggard to those who send him."[28]

But diligence in labor is its own reward and offers other benefits besides. Diligence leads to positions of leadership, inner satisfaction, increased income, honor, security, and fulfillment. Most importantly, godly diligence reflects the nature of our Creator, just as the simple industry of an ant reflects the character of its Maker.[29]

Position in vocation

In the ancient Near East, not only were there employers and employees, there were also people who worked the family business, tending vineyards or keeping sheep. Slaves worked for their masters and were taken care of in exchange. It was a slaveholding economy and masters owned many slaves. The rich owned much and worked little. And there were debtors who, if they could not repay their debts, were forced to work for their creditors. Thankfully, our culture lacks many of these injustices.

But although differences exist between the biblical context and our own, God's standards are the same. He holds all people accountable, no matter what their position in society or rank on the organizational chart. Whether a slave, an employee, a debtor, or a son working in the family business, God expects responsibility and diligence. We know from the New Testament that it is required of servants and stewards that they "be found faithful," and that even slaves should work "as pleasing Christ" rather than

28. 18:19; 10:4; 10:26.
29. 12:24; 13:4; 13:11b; 13:18b; 24:27; 31:28–31; 6:6–11; 30:25.

men. Certainly no less is required of employees today, whether they are slinging burgers at a fast food joint, or engineering mergers in a downtown high-rise. It is apparent from Proverbs that, over the long haul, "the recompense of a man's hands will be rendered to him." The words of Proverbs 22:29 paint a vivid picture of the rewards that await the faithful, diligent, hard-working employee: "Do you see a man who excels in his work? He will stand before kings; he will not stand before unknown men."[30]

But God has just as much to say about those who rule over others, supervise employees, or own businesses in which others work. God not only holds these people accountable for the way they treat others, He expects them to accurately reflect the way He treats His people! At the very least, He expects all employers and supervisors to treat their charges humanely, for if "a righteous man regards the life of his animal," recognizing that his livelihood is dependent on how well he takes care of it, surely human workers expect even better treatment! God's Word says that "like a roaring lion and a charging bear is a wicked ruler over poor people," and that "a ruler who lacks understanding is a great oppressor." Clearly there is no room in the Word of God for an employer's ill treatment of employees.[31]

The Bible offered the principle of reciprocal benefits between employer and employee long before modern labor relations experts arrived on the scene. Just as contemporary employers have discovered that better benefits and incentives produce better employees, who in turn produce better results, the sage wrote long ago, "Whoever tends the fig tree will eat its fruit; so he who waits on his master will be honored." May God produce more positive relationships between employers and employees—*especially* in Christian ministry—that reflect this timeless truth!

Honesty in vocation

Modern business knows there are many ways to turn a profit. But not all of those ways are desirable. Besides those methods that are blatantly illegal, there are many subtle ways involving treachery, deceit, and other underhanded tactics used to fatten one's wallet. This is to be expected in the world of the ungodly.

30. 10:5; 1 Cor. 4:1–2; Eph. 6:5–6; Prov. 12:14b.
31. Eph. 6:9; Prov. 12:10; 28:15; 28:16.

But how unfortunate to hear and read of so many situations in which Christians have been victimized by other Christians for the sake of financial gain!

The book of Proverbs cuts very little slack for anyone who would deal unethically, greedily, dishonestly, or even unkindly in order to reap financial reward. Many believers may honor a shrewd, ruthlessly opportunistic Christian businessman over an impoverished saint. But God's Word tells us that a poor person with integrity always is better than a wealthy person who is crooked. Those who are financially successful may feel their status makes them wise. Yet all it takes is one poor person with understanding to see right through them![32]

The Bible is even less encouraging to those who are openly deceitful or unethical. The employer who sets an example of deception can expect no better behavior from his employees. When a wicked person rises to a position of leadership, he can expect those under him to "groan," or complain. A leader who receives bribes can expect failure to be waiting in the wings. And the person who increases his wealth by dishonesty, extortion, or usury can expect to lose it sooner or later.[33]

Some of the most severe biblical warnings are reserved for those who would use their status or position as justification for considering themselves superior to others or taking advantage of the less fortunate. Those who dispossesses the poor of what little they have should think twice about the mighty Redeemer who pleads their cause. Christian businessmen should think twice about authorizing a foreclosure, repossession, or exploiting a legal loophole. Both oppressing the poor and catering to the rich for the purpose of increasing wealth is abominable to God, and ultimately brings poverty.[34]

In short, every form of dishonesty is repugnant to God. Success or affluence does not justify dishonest methods. This applies equally in providing correct information on a resumé or job application as well as an honest presentation of a corporate executive's financial statement. Nothing justifies dishonesty in one's vocation.

32. 28:4; 28:11.
33. 29:12; 29:2; 29:4; 13:11; 28:8.
34. 23:10–11; 22:16.

Direction in vocation

The books of the Bible containing the most information about correct attitudes and actions in one's vocation never differentiate between secular and sacred. Neither the book of Ecclesiastes nor the book of Proverbs treats secular work differently from Christian work. While a commitment to full-time Christian work is admirable and much needed in our world today, the truth is that every believer works full time for the Lord! According to Proverbs, every vocational decision must revolve around a desire to please God *first* and *foremost*.

That's why we should consider carefully what we plan to do with our lives. Rather than worrying about status, what our salary will be, or whether we are following popular trends in our culture, we should follow the advice of Proverbs 4:26, to "ponder the path of your feet, and let all your ways be established." The promise of God's Word is that "the righteousness of the blameless will direct his way aright." When we commit ourselves to honor God, a light in a dark world, and take every person possible with us into heaven, we will make wise choices with regard to career.[35]

35. 11:5.

CHAPTER 11

Social Wisdom

MAKING MINORITY CHOICES

AS THE WORLD'S population nears the 5 billion mark, there are many who contend that the real problem with our world is people. Or, as the old saying goes, "I love the human race—it's people I can't stand!"

In fact, it's considered philosophically fashionable in some circles today to hate the human race. Radical environmentalists argue that the world would actually be much better off if people did not populate it, or at least not in vast numbers. Animal rights activists contend that "a pig is a dog is a boy," meaning that human life is no more sacred or valuable than the life of a pig or dog. Abortionists tout their bloody cause, reasoning that murder of the unborn is the best and quickest means to realizing the utopia of zero population growth. And those who fight for so-called mercy killing claim life is not worth perpetuating if it does not meet certain standards of enjoyment.

But is the problem really people, or is the problem the *condition* of the people that populate this earth? We know from the creation account in Genesis 1–2 that God created man and woman with a capacity for a perfectly harmonious relationship—not only as man and woman, but also as cooperative partners in the administration of God's righteousness on earth. The entire human race as it existed before the first sin was in perfect agreement and without conflict.

Because of the Fall, however, mankind's ability to interact in perfect righteousness became subject to its sinful, fallen nature. Moreover, the environment was no longer under humanity's dominion, and the world became an increasingly hostile place in which to live. Most importantly, the human race became irreversibly split between those who would choose to remain in the world under Satan's dominion, and those who would choose faith in the true God and obedience to Him.

This split in humanity was seen first in Cain's treachery against Abel. More than a simple disagreement between brothers, their conflict embodied the world's natural resentment and hostility against a response of faith in the true God. Satan worked to rid the world of the only person alive who might possibly become the fulfillment of Genesis 3:15. And Cain's hatred toward his brother was the result of his hatred toward God and God's unbending truth. Because his way of self-justification was unacceptable, Cain hated God and anyone who represented Him. [1]

If Cain could speak to Abel in today's terms, he would probably call him "narrow-minded," and a "self-righteous fundamentalist." He would chide Abel for believing there is only one way to God, and condemn him as an anti-environmentalist (for making animal sacrifice). Eventually his rhetoric would claim there is no place in a civilized world for people so unbending and smug. And Cain would kill Abel.

Apart from God's intervention, every society ultimately polarizes itself into an unrighteous majority and a righteous minority.

The epitome of modern social structure began at Babel. After the earth's environment became less hospitable due to the Flood, but before the people of earth were broken into individual nations, they were united in their unbelief in the true God. Rather than choosing to live in submission to the offspring of Shem (as God ordained), they banded together in the idyllic Mesopotamian valley. There they had all they needed for food and water. And by uniting to build a city where all could live and benefit from a perfectly socialized society, they wanted to ensure their survival without dependence on God. What's more, their common religion (the "gate to god") helped fill the void left by rebellion against God. Their sheer numbers were certain to guarantee they would eventually rid the earth of those few who still held to that unpopular belief in the true God. [2]

God acknowledged that this one world society posed a genuine threat to the righteous few. Even killing off the believing remnant would be possible for the Babel-builders. So God judged

1. Gen. 4:1–8.
2. Gen. 9:25–27; 11:1–2.

them in a bloodless, but perfectly effective way—He confused their one language into many. Precisely the opposite of our *e pluribus unum* ("from many, one"), God took one and made many. At that point, the nations of the world were born, and since that time the nations have been the major vehicles through which Satan has worked to defeat the plan and purpose of God. From the time of Babel until now, the world system through which Satan attempts to effect his purposes has always been measured by the majority—a majority hostile to God's truth.[3]

All of this, then, forms the foundation of what that majority represents today. Within every kingdom, nation, or society, there is a steady movement toward a majority opinion that represents the will of the god of this age, the prince of the power of the air. Even in democracies that profess freedom, justice, and truth, eventually the will of the majority conforms more and more to the will of the personality behind the nations of the world, the same deceiver who opposed God through the vast assembly at Babel.[4]

This means that the social circles in which we live and move generally exert a continual pressure on us to be "conformed to this world." Though some well-meaning believers propose that a society can be Christianized, every attempt to found and enforce such a society is doomed to fail miserably, because of our inherent sin nature. From Solomon's Israel, to Constantine's Rome, to the Puritans' colonies, every righteous nation has ultimately fallen short of that which the King of kings will one day establish—a perfectly righteous society, or kingdom.[5]

Make no mistake—a society that includes a large number of true believers reflects its presence to a certain degree. Such a society is always preferable to a lawless, godless, or idolatrous society. However, even a society founded on a belief in the true God gradually, subtly, insidiously moves toward apostasy and the false truth of majority opinion.

What this means to believers is that most, if not all, decisions made by believers are minority choices. Depending on the moral, spiritual, and legal disposition of a culture, some decisions are less popular than others. Some believers' choices are tolerable to the culture around them, while others draw vehement opposi-

3. Gen. 11:6–9.
4. John 16:11; 2 Cor. 4:4; Eph. 2:2.
5. Rom. 12:2.

tion. But according to God's Word, every decision, every choice, every commitment a believer makes must be determined by the perfect standard of God's Word, not by the majority opinion of the surrounding culture.

SOCIAL WISDOM IN RELATION TO GOD

Proverbs offers true wisdom through the narrow path of God's righteousness over the eight-lane freeway of man's unrighteousness. Regarding social decisions, we choose God's standard, regardless of its popularity, over society's. But how do we determine what God's standard is? Is it based on what is most popular among Christians rather than non-Christians, by what is outlined in our church creed, by what is resolved during a denomination convention, or what?

Because the popularity of any viewpoint or standard can change from year to year—even in the Christian community—making social decisions according to God's opinion rather than the world's majority opinion requires a standard that does not change. We need something more sure and stable than what the media deems acceptable, or what university professors claim is politically correct. Just as an architect needs a standardized unit of measure in order to design and build a sound structure, we need a standard unit of measure in order to build solid lives. That is precisely what we find in the Scriptures. We find truth that does not change with the ebb and flow of public opinion. It is a standard that is not subject to media pressure, ecumenical councils, or the latest poll. It has its origin in God, not in the deliberations of psychologists and sociologists.

Whether we are interacting with unbelievers or other believers, our thoughts and actions must be ordered by the Word of God rather than the opinions of people. In plain language, we must be more concerned about God's opinion than people's opinions. As Paul said in reference to the unchangeability of the gospel, "For do I now persuade men, or God? Or do I seek to please men? For if I still pleased men, I would not be a servant of Christ." Paul recognized that the fear of man was as much a snare in his day as it is for Christians today.[6]

How many more Christians today would be a part of the

6. Gal. 1:10.

solution rather than part of the problem if they would simply make their social decisions based on the perfect standard of God's Word? Not only would there be an immediate, favorable effect on their lives, but they would be light and salt in a dark and decaying world.

In Proverbs, the sage emphasized that God's knowledge is far superior to the world's, and actively seeking wisdom provides an increase in successful living. "Then you will understand the fear of the LORD, and find the knowledge of God." In stark contrast to the talk-show belief that any opinion is fine as long as it draws applause from the audience, Proverbs warns:[7]

> Do not be wise in your own eyes;
> Fear the LORD and depart from evil.
> It will be health to your flesh,
> And strength of your bones.[8]

In our society, this is not a popular position to take. Many, many Christians prefer to hear that it is okay to drink freely, use crude language, be indiscriminate in what they watch, cheat on their taxes, date or marry unbelievers, and embrace popular philosophies. All because it is far more comfortable to go along with the crowd than it is to take a definite stand based on the Word of God. As a result, we tolerate today what would have been unthinkable and repulsive only a generation ago!

A survey was conducted among professing Christians and non-Christians alike in order to measure the difference between the two groups in terms of promiscuity, alcohol consumption, divorce, and other problems in our society. The survey revealed essentially *no differences* between the social behavior of those who profess to know Christ, and those who don't. Though some pessimists argue that this proves faith in Christ makes little difference in a person's life, what it actually reveals is a cultural form of Christianity that dreads, rather than advocates, socially distinctive behavior among believers.

Biblically speaking, men and women of God understand that "the wise in heart will receive commands" from God's Word. They recognize that social decisions undeniably affect one's spiritual direction. And they acknowledge that:

7. Prov. 2:5.
8. 3:7–8.

Discretion will preserve you;
Understanding will keep you,
To deliver you from the way of evil,
From the man who speaks perverse things,
From those who leave the paths of uprightness
To walk in the ways of darkness;
Who rejoice in doing evil,
And delight in the perversity of the wicked;
Whose ways are crooked,
And who are devious in their paths.[9]

Therefore godly people seek to base social decisions on what God, rather than society, deems acceptable. Rather than attempting to be politically or socially correct, they study the Scriptures in order to make biblically correct decisions. Instead of resenting God's standards as restrictive or confining, they love all of God's Word for its supernaturally wise *regulation* of life and for its *revelation* of who God is. These people are the wise in Proverbs, who live their lives in sharp contrast to the foolish. Though those who are spiritually cold or lukewarm at times imitate the walk of the wise in heart, there is a marked difference between them and the lives of the wise. The epicenter of all the wise are and do is God Himself. At the heart of the way they interact with others is a sincere desire to reflect God's image, to honor the name of the Lord, and give glory to God the Father.[10]

Because the wise made a life commitment to Jesus Christ and understand their responsibility in relation to Him, they conduct themselves as His ambassadors in a foreign land. They evaluate everyone they know, not on the basis of attractiveness or outward appearance, but on the basis of their relationship to the King. In every social encounter, the most important issue is whether a person has been reconciled to the Father through the Son.[11]

Instead of trying to find ways around the Word of God in order to *adapt* to their culture, the wise find out more about the Word of God in order to *affect* their culture. Their commitment to God's standards allows the wise in heart to be *in* the world without being *of* the world, even earning the respect of some who do not know God.

9. 10:8a; 2:11–15.
10. 2 Tim. 2:15; Col. 3:17.
11. 2 Cor. 5:20.

> My son, do not forget my law,
> But let your heart keep my commands;
> For length of days and long life
> And peace they will add to you.
> Let not mercy and truth forsake you;
> Bind them around your neck,
> Write them on the tablet of your heart,
> And so find favor and high esteem
> In the sight of God and man.[12]

According to the context of Proverbs 3:5–6, dedication to *knowing* as well as *obeying* the Word of God in every area of life, especially public life, leads to an experience of knowing the right direction and enjoying the assurance of God's approval.

> Trust in the LORD with all your heart,
> And lean not on your own understanding;
> In all your ways acknowledge Him,
> And He shall direct your paths [or literally "make your
>   paths smooth"].

In our current Christian culture many believers want smooth paths without dedication to obedience. There is more truth than fiction in the little story about the two nominal Christians adrift in a life raft on the open seas. Running low on food and water, and knowing they could not survive much longer, one of them began to pray, "Lord, if You will let us be rescued, we will never drink again. We'll stop lying to our wives. We will never cheat on our taxes again. We'll be honest in our businesses. We'll stop . . ."

Suddenly the other man interrupted, "Don't promise any more! I think I see a ship!"

We want to look like the world, act like the world, and live like the world. But when the chips are down, we want God to give us all the benefits He promises to those who ardently seek His Word, love it, and obey it! Once things are going our way again, we want to make our own rules and get on with the fun.

If we are going to be wise in relation to God, we are going to be different from the vast majority of those around us. If we are going to be wise spiritually, we are going to be different socially. A man or woman of God cannot be on fire for Jesus Christ and

12. Prov. 3:1–4.

blend in. The person who has committed his or her life to Jesus Christ will think differently, talk differently, and act differently. In fact, the person truly committed to the Lord does not look on the world with an envying eye, but longs for purity and righteous obedience to God. The committed Christian is certain of the future God promises.[13]

> Do not let your heart envy sinners,
> But in the fear of the LORD continue all day long;
> For surely there is a hereafter,
> And your hope will not be cut off.[14]

Harold Lindsell in his book *The World, the Flesh and the Devil* wrote, "It is right for the Church to be in the world; it is wrong for the world to be in the Church. A boat in water is good; that is what boats are for. However, water inside the boat causes it to sink." This accurately summarizes the essence of social wisdom in relation to God. Just as "the fear of the LORD is the beginning of knowledge," all of our social interaction—thoughts, deeds, and attitudes in the world—must *begin* with our relationship with God. His Word must be the inviolable standard of what is right and what is wrong. Rather than bringing our knowledge of God's will to the world for judgment and approval, we need to continually evaluate the world's idea of right and wrong, good and bad, acceptable and unacceptable by the perfect light of God's Word.

SOCIAL WISDOM IN RELATION TO SELF

In our egocentric, narcissistic society, the Church has been infected with the idea that self is the center of the universe. We are told, for example, that we need to learn to love ourselves before we can love other people. Erroneously based on the commandment to "love your neighbor as yourself," so-called counselors encourage believers to coddle and glorify their insecurities, wallow in their wounds, and show off their scars to one another. We are told that until we have cured ourselves of every codependency, every dysfunction, and every environmentally induced hang-up, we cannot be complete human beings who are

13. 4:26–27; 5:2; 1:4.
14. 23:17–18.

new creations in Christ. So we flock to classes, meetings, seminars, and groups designed to teach us how to probe the depths of
our hurts, *our* anger, *our* past, *our* hang-ups, *our* dependencies,
and *our* preoccupations with ourselves, rather than probing the
depths of God's sufficiency and His ability to make us new
creatures.[15]

There are definitely legitimate hurts from which some Christians need to recover by experiencing dynamic spiritual growth.
But the Bible is quite clear that we are born loving ourselves! We
do not need to learn how to love ourselves anymore than we
already do. The command to "love your neighbor as yourself,"
in fact, *assumes* human self-love to the point of using it as a
standard for loving others. Likewise, God's command for husbands to love their wives as Christ loves the Church is based on
the fact of life that "no one ever hated his own flesh, but nourishes
and cherishes it." Both as a culture and as Christ's body in that
culture, we are really into self! Let's admit it—we love to love
ourselves.[16]

Even those Christians who profess to hate themselves *must*
love themselves at least enough to clothe, feed, protect, house,
and groom themselves. Those who moan endlessly about their
self-disdain go to a great deal of trouble to find someone—*anyone*—
who will listen to *their* stories, *their* problems, *their* self-focused
observations. It has been argued that even suicide and other
self-destructive behaviors in many cases are ploys to get attention. This is not to say that those who suffer such symptoms do
not need to be set free from them, or that their disorders are not
real and problematic. However, until we recognize our addiction
to self-love as a self-centered orientation to life, we will be
spiritual, as well as social, cripples.

We must disavow the secular orientation we have learned so
well from the world. We need to freely admit that we already
love ourselves, thrive on attention, and would rather talk about
ourselves than anyone else in the world—so much so that some
of us are willing to pay hundreds of dollars in therapist fees for
the opportunity!

And we need to be aware of this preoccupation with self as just
one more symptom of the disease with which we all are afflicted—
sin. When Satan aspired to become the heir of all things the

15. Matt. 19:19, 22:39; Mark 12:33; Luke 20:27; Rom. 13:9.
16. Eph. 5:29.

Father had promised the Son, he was preoccupied with self and consumed with pride. All of his aspirations revolved around himself and placed his will above the will of God. And though he abides under God's judgment, and unavoidable eternal death, Satan's pride prevents him from believing that all of God's Word really applies to him.[17]

Fortunately, salvation through faith in Jesus Christ sets us free from that kind of deceptive domination of our thoughts. We no longer need to see ourselves as condemned to live out the effects of sin in our lives, "for the law of the Spirit of life in Christ Jesus has made me free from the law of sin and death." Now we are free to walk "not . . . according to the flesh, but according to the Spirit." In simple terms, we are free to believe that Jesus Christ has indeed made us new creations, the old things have passed away, and "behold, all things have become new." We are free to take our eyes off ourselves and to look undistracted on the Lord. And we are free to direct our concern outward toward others rather than inward toward self.[18]

According to Proverbs, this is the way of wisdom. Choosing the narrow path of righteousness over the broad boulevard of foolishness includes a genuine denial of self. The wise believer regards reproof from the Word of God without taking offense (13:18). "Whoever loves instruction loves knowledge," says the sage of those who are instructed *from God's Word,* "but he who hates reproof is stupid" (12:1).

Pride or preoccupation with self is a dead-end avenue that leads to conflict rather than spiritual growth. "By pride," we are told, "comes only contention, but with the well-advised is wisdom" (13:10). As we have already seen, the entire book of Proverbs *assumes* that all instruction, all advice, and all correction comes from the Word of God, not from personal opinion or popular thought. Therefore the sage teaches that those who continue to be preoccupied with self engage in social conflict, while those who have made a commitment to maturity accept scriptural advice and find wisdom.

In the New Testament, one group of believers was characterized by self-centeredness and internal conflicts. Paul wrote to the Corinthian church, "For it has been declared to me concerning you, my brethren [note: they were believers!], by those of Chloe's

17. Isa. 14:13–14; Ezek. 28:12–14.
18. Rom. 8:2, 4; 2 Cor. 5:17.

household, that there are contentions among you." Like many believers today who find a popular writer or speaker on whom to base their identity, the Corinthian believers were playing spiritual one-upmanship by boasting, "'I am of Paul,' or 'I am of Apollos,' or 'I am of Cephas,' or 'I am of Christ.'"[19]

Spiritually, the Corinthians were saved, but socially they were acting like children. They based their Christian experience on what the world said was true of them, not on what the Word said was true of them. Paul said that such secular wisdom is foolishness compared to the wisdom of God. As long as we try to measure and evaluate ourselves according to the world's criteria, we fall far short of God's standard. But when we acknowledge by faith that those things He says are true of us in His Word, we will begin to experience what it means to be "wise in heart" and display true biblical humility.[20]

The choice is simple. Either we can focus our attention on ourselves and stagnate spiritually, or we can think more highly of others than we do of ourselves and move on in spiritual and social maturity. Romans 12 defines spiritual and social maturity as the believer's desire "not to think of himself more highly than he ought to think, but to think soberly [that is, *realistically* in regard to God's revelation] as God has dealt to each one a measure of faith." This attitude, in turn, produces very positive results with the rest of the family of God.[21]

The Bible teaches precisely the opposite of today's philosophy of self-love. Instead, it commands us to think of ourselves in *lowliness,* not *haughtiness,* of mind. "Let nothing be done through selfish ambition or conceit, but in lowliness of mind let each esteem others better than himself. Let each of you look out not only for his own interests [since we do that automatically and naturally], but also for the interests of others. *Let this mind be in you which was also in Christ Jesus.*" True Christlikeness, which continues the way of wisdom found in the book of Proverbs, is characterized by a proper, biblical, and realistic view of ourselves. It acknowledges what Christ has done for us, leaves our old, self-consumed nature behind, and focuses on others.[22]

---

19. 1 Cor. 1:11, 12.
20. 1 Cor. 1:19–25; Prov. 16:21; 18:12.
21. Rom. 12:3, 4–5.
22. Phil. 2:3–5.

SOCIAL WISDOM IN RELATION TO OTHERS

Fulfilling the commands of Proverbs regarding social wisdom is evidence of inward godliness. It offers a wealth of information for astute believers to use in forming selfless relationships that enhance, rather than inhibit, personal growth and social harmony. Let's consider three social concerns expressed in Proverbs.

Concerning the tongue: Proverbs teaches that wise people care about what they say to others, among others, and about others. We already know from James 3:2–5 that the tongue is among the most formidable of obstacles.

> We all stumble in many things. If anyone does not stumble in word, he is a perfect man, able also to bridle the whole body. Indeed, we put bits in horses' mouths that they may obey us, and we turn their whole body. Look also at ships: although they are so large and are driven by fierce winds, they are turned by a very small rudder wherever the pilot desires. Even so the tongue is a little member and boasts of great things. See how great a forest a little fire kindles!

Proverbs taught this truth long before James: "Whoever guards his mouth and tongue, keeps his soul from troubles."[23]

Armed with this knowledge, however, we still see relationships wrecked by untamed tongues and poisonous words. Leadership groups are divided, churches are split, mission works are retired, friendships are ruined, vocational Christian workers are victimized, and ministries are damaged beyond repair, all because Christians fail to control what they say and to whom they say it.

How can those who profess to know and obey God do so much damage with their tongues? We have ignored the Bible's specific instructions about words and their power. Rather than seeking out God's wisdom concerning our speech, we continue to live out precepts we have learned from the world around us. Gossip, for example, often takes the form of a prayer request. False witness may be disguised as concern for a brother. Careless words are uttered as an honest opinion. We often cover over verbal damage with "I was only kidding." Whether spoken in

23. Prov. 21:23.

ignorance or on purpose, foolish words have the same effect—disaster!

The urge to gossip is incurable. Some people gossip from a desire to make conversation, while others gossip out of a desire to create division or strife. But all gossip is contrary to the nature and character of God. Gossip is wrong. "Wise people store up knowledge," we are told, while "the mouth of the foolish is near destruction." In other words, those who walk in God's wisdom say less than they know, while fools know far less than they say. The gossip keeps running off at the mouth. "But he who restrains his lips," on the other hand, "is wise."[24]

In our Christian subculture, however, we often get around these simple truths by sanctioning a sort of holy gossip. Holy gossip traffics in secondhand information through prayer meetings, holy huddles, or abuse of a special position in ministry. We often accept as fact any information repeated about someone else simply because it is repeated by two or three people—not because it has been verified by two or three witnesses, which is God's unbending standard for establishing a matter. We determine someone's guilt or innocence based on whispered accusations and our own "infallible" discernment, even though God's Word warns the human heart is deceptive beyond our ability to recognize it.[25]

Tragically, some Christian leaders adopt the world's belief that position, status, or wealth justifies dealing in secondhand information. Some go so far as to recruit people to be their eyes and ears. The Word of God, however, condemns holy espionage as deceptive and hypocritical, no matter how noble the motives seem to be.

Even worse are those who share and repeat malicious information. By embellishing the facts, betraying confidence, or telling only part of the story, these people manipulate information for their own purposes. They chip away at other people's lives and mock the unity Jesus Christ wants to give His children. God evaluates actions based on *motive* rather than *method*. Everyone who practices malicious gossip is a deceiver, liar, and fool. "He who has a deceitful heart," wrote the sage, "finds no good, and he who has a perverse tongue falls into evil." Such people are "like a club, a sword, and a sharp arrow," hurting other people,

24. 10:14, 19.
25. Matt. 18:16; Jer. 17:9.

slicing them up, piercing their hearts. People with malicious tongues thrive on controlling friends by starting feuds and arguments among them. "A fool's lips enter into contention, and his mouth calls for blows" (18:6). Such people are about as useful and comforting as "a bad tooth and a foot out of joint"—they bring perpetual pain to any relationship.[26]

There is little truthfulness in what these fools tell others. The more their tongue moves, the more their mouth "pours forth foolishness." They change their story to suit their audience, and think little of who they hurt or destroy. They relish inside information. Rather than concern themselves with pleasant words that bring inner satisfaction to those who hear them, they seek the kinds of juicy gossip that "are like tasty trifles," which "go down into the inmost body." In a manner that is entirely consistent with their deceptiveness, they flatter with the tongue, tailoring praise for selfish gain. And, should they be accused of gossip, these fools claim they meant nothing harmful by it, ignoring the vivid picture of Proverbs 26:18–19: "Like a madman who throws firebrands, arrows, and death, is the man who deceives his neighbor, and says, 'I was only joking!'"[27]

The book of Proverbs exhorts godly people to act and speak wisely. The ability to control our words enables us to control our lives. Just as the Scriptures tell us in James that "if anyone does not stumble in word, he is a perfect man, able also to bridle the whole body," Proverbs warns, "Do you see a man hasty in his words? There is more hope for a fool than for him."[28]

The godly know there is no such thing as an innocent rumor, and there is absolutely no excuse for repeating words that are not edifying, necessary, and true. If gossip is never repeated, it will quickly die: "Where there is no wood, the fire goes out; and where there is no talebearer, strife ceases" (26:20). Godly people know God's Word is true when it advises, "The first one to plead his cause seems right, until his neighbor comes and examines him." Therefore they stick to the scriptural standard of the testimony of two or three *eyewitnesses* (not one or two *accusers*) before they judge someone's guilt or innocence. They speak words that are a "well of life" to everyone who hears. The contrast between the foolish and the godly is as simple as Prov-

26. Prov. 17:20; 25:18, 19.
27. 14:25; 15:2b; 11:9a, 13; 18:8; 26:28; 29:5.
28. James 3:2; Prov. 29:20.

erbs 11:13: "A talebearer reveals secrets, but he who is of a faithful spirit conceals a matter."[29]

This does not mean that the godly never have anything to say. Some spiritually mature people may be quite talkative. But it is the *quality* of their words, not the *quantity,* that makes their speech worthwhile. According to God's Word, "The mouth of the righteous brings forth wisdom," again referring to the wisdom that can only come from God's Word, and, "The lips of the righteous know what is acceptable."[30]

Believing God hates a dirty mouth, and that "a wholesome tongue is a tree of life, but perverseness in it breaks the spirit" (15:4), the godly follow the admonition of Ephesians 4:29: "Let no corrupt word proceed out of your mouth, but what is good for necessary edification, that it may impart grace to the hearers."[31]

Instead of corrupt speech, those who desire to please the Lord use their words to "disperse knowledge," "deliver souls," "declare righteousness," "deal truthfully," "feed many" with God's wisdom, and generally to "speak what is right." They remember the Bible equates the importance of guarding the tongue with guarding one's life, and they work as hard to guard their words as they do to protect their lives.[32]

What would happen if Christians today took God's Word to heart and stopped all the gossiping, slander, backbiting, and whispering that goes on in our churches? A. B. Simpson once wrote, "I would rather play with forked lightning, or take in my hand living wires with their fiery current, than speak a reckless word against any servant of Christ, or idly repeat the slanderous darts which thousands of Christians are hurling on others, to the hurt of their own souls and bodies." An attitude like that could revolutionize the Church! May Christians recognize that "death and life are in the power of the tongue," and live accordingly.[33]

Concerning the unsaved

There are two biblical categories regarding those outside a relationship with God and His people—those moving toward God (through the quickening of His Spirit, in spite of their

29. 18:17; 2 Cor. 13:1; Prov. 10:11.
30. 10:31, 32.
31. 8:13.
32. 15:7; 14:25; 12:17, 22; 10:21; 16:13; 21:23.
33. 18:21.

depravity), and those moving away from Him. There are "God seekers," and "God flee-ers."

The book of Proverbs has powerful advice for people perpetually fleeing the holy scrutiny of God. It's as though the sage glimpsed our modern gangs, beer-bash fraternities, punk groups, and other unsavory subcultures. Not that the pressures of group influences and peer fear have changed much over the centuries. In the ancient Near East as in modern North America, emerging adults have always been the most susceptible to temptation and outside influence. More than anyone else they need God's no-nonsense exhortations about how and whom to choose as friends. God's advice to everyone pressured into foolish, ungodly, unrighteous behavior is simple: "If sinners entice you, do not consent!" Many emerging adults, however, know *how* to say no—it is in knowing *to whom* they should say no that problems arise. After all, the sinners Proverbs talks about are not their friends—their friends are too cool to be sinners![34]

Fortunately, Proverbs is loaded with graphic descriptions of people the wise should avoid. They are those who apply pressure to join them, rather than letting us make our own choices. They promise strength in numbers and guarantee a superior position over others who are not a part of their group. They are greedy for whatever toys they think will give them happiness. They promise that we will share in all their material happiness with them.[35]

No matter what kind of front these people put up for the sake of others, in private they have dirty mouths; despise the consistent, steady paths of righteousness; practice personal sin; do things the Bible calls evil; delight in perversity; and are deceptive toward others about the kind of lifestyle they really live. Some of these people would fit in smoothly in some churches, youth groups, or Christian schools, as well as heavy metal concerts or immoral parties. And we must beware of the sexually perverse, especially those prone to extramarital liaisons and seductive behavior.[36]

Our choice of friends must exclude those who "linger long at the wine" or regard drinking as a social event. The Bible's stand on alcohol is not popular with many believers today. Proverbs

34. 1:10.
35. 1:11, 12, 13, 19; 1:14.
36. 2:11–15; 7:6–23.

23:29–35 makes it clear that those who drink wine fermented with other ingredients to intoxicate the drinker are headed for "woe," "sorrow," "contentions," "complaints," and "wounds." In other words, anyone who drinks alcoholic beverages for social stimulus or intoxication is an unfit companion for the godly.[37]

According to Proverbs 23:20–21, the same kind of person who drinks socially shows self-centeredness in other ways, such as unrestrained gluttony leading to poverty.

> Do not mix with winebibbers,
> Or with gluttonous eaters of meat;
> For the drunkard and the glutton will come to poverty,
> And drowsiness will cloth a man with rags.

Often our response to God is like the question teenagers throw at their parents: "Don't you trust me? Don't you think I can make up my own mind?" The idea of being selective in friendships did not originate with the parents of teenagers! In Proverbs 12:26 we find that God regards the process of social selection as a serious matter indeed, and that a bad choice here can determine a long road of hardship: "The righteous should choose his friends carefully, for the way of the wicked leads them astray."

How many times have we heard testimony from convicted criminals who claimed their life's course was determined by the friends they kept when they were younger? The social, moral, and spiritual decisions made between the ages of twelve and twenty-two determine the path one chooses in life.

The Bible teaches that spiritual maturity creates a desire to select godly companions. God's Word shows the lasting effects of our friends on our lives. "He who walks with wise men will be wise," emphasized the sage, "but the companion of fools will be destroyed." Notice that it is not necessary to *be* a fool—merely associating with fools brings destruction.[38]

A notable exception to God's admonitions about avoiding the unsaved are situations where believers have the opportunity to point an unbeliever toward God. Unfortunately, some Christians use this opportunity as an excuse for continuing unedifying relationships. Teenagers go to drinking parties to be a witness, Christians date non-Christians to be a witness, Christian singles go bar-hopping to be a witness, and so on.

37. 23:29–30.
38. 13:20.

The Bible is not silent on this. We already know the wise believer avoids fools and shuns the wicked. We need to examine Proverbs' definition of the difference between someone moving away from God and someone moving toward Him. Those who "receive commands," "love instruction," "regard reproof," and generally respond positively to the message of salvation, faith, and obedience, are those in whom we may freely invest more time and energy. They respond to God in such a way they do not drag down believers witnessing to them.[39]

By contrast, those who continue to reject the Word of God and despise the righteousness of Jesus Christ must be handled with caution and wariness. It is true we should "become all things to all men" that we might "by all means save some," but our involvement with the unregenerate should never compromise our personal holiness in word and deed. According to God's Word, any association with the wicked on their terms is to be avoided.

> Do not enter the path of the wicked,
> And do not walk in the way of evil.
> Avoid it, do not travel on it;
> Turn away from it and pass on. (4:14–15)

In all of our dealings with unbelievers we need to be above reproach, impeccably honest, and discerning in all our dealings. But most importantly, we need to be continually aware of what is in the heart of those with whom we associate. And we must keep our priorities straight regarding those seeking God as well as those fleeing from Him.[40]

Generally speaking, if we are not part of the solution, we are part of the problem. If we are not missionaries, we are part of the mission field. Though God's Word never teaches *isolation* from the world, it does teach *separation* from it, and we must take this issue as seriously as the book of Proverbs.

Concerning other believers:

The farther we move along on the fast track of technology, the less personal our society becomes. Our churches are also becoming less personal. Sunday morning fellowship is considered successful when it is evaluated as entertainment with a prompt

39. 10:8; 12:1; 13:18.
40. 3:29; 4:24–27; 28:26.

dismissal! The kind of godly intimacy that sustained isolated groups of believers in past generations is absent in today's mass-media Christianity. Our houses are built closer together than ever before. But our concept of who is our neighbor is still so foggy, few of us actively work toward winning our neighbors to Christ.

The Word of God encourages us concerning relationships within the family of faith. Godly people always choose the wisdom of the wise over the foolishness of fools. But what about those times when one godly person is confronted by another with advice, counsel, admonition, correction, or rebuke? How then do we respond?

Our first reaction is to assume that we are right and the other person is wrong. However, this is just another manifestation of the old root of sin—pride. "Before destruction the heart of a man is haughty," we are told, but "before honor is humility." Pride is entirely displeasing to God, and can only lead to arguing and conflict.[41]

Openness and teachability, however, are signs of true spiritual maturity and wisdom. As difficult as it may be at times, "He who regards reproof will be honored," and "the heart of him who has understanding seeks knowledge" from God and His people. While a foolish person "does not love one who reproves him, nor will he go to the wise," "the ear that hears the reproof of life will abide among the wise." Therefore the mature in spirit listen intently to correction and advice from God's Word, rather than answering before they have heard the whole matter.[42]

We must consider two biblical cautions. First, it must be emphasized that the reproof, rebuke, or correction one believer offers to another *always* comes from Scripture. Far too many believers today have replaced a knowledge of Scripture with a knowledge of biblical principles, temperaments, personality types, or other forms of analysis and advice removed from the Word of God. While some of these theories have a grain of truth to them, how much better for Christians to major in Bible and counsel one another from its pages! There is no safer ground than the Word of God from which to edify others in the family of faith. Let's never forget 2 Timothy 3:16–17: it is "all Scripture" (not all Christian books, psychology, or Christian fads) that is "given

41. 18:12; 16:5; 13:10.
42. 13:18; 15:14; 15:12; 15:31; 18:13.

by inspiration of God, and is profitable for doctrine, for reproof, for correction, for instruction in righteousness, that the man of God may be complete, thoroughly equipped for every good work."

Finally, the spirit of correction must *always* be shared in love, edification, and humility. There is no place in the body of Christ for those who believe it is their calling to keep everyone else in line! A true friend in the family of God is faithful to correct when correction is in order, and rebukes in love. This friend speaks out of a heart of love, sensitivity, and genuine care. "A word fitly spoken," we are told, "is like apples of gold in settings of silver. Like an earring of gold and an ornament of fine gold is a wise reprover to an obedient ear." Because "counsel in the heart of a man is like deep water," it takes "a man of understanding" to "draw it out."[43]

It is a merry heart and Christian confrontation that "does good, like medicine." The rude treatment some Christians receive as a "ministry of rebuke" breaks people's spirit and "dries the bones."[44]

Proverbs teaches the same attitude of humility and love spoken of throughout the New Testament in passages like Philippians 2:1–11, Ephesians 5:18–21, and Colossians 3:16–17. If believers choose the way of wisdom through absolute submission to Jesus Christ, seek to let His Word richly dwell within them, and yield their lives to the enabling power of His Spirit, the supernatural result is loving brothers and sisters in Christ. And all will speak to one another in psalms and hymns and spiritual songs, singing and making melody in our hearts to God.

---

43. 27:5–6; 25:11–12; 20:5.
44. 17:22.

CHAPTER 12

Practical Wisdom

USING WHAT GOD HAS PROVIDED

THE STORY IS told of a Christian who lived along the floodplain of a river. And as one might expect, one day he was caught in the middle of rising flood waters. As he rushed to the highest ground he could find, he began praying and assuring himself that the Lord would save him.

Before long, a rowboat full of people came along and urged him to swim over and climb in. "Thank you very much," he said, "but no thank you. I'm a Christian, you see, and I believe the Lord is going to save me." A little while longer, the believer's faith was holding strong, but the water was up to his chest. Another rowboat happened along. Again he was urged to climb on board, but his reply was the same. "No," he said, "I'm a Christian, and I believe the Lord is going to save me."

After another hour or so, the stalwart Christian was up to his neck in floodwater. As he looked up into the sky, he saw a helicopter hovering overhead and a rope dangling down from the runners. "Hey, you!" shouted an attendant. "Grab onto the rope, and we'll pull you up!"

"No, thanks!" shouted the Christian. "I'm a Christian, and I believe the Lord will save me!"

Well, after another 30 minutes or so, the believer drowned. And, to his joy, he was transported to the glorious presence of the Lord. But the Lord could see that this gentleman was troubled, so He asked, "Son, what's on your heart?"

"Lord," he said, "I want you to know you really let me down. There I was in that flood, witnessing like crazy that You were going to save me—and you let me drown!"

"Son," replied the Lord, "what more could I do? I sent you two boats and a helicopter!"

For many believers, immersion in the floodwaters of this fallen world is a trial gladly endured with confidence that God can sustain and save us. And yet, though we may verbalize our unshakable faith to believers and unbelievers alike, we are woefully lax in availing ourselves of the lifeline of His Word. We flounder, struggle, and gasp for fresh air all because we have chosen to look somewhere besides the pages of Scripture for what we need for survival.

Paradoxically, the things we need most in our Christian lives, like prayer, obedience, witnessing, and Bible study, are the hardest elements of the Christian life to find time for. And though we claim to be living according to Christian principles and Christian values, though we seek Christian fellowship and Christian counseling, though we are a part of Christian churches and the Christian community, we spend amazingly little time in the pages of the Christian Bible.

God, of course, does not suffer loss when we fail to immerse our minds in Scripture. But we do. No matter how much biblical support a Christian book or counselor may offer, that book is not the living Word of God, and that counselor is not the Holy Spirit. Not that those things aren't *good*. Many times they are. But as our distress and broken lives tragically prove, we have chosen that which is *good* at the expense of that which is *best*. We have trusted the Lord to save us without recognizing His method for doing that is the clear instruction of His Word.

As 2 Timothy 3:16–17 tells us, "*All* Scripture is given by inspiration of God, and is profitable for doctrine, for reproof, for correction, for instruction in righteousness, that the man of God may be complete, thoroughly equipped for every good work." It would be incorrect, therefore, to propose that the clear, simple wisdom of Proverbs is *more* profitable than, say, Leviticus.

However, this is a book about the book of Proverbs, and one of our basic assumptions all along has been that Proverbs accomplishes precisely what it promises. It "gives wisdom" to the upright in heart; it can "direct your paths"; it can teach us "the way of wisdom"; and provide "strength for the upright." The real beauty of Proverbs is that we don't need to put words into God's mouth in order to get it to try and say what we want it to say. It speaks so clearly, so succinctly, so powerfully that we are left to choose either to obey it, which is the way of the wise, or to ignore it, which is the way of the fool.[1]

Since other chapters in this book have dealt with the ways in which Proverbs addresses specific areas of life—money, marriage, family, sex, and so on—this chapter will focus on the way the book of Proverbs can provide us with the resources or tools for making practical decisions in our daily walk with Christ. Based on the tools Proverbs provides, we need to live life with all the tools in the toolbox, depending on the power of the Holy Spirit for obedience. And, although these tools for practical living will be stated in the form of principles, make no mistake—a principle is *never* a substitute for the actual words of Scripture.

Let's consider, then, some of the overriding, never failing, immensely practical wisdom of Proverbs.

THE PRINCIPLE OF CAUSE AND EFFECT

Throughout Scripture we are reminded that there is a universal law of cause and effect. Our inherent sin nature, for example, is an effect of the Fall. God's kingdom plan for the ages is an effect of Lucifer's rebellion and aspiration to usurp His kingdom. Our salvation is an effect of God's perfect plan. And so on.

In Proverbs specifically, we see that many circumstances in life are the effects of observable causes. Before we look at some examples, however, we must not *assume* something as an effect of an earlier cause simply because it satisfies our personal bias or viewpoint.

For example, some people who face difficult circumstances automatically assume they are being punished for some unknown or unrevealed sin or mistake. Conversely, some people who enjoy great wealth or success assume they are experiencing the just effect of their impeccable lifestyles, or some other personal merit. Obviously, these are serious errors.

Correctly identifying some circumstances as cause and effect is a twofold process. First, we would do well to limit our understanding of cause and effect relationships to those specifically addressed by Scripture, rather than applying our own natural wisdom to such circumstances. We have extremely limited knowledge in comparison to the divine perspective. If we see an able-bodied man suffering in poverty because of laziness, we

1. Proverbs 2:6; 3:6; 4:11; 10:29.

may make a reasonable evaluation of his poverty as an effect of laziness. If, however, we see someone suffer sudden serious illness, or the loss of a loved one, or some other terrible tragedy, we would be as foolish as Job's ignorant comforters to assign some type of cause for that supposed effect. Many believers have been hurt, misled, even devastated by the well-intentioned but ignorant comfort from a fellow believer who suggested, "God must want to teach you something," or "Your faith must need building," in the response to the death of a child or the onset of financial disaster. God knows our natural tendency to try and figure out His ways. Therefore, Proverbs sternly warns, "Do not be wise in your own eyes." Instead, we are to "Fear the LORD and depart from evil."[2]

God will do what God will do, and the only issue before us is how we respond to Him. We recognize His sovereignty, and if circumstances reveal anything about sin in our own lives, we should depart from that sin. This is the lesson of the entire book of Job, and it is confirmed by Proverbs. Or, as we read elsewhere, "His ways are not our ways."

Second, we must look at those unexplained circumstances in our own lives and in the lives of others as *action* rather than *analysis*. In other words, when either tragedy or blessing befalls us or someone else, our best first response would be, "What is my responsibility now?" rather than, "How can I try and explain this?"

This means we must become more prone to *comfort* rather than *critique*. We are to respond with *encouragement* rather than *envy*. And we are to depend more on the *sovereignty of God* rather than the *speculation of man*. Our culture is inundated with the worldly philosophy that we all are victims of our circumstances, every attitude and action can be explained in terms of environment, upbringing, or some other external factor.

God's Word, on the other hand, purposefully restricts cause and effect relationships to those circumstances that have their roots in willful, observable, cognizant personal decisions. The exception to this, of course, is the ultimate cause of so many of our problems, our fallen human nature. But with regard to that, Jesus Christ offers the ultimate solution of forgiveness and the power of the Holy Spirit, combined with the guidance of His

2. 3:7

Word. And concerning all those outside influences of our past, Paul wrote without qualification, "One thing I do, forgetting those things which are behind and reaching forward to those things which are ahead, I press toward the goal for the prize of the upward call of God in Christ Jesus. Therefore let us, as many as are mature, have this mind."[3]

That brings us back, then, to recognizing that as we live our lives in view of what lies ahead, we need to remember that God does not suspend the principle of cause and effect simply because we have trusted in Jesus Christ for forgiveness. That is to say, if I as a Christian tamper with beverages that have been fermented or mixed with other elements (such as hops and barley, corn, or fruit) for the purpose of making them even more intoxicating, I can expect the *effect* of woe, sorrow, contentions (arguments), complaints, wounds without apparent cause, even the chronically red eyes of alcoholism. No argument about Christian liberty or social customs can change that principle of cause and effect. And no emotional crutch of a dysfunctional upbringing or other environmental factors can change the personal decision I make.[4]

Again, if as a believer I choose to align myself with unscrupulous businessmen who promise me a portion of their profits, I can expect to suffer the consequences God has warned us about. If I choose to ignore civil law concerning taxes, public protest, or any other matter (with the exceptions of those things God has *specifically* prohibited in Scripture), rather than recognizing that God is ultimately in control of all human government, I should expect to experience the same consequences as any other lawbreaker.[5]

On a positive note, if I choose to make a lifelong habit of seeking God's wisdom rather than foolishness, I should expect to reap the many benefits promised throughout the book of Proverbs. If I strive to excel in my work, I should expect some recognition for it along the way. If I forego my own expressions of wrath and revenge, and instead, "wait for the LORD," I should expect Him to save me in His own way, in His own time.[6]

But what does this mean to us for daily living? It means that every time we are faced with a decision to obey Him or disobey

3. Phil. 3:13b–15a.
4. Prov. 23:29.
5. 1:10–14; 21:1.
6. 22:29; 20:22.

Him, to live wisely or to live foolishly, to sin or not to sin, alongside what we already know about those things that please God and those things that don't, we add the principle of cause and effect. We know for sure that consequences will follow every action we take, every decision we make.

THE PRINCIPLE OF GOOD AND EVIL

Perhaps this seems too obvious. In our culture, however, we are continually pressured to believe that there is no such thing as good and evil—"everything is relative," as the battle cry of the 60s phrased it. It appears today that Christians are no less susceptible to this lie than non-Christians. We have succumbed to ordering our convictions according to the latest poll, and determining reality by what we see on television and read in the newspaper. Though the Church has generally held the line on the issue of abortion, we have rolled over and played dead on far too many other issues.

We have, for example, adopted the "newspeak" of our culture and now refer to homosexuals as "gay;" alcohol and drug use is "substance abuse;" immorality is referred to as being "sexually active;" alcoholic bums are "the homeless;" spiritual apathy is "burnout;" and adultery is only "an affair."

Not that we are to be insensitive and harsh toward those lost in sin. To the contrary, we are to live our lives in such a way that Jesus Christ continues to seek and save the lost through us. By the same token, however, we are to be both salt and light in a world that is rotting and dark. Jesus said, "Salt is good, but if the salt loses its flavor, how will you season it?" Salt without saltiness is worthless, just as Christians with no sense of discernment of good and evil are of little use in the world.[7]

Proverbs never compromises the existence of good and evil in the world. Violent men are "wicked," dishonesty is "an abomination to the LORD," the lazy are "sluggards," the person who spreads slander is "a fool," and the person who spreads dissension is "perverse." God clearly teaches us that the first step toward living righteously is recognizing the difference between good and evil generally—and between the *wicked* and the *righteous* specifically![8]

7. Mark 9:50.
8. Prov. 21:7; 20:10; 6:6; 10:18; 16:28.

It may be that we have heard so often the ungodly misquote, "Judge not lest you be judged" that we actually believe it means God does not care about evil or wickedness! Therefore we shrink back into our shells and fail to label sin "sin," wickedness "wickedness," and evil "evil" for fear that we will be branded as judgmental.

The point Christ was making in Matthew 7:1 was *not* that God does not care about good and evil, or that believers should not discern between good and evil. Rather, His point was that all our judgments should be based on the perfect standard of God's righteousness, not on a standard of self-righteousness. That means we submit ourselves to the same standard before Him. It also means that we recognize God's concern for the sinner, as well as His hate for the sin itself.

Amazing, isn't it, that those who are so quick to quote "Judge not lest you be judged" don't temper it with John 7:24: "Do not judge according to appearance [a standard of self-righteousness], but judge with righteous judgment [a standard of God's righteousness]"? Those who frequently quote Matthew 7:1 really aren't interested in the rest of what the Bible says. They just know they don't want anything to do with *any* judgment or *any* absolute standard of righteousness.

This is precisely the opposite of the way the godly are to live, according to Proverbs. We are to become so intimately acquainted with God's ways and wisdom that we "understand righteousness and justice, equity and every good path." We are commanded to "not turn to the right or the left; remove your foot from evil," obviously intending we understand the difference between good and evil.[9]

We are also expected to understand that a person's response to the God of the Bible is a fair indicator of whether he or she is righteous or wicked. "He who walks in his uprightness fears the LORD, but he who is perverse in his ways despises Him." We must admit that it *does* matter what someone believes about God, not just that they worship in their own way, since "the sacrifice of the wicked is an abomination to the LORD." And we must reacquaint our Christian community with the fact that true biblical faith requires we "fear the LORD and depart from evil," not as a *requirement* for knowing Him, but as a *result* of knowing Him.[10]

9. 2:9; 4:27.
10. 14:2; 15:8; 3:7b.

In short, the book of Proverbs (as well as the rest of God's Word) provides us with the tools we need for recognizing and responding to good and evil in the fallen world around us. We make evaluations and decisions concerning issues, people, philosophies, leaders, values, ideas, and every other influence we encounter based on the knowledge of good and evil. Contrary to what many have come to believe in our morally lax culture, the Christian life does not *exempt* us from living life according to God's standard of good and evil. Rather, it *equips* us to live life according to God's standard of good and evil.

THE PRINCIPLE OF THE WORLD'S INFLUENCE

We have already seen in the chapter on social wisdom that the company we keep has a profound effect on us, extending to every area of our lives. The Christian subculture in North America goes out of its way *not* to isolate itself from the world. In fact, we have become so taken with the idea of blending with our surroundings we frequently do not even take the time to be *separate* from the world, as we should be. In short, we are so fearful of being different from the world that we aren't!

One of the reasons for this is instead of realizing our purpose to spread the gospel to the remotest parts of the earth, we mistakenly believe we are here to prove that Christians can do everything better than non-Christians. Rather than introduce the world to Christ, we spend a great deal of our time introducing Christians to the world, through our Christianized version of all the world's attractions. Unfortunately, what we have to show for this "God always goes first class" philosophy is a grossly materialistic Church and a culture that is getting worse every day.

The influence of the world on believers is not static. It is always dynamic. Either believers are becoming less like the world through obedience to God's Word, or they are becoming more like the world through ignorance or apathy concerning God's Word. Either a church is reaching the world around it, or the world is reaching a church within it.

God's Word is clear that our mission in the world is to "go into" it and "make disciples of all the nations." Jesus told the disciples they were to wait in Jerusalem until they received the promise of the Father, the indwelling Holy Spirit. They wanted to know if Jesus was going to establish His kingdom at that time.

When He told them, basically, "It's none of your business," the disciples wondered why the Holy Spirit was being given *before* the establishment of Messiah's kingdom on earth. Jesus told them it was for one reason, and one reason only: "You shall receive power when the Holy Spirit has come upon you; and you shall be witnesses to Me in Jerusalem, and in all Judea and Samaria, and to the end of the earth."[11]

The indwelling of the Holy Spirit provides many benefits to believers. But the one *stated reason* the Spirit was given was to provide the power necessary for believers to be Christ's witnesses on earth. That means unless believers are witnessing, they will not experience the real purpose and power of the Holy Spirit in their lives. When we behave in a manner opposed to witnessing, as in conforming ourselves to the world, we suffer defeat, depression, aimlessness, and apathy.

The book of Proverbs warns that moving in the same direction as the world will open us up to influences that eventually overwhelm and defeat us. And though we cannot lose our salvation, we certainly lose our victory, our enjoyment of God, and even our lives! "He who walks with wise men will be wise," instructs the sage, "but the companion of fools will be destroyed." Are we as quick to teach this proverb to businessmen and homemakers as we are to teenagers? Though this does not mean that a person who comes to Christ must terminate all old relationships, it does suggest that all believers need to be careful whom they choose as close friends. "The righteous should choose his friends carefully," is the way Proverbs phrases it, "for the way of the wicked leads them astray" (12:16).[12]

At this point, let's consider the concept of going astray. Most believers look at the possibility of going astray as a temptation they can easily recognize and avoid. Scripture teaches the opposite. Going astray is like the last time you got lost while driving your car. You knew where you wanted to go, you thought you were going the right way all the time, but the next thing you knew, you were—astray. When we choose to align ourselves with the world by the way we speak, the way we act, the TV programs we watch, and the company we keep, we should not be surprised to wake up one day to find we can't get a handle on

11. Matt. 28:18–20; Acts 1:8.
12. Prov. 13:20.

our personal world. Somewhere along the way we made a wrong turn.

The allurement of the world is simple, according to 1 John 2:15–17. "Do not love the world or the things in the world. If anyone loves the world, the love of the Father is not in him. For all that is in the world—the lust of the flesh [sensual gratification], the lust of the eyes [material attraction], and the pride of life [self-satisfaction]—is not of the Father but is of the world. And the world is passing away, and the lust of it; but he who does the will of God abides forever."

We have fostered our love for the world to the point we sanctify these three areas of attraction by giving them Christian labels. We fawn over Christian celebrities; preach a gospel of success and defer to Christians in positions of status; and we flock to anyone who offers the latest innovations on God's truth. So great is our friendship with the world that we have restructured our churches modelled on corporate America. We have exchanged Christian discipleship for Freudian counseling. Our agenda for ministry is formed around social popularity, replacing worship with entertainment, and exchanging evangelism for church growth.

Whether on a personal or a corporate level, our friendship with the world today has reached epidemic proportions. It is no accident. Satan has always known believers are susceptible to the influence of majority opinion. That is why Noah alone "walked with God"; why the society of Babel represented a vast, powerful majority on earth; why Israel repeatedly succumbed to apostasy; and why the last days before the Tribulation period will be marked by widespread apostasy and ungodliness.[13]

What is the alternative for those who long to live life wisely in the counsel of God's Word? To "know wisdom and instruction, to perceive the words of understanding, to receive the instruction of wisdom, justice, judgment, and equity," no matter how unpopular or out of style it may be to those around us. We must be willing to choose the way of wisdom no matter what it costs us either socially or professionally. We must fall in love with the Word of God and spend at least as much time reading it as we do staring at cable TV or rental movies. We must believe so strongly that "righteousness delivers from death" that we pursue godli-

13. Gen. 6:9; 11:6; 2 Pet. 3:3–4.

ness and Christlikeness over wealth, success, popularity, social acceptance, or anything else the world has to offer. And we must aggressively, verbally witness to unbelievers without making the values and lifestyle of the world our own. As Proverbs sternly warns, "Do not let your heart envy sinners, but in the fear of the LORD continue all day long" (23:17). [14]

THE PRINCIPLE OF THE HEART'S DECEITFULNESS

We live in the "how to" generation of Christianity. From a simple and righteous beginning of how to know God and walk with Him, we believe we can figure out how to do everything in life. We think we can learn how to discern our own hearts and those of other people. We buy books on how to pull ourselves up by our spiritual bootstraps and overcome all the adversity in our past and present lives. We are encouraged in how to blame our present spiritual shortfalls on our parents or others; how to predict our behavior or other's actions based on their temperament or birth order; and how to force God to give us what we want by claiming certain verses of Scripture.

God must be either terribly amused or greatly saddened by all of this. Our fixation on our ability to "figure it out" is as old as the human race. Even in her unfallen state, Eve considered herself quite capable of figuring out all the angles of the serpent's temptation, and neglected to believe and obey God's revelation. It was no accident that Satan appealed to Eve through rational discussion and debate. For his part, Adam undoubtedly considered himself capable of discerning all the implications of eating the fruit, failed to obey God, and sealed the race's condemnation in sin. [15]

Since that time history constantly employed such faulty logic. Cain thought his form of religion was adequate. The earth's population in Noah's day believed they were above God's judgment. Even God's people during the period of the Judges "did what was right in their own eyes." Saul, king over Israel, frequently rationalized his own reasons for doing things, rather than obeying the voice of the Lord. It eventually cost him his rule, and his life. David, too, gave in to rationalization as he slept

14. Prov. 1:2–3; 10:2.
15. Gen. 3:1–19.

with Bathsheba, then tried to cover his tracks. And the Pharisees, who knew the Word of God perhaps better than anyone else in Christ's day, used their skills for self-analysis and self-justification.[16]

The human heart and mind, no matter how well-intentioned, are simply not capable of overcoming sinfulness to figure it out. In our day and age, we behave as though God's Word needs our help in order to change our lives. We want to depend at least a little bit on ourselves or on other people to do what God and His Word can do. And we suffer a nagging lack of spiritual growth as a result. God *never* intended us to be able to "find ourselves," "embrace our pain," or to do anything else dependent on the abilities of the human heart and mind. God warns "he who trusts in his own heart is a fool." The human heart is fallen; it is "deceitful . . . and desperately wicked" (Jer. 17:9). Our souls are not just damaged—they are dead! Our hearts don't need repair— they need replacement.[17]

Because our hearts are fallen, we suffer the same symptoms Lucifer suffered—we love to be "wise in our own eyes." We revel in discovering any new truth that adds to the revelation of God.[18]

In other words, we are all extremely susceptible to the power of suggestion. And like unbelievers who find their daily horo-scopes coming true, some believers discover all life's explana-tions in something other than the Word of God. Worse yet, some seek out counselors who twist the Word of God to conform to their own ideas.[19]

Not many years ago, a worried seminary student approached a professor and asked, "Prof, when you were in seminary, what did you do about burnout?"

"Son," replied the professor, "when I was in seminary, we didn't have to worry about burnout. It hadn't been invented yet."

Some argue that the plethora of today's psycho-emotional maladies have been around for centuries, though unrecognized and untreated. Others provide documented evidence that copy-cat disorders appear with the first announcement of their discov-ery. This is not to say that there are not *any* cases of genuine

16. 1 Sam. 15; 2 Sam. 11.
17. Prov. 28:26.
18. 26:5.
19. 30:6.

psycho-emotional disorders among the Christian population. However, the more the Christian community emulates the world and looks within the human heart for answers and explanations for various problems, the more those problems seem to multiply.

Biblical counselors agree that the more we look outward to the Word of God for solutions, the more we will begin to show signs of true Christlikeness and spiritual growth. Though a person's heart knows bitterness or joy, the heart provides no answers. Only the Word of God can do that. Of course, the heart is not passive in our Christian lives. According to Proverbs, it is a dynamic element in how we make decisions, how we respond to God and others in all the affairs of life. The key to understanding the heart, however, is understanding that it operates effectively only when it is submitted to the tutelage of the Word of God. That is why God instructs us, "Apply your heart to instruction, and your ears to words of knowledge" (again equating instruction and knowledge with God's revelation). The great benefit of submitting our hearts to the Word of God is that our hearts gain wisdom and understanding and, as a result, become more reliable guides.[20]

Unfortunately, there are those who won't believe the counsel of God's Word is the whole answer for their needs. They continue to seek attention, refusing to understand and trust in the Word of God: "A fool has no delight in understanding," we are told, "but in expressing his own heart."[21]

According to Proverbs, the purpose of seeking and gaining wisdom is that our trust may be in the Lord rather than in ourselves.

> Incline your ear and hear the words of the wise,
> And apply your heart to my knowledge;
> For it is a pleasant thing if you keep them within you;
> Let them all be fixed upon your lips,
> *So that your trust may be in the LORD.*[22]

This goes far beyond simply dealing with internal matters. The wisdom of this proverb must rule the way we handle external matters as well. "Let your conscience be your guide" may

20. 14:10; 23:12; 15:14; 16:23.
21. 18:2.
22. 22:17–19.

work well enough for Jiminy Cricket, but it leads to disaster for Christians. We are to let the perfect counsel of God's Word be our guide, "a lamp to my feet, and a light to my path." If our choice of guidance is between the revelation of God or our hearts, how could we choose any wisdom but God's? "There are many plans [or ways] in a man's heart," Proverbs 19:21 tells us, but "the LORD's counsel [His revelation]—that will stand"![23]

THE PRINCIPLE OF THE GODLY MINORITY

Throughout Scripture we clearly see those who have chosen the narrow way of God's wisdom over the broad avenue of majority opinion have *always* been the minority. Not many in our society today are described as those who follow "righteousness and mercy," who are not "greedy for gain," or do not trust in riches. Those are just a few of the characteristics of the Proverbs person. The field narrows further when we include all the qualities and character traits found in Proverbs.[24]

Obviously, no one can live up to the ideal lifestyle Proverbs advises. But we can commit ourselves to moving persistently in that direction. As we know from our understanding of the New Testament, that commitment for us begins with giving the totality of our lives to Jesus Christ. From there it involves commitment of the heart to live for Him no matter what the cost, no matter what the consequences. It also involves a commitment to obey His Word, as He enables us through the power of His Spirit.

Today, this kind of committed Christianity is a rare commodity. There are millions of professing Christians in our culture. But among those, how many are living out the kind of dedicated, committed, radical Christian life taught by Proverbs and other portions of Scripture?

The picture Proverbs provides for us is not one of a beaten-down, burdened believer who labors through each day with a do's and don'ts list in hand, carefully striving to keep all the rules and stay inside all the boundaries. Rather, Proverbs portrays a victorious, righteous, and godly life with an insatiable appetite for the wisdom and understanding of God's perfect revelation. It is a life that radiates righteousness because it reflects the very

23. Psalm 119:105.
24. Prov. 21:21; 15:27; 11:28.

nature and character of God. It is a life that loves a righteous God and His righteous Word.

Some would argue with much of what Proverbs has to say. They contend Proverbs was written to a different culture in a different time. They say we are much wiser now, and we know more about what makes us tick than the sage did in his day. They argue that this is Old Testament stuff, and that we are in the New Testament age now. But those who argue against the wisdom of Proverbs are wise in their own eyes. "There is more hope for a fool than for him."[25]

For the person who longs to live a godly life in Jesus Christ an ideal place to begin is the book of Proverbs. But such a person must not mind being part of a holy minority! Those who abhor the coarse profanity of most movies may offend believers whose tastes agree with the culture. Those who decide to take a stand against intoxicating drink might find themselves alone on a Friday night, instead of living it up with their church singles group. A businessman's stand against unscrupulous business practices may cost him his job. A politician's belief in right and wrong may cost him votes, or even his office. A teenager's commitment to chastity may mean ridicule and rejection. In other words, the believer who chooses to make the way of Proverbs a way of life can generally expect to be part of a minority of believers here on earth.

Jesus said, "Blessed are you when they revile and persecute you, and say all kinds of evil against you falsely for My sake. Rejoice and be exceedingly glad, for great is your reward in heaven, for so they persecuted the prophets who were before you." According to 2 Timothy 3:12, whether we live conspicuously for Christ and suffer some form of persecution may be a good barometer of our commitment, since "all who desire to live godly in Christ Jesus will suffer persecution."[26]

We must realize there is no middle ground for the kind of commitment outlined in Proverbs. The people of God are called to choose either the silent majority, or the vocal minority.

THE PRINCIPLE OF UNCHANGING TRUTH

If truth really *is* truth, it never changes. This is the essence of Proverbs. Truth in Proverbs is not a set of culturally conditioned

25. 26:12.
26. Matt. 5:11–12.

axioms, nor is it a collection of archaic sayings from a fundamentalist teacher. The wisdom of Proverbs is as eternal as the
God who inspired it.

Knowledge of God's Word in general, and Proverbs in particular, offers far more value for the believer than any other source
of Christian input. Christian books on the bestseller lists today
eventually go out of print as they are supplanted by niftier, more
seductive books tomorrow. The seminars and group sessions
some believers think they can't live without right now eventually
either grow old and stale, or die with those who created them.
Christian buzzwords floating around in today's Christian circles
will be long forgotten tomorrow.

If this depresses us, then we've missed the point of Proverbs
entirely! In Proverbs God provides believers of all ages with *real*
truth that will not change. It is as relevant to a Wall Street
businessman today as it was to a Jewish teenager thousands of
years ago. Has the deep pit of debt changed from then until now?
Has God changed His opinion about unethical business practices?
Have the willfully lazy and impoverished become any less ridiculous? Have the positive effects of long-sustained friendships
changed? Have the sociologists shown us anything that improves
on God's method for rearing children?[27]

No matter where we look, we can see that the truth we find in
Proverbs is genuine truth, the real thing, unchanging, inerrant,
and infallible. The only time God's wisdom is questioned is
when the world's version of truth appears more attractive, more
palatable, more popular. But if we hearken to the siren call of
unfailing faith in human achievement, we will exchange God's
unchanging truth for the version the world offers, and we will
suffer the consequences.

How much better to walk through life *assuming* the truth of
God's Word and testing every new concept in the light of His
truth, subjecting every experience, every emotion, every school
of thought *first and foremost* to the Scriptures! God's wisdom has
already promised to "give you good doctrine." Moreover, God
has promised that we will be able to understand His wisdom
without a graduate degree, a series of seminars, or an endless
continuum of expensive counseling sessions. His wisdom isn't
hidden in complex terminology and obtuse concepts. Rather,
wisdom "calls aloud outside; she raises her voice in the open

27. Prov. 6:1–5; 11:1; 26:13; 27:17; 29:15.

squares. She cries out in the chief concourses, at the openings of the gates in the city." We live out the truth of Proverbs as it is written. We discern the wicked and avoid them. We recognize the lazy as lazy and admonish them. We obey with our wills, learn with our minds, work with our hands, and treasure God's wisdom with our hearts.[28]

But we will not live out the Proverbs if we do not know them. Reading this book *about* Proverbs will not change your life. Only reading God's Word in Proverbs will do that. If you have never made it a practice to read daily in Proverbs, perhaps you should begin now, as an experiment to see what kind of effect it has in your life. If you cannot read and digest an entire chapter of Proverbs each day, try absorbing only a few verses of each chapter, say, verses 1–5. The next day, try verses 6–10, and so on through the year.

As you begin to work on this portion of God's Word, rest assured it will begin to work on you! The more you take it to heart, the more it will change your heart. And the more skillful you become at understanding what it has to say, the more skillful you will become at living life God's way. "For wisdom is better than rubies, and all the things one may desire cannot be compared with her" (8:11).

---

28. 4:2; 1:20–21.

Bibliography

Alden, Robert L., *Proverbs: A Commentary on an Ancient Book of Timeless Advice* (Grand Rapids, Michigan: Baker Book House, 1983).

Blackwood, Andrew W., Jr., *In All Your Ways: A Study of Proverbs* (Grand Rapids, Michigan: Baker Book House, 1979).

Bridges, Charles, *An Exposition of Proverbs.* (Grand Rapids, Michigan: Zondervan Publishing House, 1959).

Briscoe, Jill, *Queen of Hearts: Role of Today's Woman* (Old Tappan, New Jersey: Fleming H. Revell, 1984).

Brock, Fred R., Jr., *Practical Pointers from Proverbs.* (Regular Baptist Press, 1981).

Brown, Francis, et. al., *A Hebrew and English Lexicon of the Old Testament.* (Oxford: Clarendon Press, 1907).

Brownville, C. Gordon, *Practical Proverbs for Everyday Christian Living.* (Grand Rapids, Michigan: Zondervan Publishing, 1942).

Cory, Lloyd. *Quotable Quotations.* (Victor Books).

Drakeford, Robina and John W., *In Praise of Women* (San Francisco: Harper & Row, 1980).

Draper, James T., *Proverbs: The Secrets of Beautiful Living* (Wheaton, Illinois: Tyndale House Publishers, Inc., 1971).

Eims, LeRoy, *Wisdom from Above for Living Here Below* (Wheaton, Illinois: Victor Books, 1978).

Horton, R. F., *The Expositor's Bible,* Vol 4: *The Book of Proverbs* (New York: A.C. Armstrong and Son, 1898).

Hubbard, D. A., *International Standard Bible Encyclopedia,* Vol. III. *Book of Proverbs,* 1988 ed.

Ironside, H. A., *Notes on Proverbs* (New York: Loizeaux Brothers, ND).

Jeffrey, James, *The Way of Life* (Cincinnati, Ohio: Jennings and Graham, 1904).

Jensen, Kenneth L., *Wisdom: The Principal Thing* (Seattle, Washington: Pacific Meridian Publishing Co., 1971).

Jensen, Irving L., *Proverbs* (Chicago: Moody Press).

Jeremiah, David, *The Wisdom of God* (Milford, Michigan: Mott Media, ND).

Johnson, John E., "The Contribution of Proverbs to Ethics." Th.D. Dissertation, Dallas Theological Seminary, 1984.

Kaiser, Walter C., Jr., *Toward an Exegetical Theology: Biblical Exegesis for Preaching and Teaching* (Grand Rapids, Michigan: Baker Book House, 1981).

Kanengieter, Marvin W. and Quinlan, Edith, *Looking at Life's Relationships* (Denver, Colorado: Baptist Publications, 1973).

Keil, C. F. and F. Delitzsch, Trans. by James Martin. *Commentary on the Old Testament*, Vol. VI. *Proverbs* (Grand Rapids, Michigan: Eerdmans Publishing, 1973 reprint).

Lange, John Peter, Trans. by Philip Schaff, *Commentary on the Holy Scriptures,* Vol. 9 *Psalm-Song of Solomon* (Grand Rapids, Michigan: Zondervan Publishing House, 1960).

Larson, Paul E., *Wise Up and Live* (Glendale, California: Gospel Light/Regal Books, 1974).

Morgan, D. F. *International Standard Bible Encyclopedia,* Vol. IV, *Wisdom of Solomon*, 1988 ed.

Oesterley, W. O. E., *The Book of Proverbs* (London: Methuen & Co., Ltd., ND).

Scott, R. B. Y., *The Way of Wisdom in the Old Testament* (New York: Macmillan Company, 1971).

Theological Wordbook of the Old Testament, R. Laird Harris, editor et. al. (Chicago: Moody Press, 1980).

Thomas, David., *Book of Proverbs* (Grand Rapids, Michigan: Kregel Publications, 1982).

Von Rad, Gerhard, *Wisdom in Israel* (Nashville: Abingdon Press, 1972).

Whybray, R. N., *Wisdom in Proverbs* (Naperville, Illinois: Alec R. Allenson, Inc., 1965).

Wiseman, D. J., Gen. Ed., *The Tyndale Old Testament Commen-*

taries, Vol. 11, *The Proverbs*, by Derek Kidner (Downers Grove, Illinois: InterVarsity Press, 1964).

Woodcock, Eldon, *Proverbs: A Topical Study* (Grand Rapids, Michigan: Lamplighter Books, 1988).

About the Authors

H. Wayne House is a popular seminar speaker, debater, and lecturer on law ethics, social issues, theology, and biblical studies. He holds the B.A. degree from Hardin-Simmons University, the Master of Divinity and Master of Theology from Western Conservative Baptist Seminary, the Master of Arts from Abilene Christian University, the Doctor of Theology from Concordia Seminary, St. Louis, and the Juris Doctor from O. W. Coburn School of Law. He has been professor of theology and ethics at Dallas Theological Seminary and is Visiting Professor of Law at Simon Greenleaf School of Law and Regional Director with the Institute for Christian Apologetics.

Dr. House has published numerous articles in publications such as *Bibliotheca Sacra, Concordia Journal, Bible Expositor and Illuminator,* and *Memphis State University Law Review,* and a number of books, including *Civilization in Crisis, The Role of Women in Ministry Today, Divorce and Remarriage: Four Christian Views,* and *Christian Ministries and the Law.*

He lives in Salem, Oregon, with his wife, Leta, and their daughter and son, Carrie and Nathan.

Kenneth M. Durham is a professional writer, editor, and communicator whose work has appeared in Christian and secular publications over the past sixteen years. He holds the B.A. degree in journalism from California State University at Long Beach, as well as the Master of Theology and Master of Arts in Christian Education degrees from Dallas Theological Seminary, where he also was editor of Dallas Seminary's *Kindred Spirit* magazine.

Mr. Durham's work has appeared in *Worldwide Challenge, World Vision, Moody Monthly* and *Discipleship Journal,* as well as in several large metropolitan daily newspapers and national magazines. His published efforts also have included Christian education materials and expository devotionals for national distribution.

He lives in Colorado Springs, Colorado, with his wife, Mary-Good, and their five children: Dallas, Kala, Denver, Austin, and Malia.